CONTENTS

LIST OF TABLES

PREFACE

Students of economics often reach the end of their courses with only the most basic knowledge of the financial system. The macro-economic models they meet concentrate on saving, investment, money and 'the' rate of interest. The entire range of non-monetary financial instruments is represented by long-term securities. The only financial institutions worthy of detailed attention are banks, some of whose liabilities happen to be money, with other institutions considered only in so far as their activities complicate the tasks of the monetary authorities. While bond-holders' attitudes have a crucial influence in the Keynesian model, the financial system itself is down-graded – it is the level of income, rather than the interest rate, which brings saving and investment into balance, and the rate of interest depends only on the demand and supply of money.

This comparative neglect of the internal workings of the financial system contrasts with a high level of public concern. Financial institutions have always been in the public eye and frequently attract politicians' attention. The availability of finance, the terms which lenders demand before parting with their funds, and the economic power wielded by large financial institutions are matters for controversy. Public debate, however, is seldom founded on a deep understanding of how the financial system works, partly due to the complex nature of the system itself and partly to the reticence of its practitioners.

The evidence submitted to the Wilson Committee (Committee to Review the Functioning of Financial Institutions) did much to overcome this reticence, and the Committee's report contained an authoritative account of many important aspects of the UK financial system in 1980. While some people will disagree with the Committee's recommendations, there is now less excuse for ignorance and misunderstanding. Nevertheless the report does not pretend to go into the theory of the system in any detail, and the treatment is selective, linked to the questions the Committee was asked to consider, rather than comprehensive.

My object in this book has been to provide a complete account of the working of the financial system in the UK at a level which is suitable both for students with only a basic course in economics behind them and for informed laymen or people embarking on a career in the financial sector. I have tried to put the emphasis on *behaviour* – what motivates the actors in the financial system, why they behave as they do, what constraints influence the decisions they take – rather than on detailed descriptions; these can be found elsewhere, as for example in Jack Revell's excellent book, *The British Financial System*. I have also attempted to provide an evaluation of the efficiency of the financial system in Britain, and to consider some issues of current interest.

The framework around which the book is organized is the flow-of-funds table. This is introduced in Part I in the context of a brief overall view of finance in the UK. The sectors are discussed in Part III and the institutions and markets in Part IV.

Part II, which precedes the institutional material, deals with the theory of financial systems. It is the most technical section of the book; readers who are prepared to take on trust the important part played by financial institutions and markets in mobilizing saving and stimulating productive investment may choose to skip the indifference curve analysis in Chapter 3. Chapter 4 deals with asset transformation in a non-technical fashion and Chapter 5 contains a loanable funds model of interest rate determination. I have not entered into the debate concerning stocks and flows, nor attempted to reconcile loanable funds with Keynesian interest theory – though the possibility that interest rates may fail to balance saving and investment at a high level of income is discussed later.

Parts III and IV draw upon this theory to explain the behaviour of the participants in the financial system. The importance of structural and legislative factors is emphasized, as well as the market considerations, which are usually more central to economic models. Some issues concerning the needs of particular sectors or the facilities provided by the financial institutions are discussed in the relevant chapters.

Part V contains three chapters on broader issues: first, the efficiency of the system as a whole and its success in meeting the demands which fall upon it; secondly, the effects of inflation and possible remedies for the difficulties it causes; thirdly, the thorny questions of whether, and if so what, changes in the financial system are needed in order to promote industrial investment in the UK.

Some, but not all, of these issues were considered in the report of the Wilson Committee. My work on the book has arisen naturally out of my service on that Committee, and I acknowledge my debt to my colleagues – not least to those with whom I frequently disagreed. I am also indebted to colleagues at the University of Strathclyde, particularly John Harvey for the many helpful suggestions he made, and Dick Davies who cast an informed eye over a key chapter. Neither is responsible for any heresies or errors that remain. My greatest debt, however, is to my secretary, Jean Paterson, who worked tirelessly at successive drafts and without whose dedication the book could not have been completed at this time.

A.D.B.
May 1981

PART I INTRODUCTION

This Part is intended to provide the reader with the background knowledge required for the more detailed discussion which follows in the rest of the book. The first chapter is an introduction to the functions of financial systems in economies, their importance, and the ways in which they perform their tasks. The second provides a bird's-eye view of the UK financial system, focusing on the salient features. Attention is drawn to the sizes and importance of the major institutions, the levels of saving and investment in the economy and the sectors in which they are found, and the financial channels through which savings flow on their way to investors. The flow-of-funds framework is introduced as a means of providing a coherent description of financial activity, and as the organizing framework for later chapters.

1   THE FINANCIAL SYSTEM

Everyone has some contact with the financial system. We are all aware of financial institutions like banks, building societies, and insurance companies, each providing in its own way for some of our everyday needs – for example, payments facilities through banks, convenient savings and access to home loans by building societies, and car, house, or life insurance. Other financial institutions, such as investment trusts, development capital companies, and the National Enterprise Board – to name only a few – are less well known and carry out more specialized functions. Most people also know something about financial markets, like the Stock Exchange where securities are bought and sold, though comparatively few are directly concerned with their activities. Again, there are other important but less familiar financial markets, like the money market in which large sums are borrowed and lent for very short periods, and the foreign exchange market in which dealings in foreign currencies take place. All these financial institutions and markets fit together into a network which comprises the financial system.

The quality of the services provided by the financial system affects the performance of the economy as a whole. The most basic function of any financial system is to facilitate payments in the economy. Normally the responsibility for providing the necessary facilities falls on the note-issuing authority – the government or the central bank – and the commercial banking system. Satisfactory payments facilities are something which we are inclined nowadays to take for granted, but productive economic acitivity is dependent on their existence, and indeed on traders having reasonable access to short-term credit facilities.

Important as payments facilities are, they will receive relatively slight consideration here, because a properly developed and smooth-running financial system can do much more for the economy. It raises the levels of saving and investment and provides incentives for the allocation of the available resources to those uses where they are likely to give the highest returns. The financial system thus facilitates effective capital accumulation, one of the major engines of economic growth, and it is the saving/investment aspect which will be the focus of our attention.

How well the financial system of a country satisfies the needs of users is a matter for public concern. By their very nature financial institutions attract criticism: bankers would not be doing their jobs if they did not turn down some requests for loans, and those who are denied funds sometimes feel hard done by and are vociferous in their complaints. The control which financial institutions wield over very substantial sums of money also attracts the attention of governments, partly because they may see irresistible opportunities to secure cheap finance for favoured borrowers (notably governments themselves), and partly in view of the economic power attached to control of finance. Official enquiries into the financial system are therefore not uncommon. The most recent British enquiry was the Wilson Committee on The Functioning of Financial Institutions, which reported in 1980.[1] It had broad terms of reference, with special attention being given to the finance of industry and trade. In Australia, the Campbell Committee[2] is conducting a similar investigation, though its main thrust is on the extent of government regulation in the system. In Germany the Gessler Committee[3] recently examined the structure and activities of the banking system, with a particular concern for the influence which the banks' central position in the financial system gave them over industrial companies. There are many other examples. But whatever the particular slant of each enquiry, the objects are generally to ascertain whether the organization of the financial system and the practices of its institutions are in accordance with the current needs of society, and to make recommendations for improvements.

Any evaluation of the financial system should be founded on an understanding of its functions within the economic system as a whole, and the means by which these can be carried out. This must be complemented by a knowledge of users' requirements, of the behaviour of institutions, and of the market practices. Moreover, institutions and markets cannot be viewed in isolation, for it may not be important that one category of financial institution makes no provision for certain needs if these can be satisfied elsewhere in the system. What matters is not the shapes of the individual pieces, but how well the jigsaw fits together and the quality of the picture that emerges.

THE PARTICIPANTS IN THE SYSTEM

The participants in the financial system can be classified into five
broad groups: savers, investors and other borrowers, financial intermediaries, brokers and advisers, and regulators. At one edge of the
financial system are the *savers*, i.e. those whose current spending is
less than their income and who have money available to lend to
others. Opposite them are the *investors*, who want to borrow money
in order to buy capital goods or increase the scale of their business,
and other borrowers who want to spend more than their incomes.
In between lie the financial institutions and markets. Ensuring that
money flows smoothly from savers through institutions and/or
markets to investors is an important function of the financial
system. It is the ultimate savers and ultimate borrowers who are,
as it were, on the periphery of the financial system, whose needs it
serves and who provide the rationale for its existence.

Nevertheless, a good deal of the business of financial institutions
and activity in financial markets is generated, not by new saving and
investment, but by rearrangements of existing savings or changes in
the form of existing borrowings. People shift money from bank
accounts to building societies or vice versa, and firms raise new long-
term capital in order to pay off short-term debts. Moreover, investors
do not always need to borrow in order to finance expenditure; they
may choose instead to run down savings accumulated from earnings
previously, or they may use balances obtained by borrowing on other
occasions. By permitting economic agents to organize their financing
in a flexible manner, the financial system helps to make all this
possible.

Financial intermediaries are institutions which attempt to serve
the needs of both lenders and borrowers. As we shall see later the
forms in which savers wish to hold their savings, for example bank
deposits, frequently differ from the ways in which borrowers would
like to obtain their funds, for example long-term loans. Financial
intermediaries are often able to reconcile these divergent requirements. In addition they provide a variety of specific services which
savers and borrowers value in their own right. Examples are money
transmission facilities and advice on corporate finance in the case
of banks, and life assurance cover in the case of insurance companies.
Moreover, while there is nothing to prevent savers and investors from
dealing directly with each other if they wish, the existence of financial institutions makes direct contact unnecessary, since both groups
can deal with the intermediating institutions.

In a competitive financial system (like that in Britain) institutions compete for business in broadly construed 'markets' for saving and lending business; they seek to attract funds from savers and supply funds to borrowers. But there are also *organized* markets, which provide facilities for economic agents to borrow and lend or to buy or sell securities. The main role of *brokers and advisers* is to help these organized markets to function properly. Brokers and advisers provide information to participants in the markets, and attempt to ensure that lenders and borrowers, buyers and sellers, have the facts they need to strike a fair bargain. They also perform the vital task of putting actual lenders and borrowers in touch with each other – for example, the money-market broker brings together the lender who has money to spare with the borrower who wants it temporarily. By obviating the need for individual borrowers or lenders to search out counterparts themselves the brokers substantially reduce the transactions costs involved in borrowing and lending. In some markets there are also professional dealers, whose function is to ensure that lenders and borrowers are always able to find a counterpart for their deals.

Historical experience in many countries has shown that where large sums of money are involved in financial markets there is a considerable danger of fraud or other malpractices. Most countries therefore need *regulators*, who control their financial institutions and regulate dealings in securities markets with the objects of ensuring that the financial institutions are able to honour their commitments, that people have access to relevant information before they enter into contracts, and that dealing in securities is fair. These rules come under the general heading of *prudential* regulations. But more general *economic* controls are also needed. Sharp expansions or contractions of activity in financial markets are often associated with booms and slumps in the economy at large, and the intimate connection between money, credit and economic stability compels countries to curb the expansion of credit in some periods and to stimulate it in others. Economic controls may also be required to guard against monopolistic structures or practices in the financial system.

FINANCIAL INSTRUMENTS

The financial system deals in financial instruments or claims. These are all more or less sophisticated forms of IOUs – they are an asset of one party and a liability of another. In most instances the former party is entitled to repayment at a specified time, and also receives a promise of some interest, share of profits, or other service as compensation for his loan. For example, deposits and liabilities of banks or other institutions, are generally repayable on demand or in the fairly near future, and usually bear interest. Loans and often liabilities of ultimate borrowers, are usually repayable by the end of some predetermined period, and carry an obligation to pay interest. And ordinary shares are liabilities of firms, which confer on their owners the right to a share of the profits earned but, in contrast with loans, do not have to be repaid. Although a wide variety of financial instruments exists, differing significantly in detail, the major distinctions rest on three characteristics – risk, liquidity and susceptibility to loss of value due to inflation.

A distinction can be drawn between on the one hand deposits and loans, which are generally made only if repayment of capital and interest is confidently expected, and on the other company shares, which are claims to a share of the surplus incomes after prior claims have been met. People think of their deposits with financial institutions as safe,[4] and loans are usually secured on assets or made conditional on the borrower's financial performance, to give the lender added confidence in the safety of his funds, though there is usually some small chance of partial or total loss. The *risk* of loss, and conversely the possibility of gain, is heavily concentrated on equity assets, mainly the ordinary shares of companies. The shareholder is entitled to his share of the company's profits but must also accept the chance of experiencing some loss. Indeed, for reasons discussed in Chapter 7, the effects on the shareholder of success or failure of a company are magnified if the company has loans outstanding as well as ordinary shares.

Liquidity refers to the ease and speed with which savings in nonmonetary form can be turned into cash, and reflects both the *maturity* of financial instruments and their *marketability*. By maturity we mean the time which elapses before a deposit or loan is due to be repaid. Deposits which are repayable on demand have a short maturity, mortgage loans due for repayment after 25 years a long one. Thus maturity covers a very wide range, and the shorter is the maturity of a deposit or loan the greater is its liquidity. But assets which are marketable may also be liquid, even if they are not automatically repayable in the near future. For example, ordinary shares in many companies can be sold at short notice and their value turned into cash, though at a price which is uncertain. Not all assets are marketable – fixed-term deposits are an example – and in other cases the ease of selling and ability to obtain a reasonable price may be in doubt. A house may be for sale for many months and the price received will be a matter for negotiation. The existence of an organized market for an asset and the ability to deal at short notice therefore adds to the asset's liquidity.

The third distinguishing characteristic of financial instruments is their susceptibility to loss of value due to a rise in the general price level – *real value certainty.* Neither deposits nor loans, whose values are fixed in money (or *nominal*) terms, provide their holders with protection against price-level changes. Ordinary shares stand a good chance of doing better on this score, because profits can be expected in the end to rise roughly in line with the general price level, though there may be prolonged periods when this does not hold good. Indeed, over a long period, probably the safest asset to hold in real terms is a physical asset, property, rather than any form of financial instrument.

SAVERS AND INVESTORS

In developed economies decisions to invest are often taken separately from decisions to save. The investor may be a company manager who wishes to expand the activities of the firm by which he is employed, while the saver may be a private individual who wishes to put some money aside for his retirement. Even when saving and investment are carried out by the same economic agent, the timing is usually different, with saving either preceding the investment which is to take place, or occurring afterwards as debts are gradually repaid. Moreover, the acts of saving and investment are also often far apart in space. British savings in the nineteenth century helped to finance the construction of the US railroads, just as in more recent times US saving has helped to pay for the development of North Sea oil, and saving by oil-rich countries in the Middle East is currently being used to finance investment in many other countries.

There are of course important exceptions. The businessman who ploughs his profits back into the business is saving and investing simultaneously, and the same is true of the large company which holds down its dividends in order to retain profits for investment. A substantial part of company investment is in fact financed in this way, with funds put aside for depreciation being used to replace capital equipment as it wears out or to finance new investment. Nevertheless, a high proportion of saving is not employed directly or immediately by the saver himself, and is made available to investors elsewhere.

Savers' objectives are varied. Some people save for short periods merely as a means of levelling out their income and consumption patterns, or they save up for some specially heavy expenditures, such as presents at Christmas or a holiday. Others have motives directed to longer-term needs, of which the most important is saving for retirement. Firms save to finance future investment or to provide a cushion against the possibility of adverse business conditions. Governments may add to saving through the tax system if they anticipate that there will be a shortage of saving in the economy as a whole and decide to compel people to save more (through the fiscal system) rather than curtail investment.

Their motives for saving have a bearing on the characteristics of the financial instruments which people wish to hold. First and foremost people look for *safety*; they wish to be sure that their savings will not be lost. Security of money value is important for many asset holders, and it is comparatively easy to ensure that savings will not lose their value in this sense; but the objective of securing the real value of saving is difficult to attain in periods of inflation, when the real value of monetary savings is eroded by rising prices.

Secondly, most firms and many individuals want a large part of their savings to be readily available. This means that *liquidity* is vitally important; the maturity of the assets which they hold must be short or good markets must exist in which assets can be sold so that cash can be raised if necessary. In consequence, savers have a strong demand for deposits and short-term loans. There are, however, very important exceptions to this preference for liquidity: savings built up for retirement, for example, will often not be required until many years have elapsed, and do not need to be held in a liquid form. Long-term loans, and assets which provide some protection against inflation, may be suitable for this purpose.

Thirdly, savers seek a *yield* (income) on their assets. For most, this ranks well behind safety and liquidity. But in choosing between financial claims which are similar in other respects savers can generally be expected to select that which offers the higher yield. Some savers are also prepared to hold risky financial assets, like ordinary shares, if the return[5] they hope to earn is sufficient to compensate them for the risk of loss.

Investors' needs are very different. The bulk of physical investment is durable, generating a flow of earnings which permits its value to be recovered gradually and over a long period. Much of it is specialized and could be sold only at a considerable loss. Moreover investment is an inherently risky activity, and the investor can never be certain about the income which an investment is likely to produce. The rents on commercial properties may not rise as has been antici- pated, the market for a new product may be misjudged, or the costs involved in production may turn out higher than expected.

The characteristics which investors seek in the liabilities they issue reflect these features of physical investment. Ideally, they prefer to issue long-term liabilities, like long-term loans, reflecting the extended period over which many investments pay for themselves. Since the profitability of investment is uncertain it is essential for part of their liabilities to have the form of equity capital, to be remunerated in a way which reflects their profitability. Finally, other things equal, investors wish to pay as little as possible for the funds they obtain.

FINANCIAL INTERMEDIARIES AND MARKETS

The separation of saving from investment and the differing and conflicting requirements of savers and borrowers create opportunities for financial institutions. They perform a variety of functions, including; mobilizing saving, encouraging investment, transforming maturities, averaging and transforming risks, reducing information and transaction costs.

Financial intermediaries *mobilize saving.* They draw attention to the benefits of saving, stressing for example security in the case of life insurance and safety combined with income in the case of building society deposits; in so doing they change people's attitudes, and raise the level of saving in the economy. Moreover they encour- age people to save, and to do so through the financial system, rather than by buying land, jewellery, or some other more tangible assets; pension funds, for example, enable people to convert present into future income without becoming directly involved in productive investment themselves. Many financial institutions also collect the comparatively small savings of individuals and make them available in large sums to borrowers; the savings of many individual building society depositors are required to make up each single mortgage loan; the liquid funds of a large number of firms and individuals are needed to supply a bank loan sufficient to finance a large indus- trial investment project; and the pension contributions of many working people are put together by a pension fund to provide money to a property development company. Investment, which is on a comparatively large scale, requires access to funds gathered together from many sources.

While many of the financial institutions set out actively to stimulate saving they often take a more passive stance on the lending side of their business. They facilitate, rather than directly *encourage*, *investment*. This is certainly the case for long-term investment institutions like insurance and pension funds, which buy and sell securities in the financial markets. It is less true of banks, some of which put a considerable effort into marketing their loan facilities and, particularly with corporate customers, encouraging clients to go ahead with developments which create a need for finance. However, as a general rule institutions respond to the demand for funds and influence demand by varying the price at which they are prepared to supply funds or the terms attached to loans, rather than attempt to persuade customers to take on additional spending commitments. Their role in encouraging investment is therefore mainly indirect – by providing funds at a price that is lower and on other terms which are more favourable than borrowers could negotiate if they had to seek funds directly from savers themselves.

One way in which financial institutions improve the terms facing borrowers is by *transforming maturities* – they provide liquid liabilities which meet the needs of savers whilst employing their funds in the longer-term financial instruments which are more convenient for borrowers. Deposit-taking institutions like banks and building societies are able to do this because, although some individual depositors may be reducing their deposits, others will simultaneously be adding to theirs, and the institutions can rely on a considerable degree of stability in their deposit-base as a whole. It is therefore legitimate for them to regard at least a proportion of their deposits as available for long-term loans. Moreover, the existence of organized markets in which they can bid for large deposits provides banks with the assurance they need to make loan commitments.

Most financial institutions issue liabilities which are comparatively safe, but hold amongst their assets instruments on at least some of which there is a possibility of loss. To do this they *average risk* and *transform risk* by taking the residual risk of loss on their own equity capital. For example, by making a large number of loans, and spreading them over a wide range of activities, banks try to ensure that their overall loss experience is small. They attempt to allow for losses in the charge they make for loans, and if this allowance is insufficient their own capital is available to absorb any further losses before the funds supplied to them by depositors are at risk. Life insurance companies hold a much greater proportion of risky assets than banks, and the possibility of capital gain or loss on individual assets is also higher. But they too are able to offer life insurance policies with a guaranteed minimum value and to protect their policyholders from undue risk. Indeed, by holding different types of assets in their portfolios – bonds, ordinary shares and property – and by diversifying their holdings within each category, they are able to eliminate much of the risk involved in financial investment.

For the private individual, holding the liabilities of ultimate borrowers himself involves substantial costs. These *information and transaction costs* are much lower for financial institutions. For example, the individual with funds to lend is not usually in a position to assess accurately the value of a house on which a mortgage loan is secured, but the building society specializing in this type of lending can do so easily. Moreover the legal documentation which is required can be prepared with much less effort by the specialist for whom it is an everyday occurrence. Through their network of branches and agencies building societies are also in a position of make contact with depositors and borrowers, whereas the private individual might have considerable difficulty in finding a suitable mortgagee. Turning to stock-market investments, unless the private investor has a really substantial amount of money to invest, he faces proportionately high transactions costs if he wishes to buy or sell ordinary shares. It makes sense, therefore, for him to invest through an intermediary like a unit or investment trust, which, by dealing in large amounts, incurs proportionately lower costs.

While financial intermediaries usually perform one or more of these functions, they also provide a variety of other services, which may indeed be their *raison d'être*. For example, life insurance companies provide insurance against the risk of early death (life policies) or prolonged life (annuities); banks provide money transmission services which allow people to make payments easily; and investment and unit trusts seek to offer expert investment management, which removes from the individual the need to monitor continuously the progress of the companies whose shares he holds. All these services are important in their own right.

The organized markets provide alternative and complementary mechanisms to financial intermediaries for meeting the needs of savers and borrowers. Organized markets *provide liquidity*, because they make it easy for the saver to sell a financial instrument before it reaches maturity. Thus what is a long-term liability for a borrower becomes liquid in the hands of the holder. Organized markets *mobilize saving* and allow large sums to be borrowed. Through the new issue market firms or the government can raise very large sums of money, drawing at the same time on the savings of a host of individuals and financial institutions, each of whom can provide only a small proportion of the total that is required. Organized markets help to *disseminate information* and ensure that those who participate in the markets as buyers or sellers are well-informed. This means, for example, that share prices will reflect an up-to-date assessment of the performance of the companies concerned, and that even the less well-informed investor may therefore expect to be able to deal at a fair price. Finally, organized markets *reduce transactions costs*, because a mechanism for bringing buyers and sellers together is created. Examples of organized markets are the new issue market, which helps companies or the government to raise new capital, the stock market where trading in existing securities takes place, and the money market which facilitates short-term deposit-taking and borrowing in large amounts.

It is important to observe that markets do not just happen – they need some form of organization. Thus issuing houses and stockbrokers help to organize the new issue market; the Stock Exchange consists of stockbrokers, through whom clients deal, and 'jobbers' whose function is to act as the counterpart of buying and selling orders and to quote prices continuously; and the money market has money-brokers who bring borrowers and lenders together and institutions such as the Discount Houses which act as dealers in a variety of short-term securities. Without these specialists savers would be likely to experience difficulty both in finding buyers for securities they wished to sell and in ensuring that they received a fair price for their assets, which would therefore lose liquidity. Borrowers would find equal difficulty in gaining access on reasonable terms to the funds they required.

RATES OF INTEREST AND OTHER TERMS

The prices prevailing in financial markets and the rates of return on financial instruments have important economic functions. They help to allocate resources in the economy and they play a significant part in achieving macroeconomic balance – balance between saving and investment overall at a satisfactory level of economic activity.

At this point it may be helpful to digress briefly to draw attention to the relationship between the prices of assets and their *rates of interest*. A financial asset is a claim to a stream of income in the future, the interest on the asset. The rate of interest, or yield, on a security is simply the income per period expressed as a percentage of the price of the asset. Thus if; Y is the income in some period, P is the price of the asset, r is the rate of interest for the period

$$r = \frac{100Y}{P} \text{ per cent.}$$

It is clear that there is an inverse relationship between P and r; for any given income, Y, the higher is P the lower is r.

This connection is reflected in the behaviour of asset prices and interest rates in the financial system. People can choose between holding securities directly and lending to institutions, firms can choose between issuing securities in the financial markets and borrowing from institutions, and the rates of interest and asset prices affect their decisions. If deposit interest rates rise people will be less inclined to hold securities unless security prices fall to offer an equivalent yield. If companies are actively seeking funds, this will tend simultaneously to increase the supply of securities in the markets, so lowering security prices, and to raise the rate of interest charged for bank loans. Interest rates and asset prices therefore tend to change together (though in opposite directions).

In a market economy prices are at the centre of the process of resource allocation. People with resources are persuaded by a high price to make them available to others; and the limited supply of resources goes to those who are willing to pay the prevailing price for them. Economic agents, whether sellers or purchasers, respond to impersonal market incentives. This applies to capital markets, where securities are bought and sold, and to a lesser degree to financial institutions, which have to compete for funds and vary their own charges for loans in line with what they themselves have to pay. The rates of interest charged by lenders also normally reflect the risk of loss, so that when risk is high borrowers pay more.

Nevertheless there is a sense in which the financial system allocates funds more directly and in a less impersonal fashion. Lenders and financial investors do not automatically provide funds to all potential borrowers who claim to be able to pay the going rate. Lenders make their own assessment of the probability of loss, and refuse funds in those cases where they think the risk is too high. Moreover, particularly when credit is tight, lenders may choose to ration funds – to lend to some customers, but decline requests from others who satisfy all the appropriate risk criteria.

Non-competitive features of the financial system such as these affect the efficiency of resource allocation. When allocation of funds amongst those borrowers who satisfy the appropriate risk criteria is by price, there is a presumption that funds will go to those who are able to pay most for them and that resources will be channelled into those areas where they are likely to prove most productive. In this sense allocation through the price system is 'efficient' and rationing by institutions detracts from efficiency. But this concept of efficiency does presuppose that the value of an investment is reflected in ability to pay for funds, and it can be argued that the ability to pay the going rate and meet the risk standards set by the institutions may not always be appropriate criteria for deciding who should get funds.[6]

The prices of financial assets and rates of interest also act to equate the supply of saving with the demand for investment in the economy as a whole. Just as the price of the shares of some company will rise if demand is greater than supply, so the prices of securities generally rise when there is excess demand in securities markets. The same principle applies to institutions. If building societies fail to attract sufficient deposits to meet the demand for loans they may react by raising both their deposit and mortgage interest rates. By offering to pay more for deposits they attract a higher proportion of the available saving, and by raising their lending rates they curtail the demand for funds. Thus supply and demand come into balance. The behaviour of banks is very similar. If the demand for bank loans increases and the banks are short of funds, they too offer more for deposits and raise the interest rates on their loans accordingly. The process may take a little time because financial institutions may prefer not to change their interest rates at first, but instead offer other inducements to savers or alter other terms of lending in a way intended to keep their liabilities and assets in balance. But while the change in interest rates required to balance supply and demand may be delayed it does usually take place eventually.

The role of the financial system in balancing saving and investment in the economy is controversial, and the mechanism is in fact rather complex. A discrepancy between the desired levels of saving and investment may have repercussions on economic activity, which would feed back into saving and investment themselves, and conditions in financial markets are also influenced by changes in the form in which people want to hold their assets and by the amount of money which is available – factors which may all interfere with the ability of rates of interest to carry out their equilibrating function.[7]

NOTES

1. See Cmnd 7937.
2. See *Australian Financial System: Interim Report of the Committee of Inquiry*, Australian Government Publishing Service, Canberra, May 1980.
3. See *Grundsatzfragen der Kreditwirtschaft - Bericht der Studienkommission*, Schriftenreihe des Bundesministeriums der Finanzen, Heft 28, Wilhelm, Stollfuss Verlag, Bonn, 1979.
4. One of the functions of prudential regulation is to ensure that they are not disappointed.
5. Including capital gain as well as income.
6. The role of rates of interest in resource allocation is discussed further in Chapters 5 and 15.
7. This question is discussed further in Chapter 15.

2 FINANCE IN BRITAIN

In this chapter we shall look briefly at the structure of the British financial system today, which reflects the ways in which savers hold their financial wealth and the nature of the liabilities which borrowers have issued in the past. We shall then go on to examine three aspects of the process by which saving is channelled to investors through the financial system: first, the amounts of savings and investment that go on in the economy, then the question of who saves and who invests, and finally, the flows of funds through financial institutions and markets as money passes on its way from savers to investors. At this stage we do no more than sketch the outline of the picture in order to draw attention to the salient features; more detailed discussion and analysis will be found in subsequent chapters.

INSTITUTIONS AND MARKETS

Tables 2.1 and 2.2 contain figures which show the size of some of the more important financial institutions in Britain. Deposit-taking institutions, whose liabilities are usually short-term and liquid, control much the same volume of funds[1] as the investing institutions, whose liabilities are generally of a longer-term nature, in both cases amounting to a little under £100 billion[2] – about 50 per cent of GDP at market prices. Table 2.1 shows that banks are the most important category of deposit-taking institutions, but building societies run them a close second so far as sterling deposits are concerned. (Banks are also heavily engaged in foreign currency operations.) While the Trustee Savings Banks and the National Savings Bank are much smaller than either banks or building societies, they deal nevertheless with substantial volumes of funds and account for a little under 10 per cent of the total. Deposit-taking institutions are discussed in Chapter 10.

TABLE 2.1   SELECTED DEPOSIT-TAKING INSTITUTIONS, STERLING DEPOSIT LIABILITIES,[1] END 1979

	(£ billion)
Banks in the UK	46.2
Building societies	42.8
Trustee Savings Banks	5.8
National Savings Bank	3.4
Total	98.2

Source:Financial Statistics, April 1981
[1] To non-bank UK residents. Figures for banks are at 12 December

TABLE 2.2   INVESTING INSTITUTIONS, ASSETS, END 1979

	(£ billion)
Insurance companies	52.8
Self-administered pension funds	34.4
Investment trust companies	5.8
Unit trusts	3.3
Total	96.3

Source: Financial Statistics, April 1981

Insurance companies and pension funds dominate the investing institutions, accounting together for over 90 per cent of their total assets. The insurance companies are the largest category, but a significant proportion of their assets is held in respect of pension business. Self-administered pension funds have grown rapidly in recent years, and in terms of the new money they make available for investment have now overtaken the insurance companies. Investment and unit trusts managed asset portfolios amounting to over £9 billion at the end of 1979, with a considerable emphasis on investment in foreign securities. Recently, however, they have not been an important medium for channelling new saving into investment in the UK. The investing institutions are discussed in Chapter 11.

Table 2.3 illustrates the scale of securities markets and sterling money markets – markets for certain short-term financial instru-

TABLE 2.3   SECURITIES AND MONEY MARKETS

	(£ billion)
UK public sector stocks[1]	
British Government and Government guaranteed	70.7
Local authority and public bonds	2.6
UK companies[1]	
Loan capital and preference shares	4.6
Ordinary shares	85.9
Sterling money markets[2]	44.8

Sources: Stock Exchange Fact Book; Wilson Committee Report, Table
3.70
[1] End 1980, at market value
[2] End 1979

ments – in the UK; these are considered more fully in Chapter 12. The market for fixed interest securities is dominated by government stocks, which comprised over 40 per cent of the total market value of UK securities on the Stock Exchange at the end of 1980. By comparison, local authority bond and company loan (and preference share) capital are very small beer. Ordinary shares of UK companies accounted for over 50 per cent of the total.

Table 2.3 also shows the importance of the sterling money markets. Much of the business in these markets takes place between financial institutions, but banks could not function as they do in the absence of these markets, and the instruments dealt in are significant sources of funds for some borrowers (e.g. local authorities) and represent highly liquid assets to their holders.

Tables 2.1 to 2.3 do not cover by any means all of the financial instruments or financial institutions in Britain. Notes and coin, non-marketable central government debt, and longer-term local authority loans and mortgages held by the private sector amounted to over £30 billion at the end of 1980; and sterling loans to the private sector by banks and building societies added up to almost £100 billion at that time – more than the market value of all the fixed-interest securities on the Stock Exchange. Moreover, there are other more specialized institutions which attempt to meet specific needs, and which may be of great importance for certain categories of borrower, some of these special credit institutions are considered in Chapter 13.

SAVING AND INVESTMENT IN BRITAIN

We turn now to consider the part played by the financial system in the saving/investment process. Table 2.4 shows that since the mid-1970s saving and investment in Britain has typically absorbed less than 20 per cent of GDP.[3] There have been considerable fluctuations from year to year but on average during this period investment exceeded saving by about 1 per cent of GDP, giving rise to borrowing from abroad.[4] Taking the period since 1973 as a whole investment was at much the same level as the preceding 10 years, while saving was a little lower than its earlier level.

Variations in saving and investment from one year to the next have been associated with general economic conditions. For example, saving fell very sharply between 1973 and 1974; the rise in commodity prices, particularly the oil price, at that time, caused an adverse movement in the terms of trade and led to a reduction in Britain's income. In an effort to avoid unemployment the government took action to maintain consumption and investment and relied on overseas borrowing to finance the balance of payments deficit. Saving fell further in 1975 but since then there has been some recovery, though saving has not yet returned to the level of the

TABLE 2.4   SAVING AND INVESTMENT IN THE UK, 1973–80

	(Per cent of GDP at market prices)	
	Saving[1]	Investment[2]
1973	21.5	21.5
1974	17.6	21.9
1975	16.2	18.1
1976	17.3	19.7
1977	18.4	19.3
1978	18.8	18.8
1979	18.5	19.1
1980	17.6	15.9

Sources: Blue Book, 1980; *Economic Trends*, April 1981
    [1] After deducting stock appreciation but before providing for depreciation and additions to reserves
    [2] Gross domestic fixed capital formation *plus* value of physical increase in stocks and work in progress

early 1970s. Investment in 1973 and 1974 was very high by historical standards, but fell back subsequently, partly as a result of
economic policies directed towards eliminating the balance of payments deficit, curbing inflation and controlling public sector borrowing, and partly as a consequence of the deteriorating business
outlook. The investment collapse in 1980 reflects the massive reduction in stocks which occurred in that year as companies struggled to
conserve cash and remain solvent.

Saving and investment in Britain have been rather low by international standards, as Table 2.5, which shows figures for other major
developed countries, demonstrates.[5] Although investment was even
lower in the USA, the British figures are significantly less than those
of our three largest European counterparts, and far below those of
Japan. The relatively low share of GDP devoted to investment in this
country is certainly linked to our comparatively poor economic
performance.

TABLE 2.5   SAVING AND INVESTMENT IN MAJOR
DEVELOPED COUNTRIES, 1973–77

	(Per cent of GDP at market prices)	
	Saving[1]	Investment[2]
UK	17.0	20.0
USA	17.3	17.8
Japan	32.6	33.6
France	21.1	24.5
Germany	23.6	22.3
Italy	21.8	23.0

Source: Wilson Committee Report, Table 3
[1] Gross saving, before deducting capital consumption
[2] Increase in stocks *plus* gross fixed capital formation

SAVING AND INVESTMENT BY SECTOR

For many purposes it is convenient to divide the economy into
sectors, whose functions differ or whose activities are governed by
different considerations. We shall employ a five sector classification;
personal sector (households etc.), industrial and commercial com-

panies, financial companies and institutions, public corporations, general government (central government and local authorities). The needs and financial behaviour of these sectors will be discussed at much greater length later, but at this stage a brief description of the contribution of each sector to saving and investment in the economy, and of the financial flows between, them will help to set the scene.

TABLE 2.6   SAVING AND INVESTMENT BY SECTOR, 1973-80

	Saving[1]				Investment[2]			
	1973-77 average	1978	1979	1980	1973-77 average	1978	1979	1980
Personal sector	7.7	8.6	9.6	10.6	3.0	3.3	3.5	3.1
Industrial and commercial companies	6.5	7.6	5.7	3.7	7.4	7.7	8.0	5.0
Financial companies and institutions	1.4	1.5	1.9	2.5	1.6	1.9	2.0	2.1
Public corporations	1.9	2.4	1.9	2.0	3.5	3.0	3.0	3.2
General government	0.7	−1.4	−0.6	−1.1	4.6	2.9	2.9	2.6
Total	18.2	19.1	18.5	17.7	20.2	18.8	19.4	16.0

(Per cent of GDP at market prices)

Sources: Blue Book, 1980; *Economic Trends*, April 1981; *Financial Statistics*, April 1981
    [1] Saving, after deducting stock appreciation, but before providing for depreciation and additions to reserves, *plus* net capital transfers
    [2] Gross domestic fixed capital formation *plus* value of physical increase in stocks and work in progress

Table 2.6 shows how saving and investment have been divided between these sectors in recent years. The personal sector, which includes unincorporated businesses and non-profit making institutions as well as households, is the most important source of saving in the economy. In the period 1973-77 personal sector saving amounted to nearly 8 per cent of GDP, and it has climbed to over 10 per cent more recently. The sector's investment needs, which include owner-occupied housing and the buildings, plant and equipment required by the business component of the sector, have been much more modest at only about 3 per cent of GDP.

Industrial and commercial companies are also usually responsible for a substantial part of the economy's saving, though their contribution has been eroded by declining profitability, and has now fallen to a very low level; what remains consists largely of funds set aside for depreciation on existing capital equipment. Until the early 1970s there was a fairly close balance between saving and investment in this sector, but investment – a little over 35 per cent of the total for the economy – now exceeds saving.[6]

Partly as a result, financial companies and institutions – particularly the banks, insurance companies and pension funds – have come to occupy a more prominent role, as *real*[7] investors in the economy. A growing part of their assets in recent years has consisted of property, which is rented to other companies, public corporations or the government, and plant and equipment which is leased to these users in a similar fashion. Although some of their investment is for their own use, e.g. offices and computing equipment, the bulk is employed elsewhere in the economy; real investment by financial institutions has doubled from 1 per cent of GDP in the decade before 1973 to about 2 per cent now.

Public corporations include the nationalized industries and certain other publicly-owned enterprises. Their profitability, and hence their saving, varies enormously from one to another. For example, the British Gas Corporation currently makes large profits, whilst the British Steel Corporation makes losses. Overall their profitability is influenced by their own efficiency and by government policy with regard to their objectives and responsibilities. In recent years, at about 2 per cent of GDP, their contribution to saving has not been large and has in fact been less than the amounts required for depreciation[8] on their assets. Their contribution to investment has been more substantial, and would have been higher if it had not been curbed by government policy.

General government consists of the central government and local authorities. In the recent years general-government saving has been negative; while local authorities have a small current account surplus (i.e. saving) this has been more than offset by dis-saving by the central government. The government saves if tax revenue exceeds its current expenditure. In the decade up to 1972 central government saving averaged nearly $3\frac{1}{2}$ per cent of GDP, but since then it has fallen away for several reasons. The most important are the government's desire to stimulate the economy, which led it to cut taxation and increase expenditure in the early 1970s; political pressures for higher government current expenditure, together with an inability to control expenditure effectively; and a reluctance to raise taxation correspondingly. In the years from 1973 to 1977, at 4.6 per cent of GDP, the general government accounted for over 20 per cent of investment, but since then cuts in spending programmes have brought about a sharp reduction. About three quarters of the investment is carried out by local authorities – for example housing schemes, water and sewage facilities, and other aspects of infra-structure for which they are responsible. Central government investment too is largely concerned with the nation's infra-structure.

The separation of saving from investment emerges clearly from these figures. Saving by the personal sector in 1980 was $7\frac{1}{2}$ per cent greater than that sector's own investment needs. The three enterprise sectors together – industrial, commercial and financial companies and public corporations – had saving amounted to only just over 8 per cent of GDP, but their combined investment came to over 10 per cent of GDP, so that their saving provided for only about 80 per cent of their investment. The general government made no contribution to its own investment from saving, but had to draw on savings generated in other sectors to finance consumption spending.

The conditions shown in Table 2.6 are not necessarily immutable or permanent. Saving by the personal sector has in fact risen very substantially since the early 1970s, and with it the excess of saving over investment. And while local authorities have always borrowed to finance the greater part of their capital needs, the central government used to finance its own capital expenditure out of revenue, and have something over to lend to local authorities or public corporations. It is by no means impossible that the former patterns of saving and investment in the economy will re-emerge in future, or that industrial companies and public corporations, rather than the rest of the government, will become the principal users of the personal sector's saving.

FINANCIAL SURPLUS OR DEFICIT

When an economic agent (for example a household, firm or government authority) has saving which exceeds its investment we say that it has a *financial surplus*; even if all its investment was financed from its own saving there would be a surplus over to be used to acquire financial assets or repay debts. In the contrary case, when investment exceeds saving, we say that the agent has a *financial deficit*. Thus in

Table 2.6 the excess of personal sector saving over investment is a measure of the personal sector's financial surplus.

The surpluses and deficits (which have a negative sign) for all the sectors for 1973–80 derived from Table 2.6 are shown in Table 2.7, which also includes the 'overseas sector'. This shows the extent to which the UK increases its indebtedness to the rest of the world (i.e. the overseas sector has a financial surplus) or builds up its claims on other countries.[9, 10] Table 2.7 shows clearly the importance of the personal sector as a source of finance for other sectors in the economy, as well as the dominant position of the public sector (public corporations and general government) as a net borrower.

TABLE 2.7   SECTOR FINANCIAL SURPLUSES AND DEFICITS IN THE UK, 1973–80

| | (Per cent of GDP at market prices) | | | |
| | Financial surplus/deficit | | | |
	1973–77 average	1978	1979	1980
Personal sector	4.7	5.3	6.1	7.4
Industrial and commercial companies	−0.9	0.0	−2.3	−1.2
Financial companies and institutions	−0.2	−0.4	−0.1	0.4
Public corporations	−1.6	−0.6	−1.1	−1.3
General government	−3.9	−4.3	−3.2	−3.7
Overseas sector	1.6	−0.4	0.9	−1.2

Sources: Blue Book, 1980; *Financial Statistics*, April 1981, Table 1.1

The sectors' financial surpluses and deficits provide some indication of the extent to which the financial system has the task of shifting funds between broad sectors of the economy. For that reason they are important. But they do not tell the whole story, because funds also have to be transferred between lenders and borrowers within each sector, and because a great deal of financial activity is caused when people rearrange their assets or liabilities. For example, a very high proportion of households' investment in owner-occupied housing depends upon mortgage borrowing, so that the savings of some are being channelled through the financial system to provide funds for others within the same sector. Again, although self-financing is much more prevalent amongst enterprises, the deficit of the industrial and commercial companies sector as a whole is made up from surpluses of some companies outweighed by deficits of others, so that in this sector too financing activity greatly exceeds the net deficit of the sector as a whole. Within the public sector, however, financing is much more highly centralized, with the saving of some public sector entities being made available for investment by others without passing through the financial system. The deficit of the public corporations and general government together is therefore a reasonably good indicator of their demands upon financial institutions and markets.

TRANSACTIONS IN FINANCIAL ASSETS - THE FLOW OF FUNDS TABLE

An economic agent's financial surplus/deficit provides a link between the agent's saving and investment in physical assets on the one hand and its transactions in financial assets on the other. An agent with surplus saving is in a position to acquire additional financial assets or to repay debt, while an agent with a deficit must either borrow more or reduce financial asset holdings. We can show this schematically as follows:

Saving − investment = Financial surplus

= Increase in financial assets
    − Increase in financial liabilities

= Net acquisition of financial assets

For the purpose of this equation a deficit is treated simply as a negative financial surplus, and decreases in financial assets or liabilities are treated as negative increases.

Table 2.8 shows an illustrative example. Suppose a company has saving of £100 000 and investment of £200 000 in a year, and suppose that its financial assets and liabilities consist of bank deposits and loans respectively. The upper part of the table shows that its financial surplus is − £100 000, i.e. it has a financial *deficit* of £100 000.

There are a number of ways in which it can arrange its finances, of which two are shown in the lower half of Table 2.8. Example A shows the company as *increasing* its bank deposits by £50 000 (investment in new activity may well entail an increase in liquid assets), so that loans have to rise by £150 000, to match the financial deficit and increase in assets. Alternatively (example B) the firm might have financed the deficit by running down bank deposits (− £50 000) and borrowing only £50 000. In either case the *net* acquisition of financial assets is − £100 000 (increase in assets *less* increase in liabilities), equal to the financial surplus for the firm. The financial surplus provides a constraint which the company's financial transactions are bound to satisfy.

TABLE 2.8   SAVING, INVESTMENT AND TRANSACTIONS IN
FINANCIAL ASSETS AND LIABILITIES

		(£ thousand)
Saving		100
less Investment		− 200
Financial surplus		− 100

	A	B
Change in bank deposits (asset)	50 (increase)	− 50 (decrease)
less Change in loans (liability)	− 150 (increase)	− 50 (increase)
Net acquisition of financial assets	− 100	− 100

A picture of the financial activities of each sector can be obtained by listing its transactions in all the available financial assets and liabilities; taken together these must, of course, be consistent with the sector's financial surplus or deficit. This procedure can be carried out for every sector in the economy – the financial instruments employed in the economy have to be classified into a limited number of categories, such as bank deposits or loans for house purchase, and the transactions by all the sectors in each of the categories have to be shown. A table in which the rows show categories of financial instrument and the columns show the sector's transactions in each instrument is called a *flow of funds table*. The flow of funds table then presents a complete and consistent statement of the financial transactions between the sectors of the economy.

Table 2.9 is an example of a flow-of-funds table, which shows the flows of funds in the UK during the years 1976–80, expressed as percentages of GDP. The sectors are familiar, although public

TABLE 2.9   FLOW OF FUNDS, 1976-80

(Per cent of GDP at market prices)

	Personal sector	Industrial and commercial companies	Public sector	Banking sector	Other financial institutions	Overseas sector
Notes and coin	0.3	0.3	-0.6	–	–	–
Bank deposits	2.1	1.0	0.1	-4.3	0.5	0.6[1]
OFI deposits	3.6	–	–	–	-3.5	-0.1
Life assurance and pension contributions	4.6	–	-0.2	–	-4.5	–
Public sector debt	1.6	0.2	-5.8	0.6	3.0	0.4
UK company securities						
Capital issues	–	-0.5	–	-0.2	-0.1	–
Other transactions	-1.0	0.4	0.1	–	0.9	0.3
Bank lending	-1.1	-2.3	–	3.9	-0.5	–
Loans to house purchasers	-3.2	–	0.1	0.2	2.9	–
Other loans	-0.3	-0.1	0.1	–	0.3	-0.1
Overseas securities	-0.1	0.4	–	0.2	0.5	-1.0
Investment abroad (net)	–	0.3	0.1	–	0.1	-0.5
Trade and other credits	-0.1	-0.2	0.5	–	-0.2	-0.1
Official currency financing	–	–	0.6	-0.1	–	-0.5
Unidentified	-0.9	-0.3	–	–	–	0.9
Financial surplus	5.7	-1.0	-4.9	–	0.9	-0.1

Source: Financial Statistics, April 1981, Tables 1.6–1.11 (amended)
[1] Deposits from overseas less bank lending overseas

corporations and general government have been grouped together as the public sector, because so much of their financing is centralized, and the financial companies and institutions sector has been divided into the banking sector and other financial institutions (OFI).

With so many different financial instruments it is inevitable that there should be some degree of grouping in the figures. Thus, for example, all OFI deposits – e.g. building society deposits and Trustee Savings Bank deposits – have been aggregated together. Nevertheless the table does show major distinct categories of liquid savings, contractual saving instruments (life assurance and pension contributions), a variety of forms of borrowing, transactions connected with overseas investment and the management of the foreign exchange reserves (official currency financing). The bottom line shows the financial surpluses and deficits derived from the national income accounts, and the discrepancies between the estimates of transactions in financial assets and these totals are included in the 'unidentified' row.

Since the flow of funds table is a complete description of financial transactions all identified transactions of each sector must be allocated to one or other of the rows in the table. Acquisitions of assets or reductions in liabilities are shown as positive, and reductions in assets or increases in liabilities are negative. Since each *column* shows the transactions for one sector, the sum of the transactions items – the net acquisition of financial assets – is of course equal to the financial surplus or deficit for that sector.

Each *row* of the table shows the transactions by all of the sectors in that particular category of financial instrument. The sum of all the entries in each row is therefore normally zero, because financial instruments are simultaneously liabilities of their issuers and assets of their holders. For example, if the personal sector increases its holdings of bank deposits as an asset (a positive entry in the bank deposits row), banks must at the same time be increasing their liabilities to the personal sector (an equal negative element in the deposits entry for the banking sector). However, there are some exceptions to this rule in the table: under UK company securities the counterpart to 'capital issues' appears under 'other transactions', so the two rows together add to zero; and since the sum of the financial surpluses of all the sectors is (minus) the residual error in the national income accounts,[11] the bottom row does not add to zero and the second-last row ('unidentified') sums to the same total.

The flow-of-funds table helps us to pick out some of the major characteristics of finance in the UK.

Several aspects of the personal sector's financial transactions are

worth commenting on. The personal sector in this period put 6 per cent of GDP per year into highly liquid assets, like notes and coin, bank deposits, and deposits with OFIs. Part of the personal sector's acquisitions of public sector debt (1.6 per cent),[12] e.g. national savings and some securities, can also be regarded as highly liquid. At 4.6 per cent contractual saving through life assurance and pension contributions was also very substantial. But the personal sector sold UK company securities amounting to 1 per cent per year, borrowed heavily for house purchase (3.2 per cent) and also borrowed a significant amount from the banks for a variety of other purposes (1.1 per cent).

Although industrial and commercial companies (the company sector) had a financial deficit of 1 per cent over this period they nevertheless built up their liquid assets (notes and coin, bank and OFI deposits, and public sector debt) by $1\frac{1}{2}$ per cent. Their main source of funds was borrowing from the banks – 2.3 per cent per year. Some companies also raised funds through capital issues of ordinary shares or other securities (0.5 per cent), but companies as a group spent much the same amount on buying the securities of other companies during takeovers and mergers (0.4 per cent); consequently, in aggregate, companies put nearly as much money back into the UK capital market as they drew from it. Companies also used a considerable amount of money to purchase overseas securities (0.4 per cent), and direct investment abroad also exceeded the inflow of funds for direct investment to UK companies by 0.3 per cent.

Turning to the public sector, three points are worth noting. First, the public sector is a lender to other sectors, as well as being an important borrower; for example, in the period shown loans for house purchase and other public sector loans each amounted to an average of 0.1 per cent per year – and they were considerably higher in earlier years. This lending has to be financed, which means that the public sector borrowing requirement (PSBR) is generally greater than the public sector's financial deficit.

Secondly, the public sector may also have to borrow to finance an increase in the foreign exchange reserves (or reduce its borrowing if the reserves fall) – during this 5-year period official currency financing added 0.6 per cent per year to the funds that needed to be raised. Thirdly, the result of the sector's financial deficit and these other requirements was that the public sector had to borrow nearly $6\frac{1}{2}$ per cent of GDP per year by issuing notes and coin, and 'public sector debt' – non-marketable debt, such as national savings certificates, and gilt-edged and other securities.

TABLE 2.10   FLOW OF FUNDS, 1980

(£ billion)

	Personal sector	Industrial and commercial companies	Public sector	Banking sector	Other financial institutions	Overseas sector
Notes and coin	0.4	0.4	– 0.4	– 0.3	–	–
Bank deposits	6.6	3.0	0.4	– 12.1	1.6	0.5[1]
OFI deposits	7.8	–	–	–	– 7.8	–
Life assurance and pension contributions	10.7	–	– 0.3	–	– 10.4	–
Public sector debt	3.6	0.4	– 13.7	2.7	5.5	1.5
UK company securities						
Capital issues	–	– 1.3	–	– 0.4	–	–
Other transactions	– 1.8	0.4	0.2	0.2	2.0	0.9
Bank lending	– 3.0	– 6.6	–	10.3	– 0.6	–
Loans to house purchasers	– 6.9	–	0.5	0.6	5.8	–
Other loans	– 0.4	– 0.5	0.4	–	0.6	– 0.1
Overseas securities	– 0.1	1.2	–	0.9	2.3	– 4.2
Net investment abroad	–	0.2	0.3	0.1	0.2	– 0.9
Trade and other credits	0.6	0.5	– 0.8	–	– 0.7	0.3
Official currency financing	–	–	1.5	– 0.8	–	– 0.7
Unidentified	– 0.8	– 0.4	1.0	1.2 (Banking and OFI combined)		0.1
Financial surplus	16.6	– 2.8	– 11.0	0.9 (Banking and OFI combined)		– 2.7

Source: Financial Statistics, April 1981, Tables 1.6–1.11 (amended)

[1] Deposits from overseas less bank lending overseas

Deposits with the banking sector[13] during this period rose very rapidly, by 4.3 per cent per year, though part (0.6 per cent) consists of deposits from overseas which were employed in lending in this country. Loans to the private sector (bank lending and loans for house purchase), at over 4 per cent, absorbed the bulk of the increase in deposits with most of the balance providing finance for public sector borrowers. Banks are, however, the residual lenders in the economy, and the division of their assets between sectors can vary substantially from year to year.

The increase in OFI liabilities takes two main forms – deposits, and the liabilities of life assurance and pension funds. A high proportion of the personal sector's OFI deposits (3.6 per cent) was channelled back (via building societies) into loans for house purchase (2.9 per cent), while most of the balance was invested in public sector debt. Government debt also attracted a substantial part of the resources at the disposal of the life assurance and pension funds, but these funds were also important buyers of UK company and overseas securities (0.9 per cent and 0.5 per cent respectively).[14]

The figures for the overseas sector show the inflow of money through the banks (bank deposits at 0.6 per cent) and into public sector debt (0.4 per cent). Overseas investors bought UK company securities amounting to 0.3 per cent per year, but sold foreign securities to UK investors equal to an average of 1 per cent. Investment abroad (−0.5 per cent) is the difference between foreign investment in UK companies, averaging over 1 per cent per year, and UK investment in foreign companies which came to about 1.5 per cent year.

Table 2.10 shows the flows of funds for 1980 (the figures are in £ billions). The broad pattern of financing is very similar to that of the previous 5 years, though, since every year has its own special conditions, there are of course differences in detail. Particularly striking features are the very high level of bank lending to industrial and commercial companies (£6.6 billion, or 3 per cent of GDP), and the massive purchases of overseas securities by these companies (£1.2 billion), banks (£0.9 billion) and other financial institutions (£2.3 billion). This reflected the abolition of exchange controls on capital transactions in the previous year and the high exchange rate for sterling which made overseas assets appear cheap.

NOTES

1. Leaving the foreign currency operations of the banks aside.
2. Throughout this book the term, billion, means a thousand million.
3. So far as possible throughout this book saving and investment are measured

after deducting stock appreciation, which is largely a consequence of inflation and is automatically absorbed by the increased value of stocks.

4. A shortfall in domestic saving is reflected in a balance of payments deficit on current account. The statistical estimates of saving and investment are also usually slightly different as a result of errors and omissions in the figures – the residual error in the national income account.
5. The figures for the UK are computed on a slightly different basis from those in Table 2.4 to ensure comparability with other countries.
6. The comparison between saving and investment is complicated by the treatment in the national income accounts of unremitted profits earned abroad. When allowance is made for this the excess of investment over saving is increased.
7. I.e. as owners of physical assets themselves, rather than lending their funds or investing them in securities.
8. Calculated at replacement cost.
9. The financial surplus of the overseas sector is therefore equal to the current balance of payments (with sign reversed) adjusted for capital transfers.
10. The sum of the sector surpluses and deficits in each year should in principle be zero, since total saving (including the net acquisition of foreign assets) must equal total investment. In practice there is a discrepancy, equal to the residual error in the national income accounts.
11. See footnote 4 above.
12. Figures are percentages of GDP.
13. Most overseas depositing and lending activities of the banks have been netted out of the figures. Deposits of the overseas sector measure deposits less loans.
14. About 20 per cent of their funds were also invested in property. This does not appear explicitly in the flow-of-funds table.

PART II THEORY OF THE FINANCIAL SYSTEM

In Part II our task will be to examine in greater depth the means by which the financial system influences saving and investment in the economy. Borrowers and lenders, sellers and buyers of securities, have access to markets for funds in the broad sense, i.e. they can issue liabilities or acquire financial assets on 'market' terms. This does not mean that all vestiges of monopoly power are ruled out, or that the market is free of government intervention; the rate of interest charged to a borrower is likely to reflect the strength of competition amongst lenders for his business, regulations which affect costs, and government subsidies. But access to markets does imply that the rates of interest charged to individual borrowers or paid to lenders are not *arbitrary*, that economic agents in similar situations are accorded the same treatment, and that borrowers and lenders have some choice regarding their sources or uses of finance.

For the first part of the analysis we shall focus on 'the' rate of interest as the price which balances the supply of funds with the demand in financial markets. This single rate is a simplification for the range of rates of interest attached to different financial instruments. The relationship between the rates on different instruments – the *structure* of interest rates – will be discussed later, but changes in the supply or demand for funds overall have a pervasive influence on financial markets so that there is a tendency for interest rates to follow a common trend when demand or supply conditions change. Hence initially we shall suppose that all interest rates move together.

In the following three chapters we examine a number of aspects of the financial system. We begin in Chapter 3 by considering the ways in which financial institutions and markets help to mobilize saving in the economy and channel savings to those who are likely to make best use of them. Asset transformation, the task of transforming risky and illiquid liabilities into safe and liquid assets, and cost reductions are the subjects of Chapter 4. In Chapter 5 we look further at the factors which determine the level of 'the' rate of interest, at the structure of interest rates, and at the influence which the financial system has on the allocation of resources in the economy.

3 MOBILIZING SAVING

In Chapter 1 we drew attention to some of the ways in which financial institutions and markets promoted saving and investment. It was partly a matter of improving the opportunities available to savers, who, as a result of the financial system, were able to obtain higher yields on their savings and to hold them in safer and more liquid forms; partly of altering savers' preferences, so that saving ranked higher in their list of priorities; and partly of giving potential investors access to funds on the scale they required, at a cost which they could afford, and on terms which were acceptable to them. In this chapter we consider the mobilization of saving – the functions of providing facilities for saving, of gathering savings together, and of making saving available to investors.

In what follows we shall assume that saving and investment are brought into balance in the market for funds, as illustrated in Figure 3.1. The level of saving, S, is assumed to increase and of investment, I, to fall as the rate of interest, r, rises; the justification for these assumptions will emerge later. In Figure 3.1 the equilibrium level of saving and investment is OA, and the equilibrium rate of interest is r_0. Anything which shifted the saving schedule to the right would raise the equilibrium level of saving and investment and lower the rate of interest (e.g. an increase in desired saving represented by a shift in the savings schedule from S to S' would increase actual saving and expand investment to OA$'$ and lower the rate of interest to r_1), and anything which shifted investment to the right would also increase saving and investment but raise the rate of interest (e.g. a shift from I to I' would increase saving and investment to OA$''$ and raise the rate of interest to r_2); and vice versa for leftward shifts in the saving and investment schedules.

We shall begin by investigating saving and investment in a rudimentary economy in which individuals are unable to borrow or lend and are therefore constrained by their own incomes and the investment opportunities open to them. We shall then consider the effect

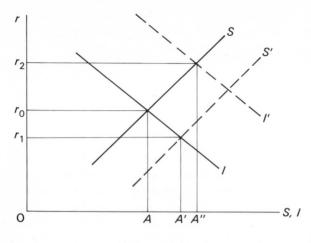

Fig. 3.1

on savers of breaking this budget constraint by allowing them to purchase financial assets or to borrow at some given rate of interest, and we shall examine how this aspect of financial institutions' activities influences the propensity to save. After that we shall turn to investors, the main borrowers of funds, and investigate the effects of giving them access to whatever funds they can usefully employ at the going rate of interest. Finally we shall draw the threads together to see how saving, investment and the rate of interest are affected by the existence of a financial system.

SAVING AND INVESTMENT IN THE ABSENCE OF A FINANCIAL SYSTEM

Consider first an economy without financial institutions or markets. No actual economy is as poorly endowed with financial opportunities as this,[1] but it is nevertheless useful to examine the factors which would influence saving and investment in a very simple, hypothetical economy. We shall work with a two-period model, and we shall assume that every economic agent is both a producer and a consumer. As a producer he has to choose between using resources to produce consumption goods in the first period, or for investment in order to augment the output of consumption goods in the second. As a consumer, he has preferences concerning the time-pattern of his consumption; if he chooses to consume less today it is because he expects to be compensated by a higher level of consumption to-morrow. We assume further that if he neither invests nor disinvests our economic agent will have a given output of consumption goods (or endowment of income) in each period. The decisions taken by the economic agent will depend upon; the *income* from existing resources in the two periods, the *opportunities* to vary the pattern of consumption between the two periods by investment or disinvestment, the agent's *preferences* relating to consumption levels in the two periods.

The income from existing resources and opportunities of changing the pattern of income through investment or disinvestment are illustrated in Figure 3.2. The point A, with incomes OY_1 and OY_2, shows the income in periods 1 and 2 respectively. PP' is a production possibility curve which shows the terms on which, through investment, consumption can be transferred between the two periods; by giving up some of the consumption available in period 1 the economic agent is able to increase his consumption in period 2.[2] If he chooses to move to point B this means that his consumption in the first period is OC_1, and in the second is OC_2. That part of his endowment of income which is not consumed in period 1 is his saving – C_1Y_1 in Figure 3.2 – and this is also a measure of his investment. As a result of saving C_1Y_1 he is able to add C_2Y_2 to his consumption in period 2.

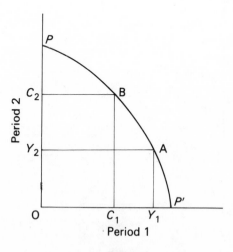

Fig. 3.2

Notice that the ratio of C_2Y_2 to C_1Y_1 decreases as C_1Y_1 increases; as the level of investment rises the marginal return to investment normally falls. The return to investment can be expressed as a rate of interest, r. The additional consumption gained as a result of investing C_1Y_1 in period 1 is $(Y_2C_2 - C_1Y_1)$, so that

$$r = (Y_2C_2 - C_1Y_1)/C_1Y_1$$
$$= (Y_2C_2/C_1Y_1) - 1$$

or

$$Y_2C_2/C_1Y_1 = 1 + r$$

Y_2C_2/C_1Y_1 is simply the average slope of PP' between A and B, showing that the slope of the production possibility curve is equal to $(1+r)$. In this instance r can be either positive or negative.[3]

Economic agents have preferences regarding the time-pattern of their consumption, and these preferences can be represented by an *indifference map*, as in Figure 3.3. Each curve represents combinations of consumption in the two periods, between which the individual is indifferent. Thus since the points X and X' lie on the same indifference curve (I_1) this implies that the individual is equally happy with consumption OC_1 in period 1 and OC_2 in period 2 as he would be with consumption OC_1' and OC_2' in the two periods respectively. Any point on a higher curve, such as I_2 is preferred to

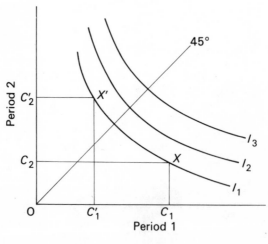

Fig. 3.3

any point on a lower. If the needs of the economic agent in the two periods are perceived to be the same, the curves will be symmetric about the 45° line; and they will also be convex to the origin because the consumer will be willing to depart from an equal consumption pattern only if the increased consumption of one period is sufficient to compensate him for the reduction in the other.[4]

The preferences and opportunities of economic agents can be put together to show what combination of consumption in the two periods he will choose, and this is done in Figure 3.4. Given his income A, the production possibility curve PP' shows the maximum achievable combinations of consumption in the two periods, and the preference map indicates that the highest attainable indifference curve is I_2, where the agent is at point B on PP'. At this point consumption will be OC_1 and OC_2 in periods 1 and 2 respectively. Since income in the first period is OY_1 saving (consumption forgone) amounts to C_1Y_1, and this is invested to produce output of Y_2C_2 in the second period. The implied rate of interest on saving is therefore $[(Y_2C_2/C_1Y_1) - 1)]$.

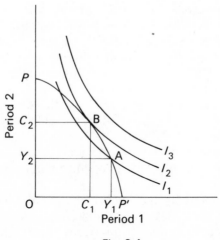

Fig. 3.4

There is no reason to believe that the production opportunities or preferences of all the economic agents in a rudimentary economy of this kind would be identical, and, with lending and borrowing ruled out, each agent would have to make the best of his own position. This means that the implied rates of return on investment would vary, agent to agent, according to each agent's own production possibilities and preferences. There would be no possibility of transferring resources from those agents who could only achieve a low rate of return on investment to those who were able to invest more productively. Moreover, in practice many individuals have very limited opportunities for carrying out real investment projects, almost to the point where no such opportunities may exist at all. In a rudimentary economy such an individual would be constrained to have a time-pattern of consumption which was the same as that of his income, i.e. he would be constrained to remain at point A on indifference curve I_1 in Figure 3.4.

THE RATE OF INTEREST AND SAVING

Now consider the effects of creating a financial system which allows lending and borrowing to take place. For this purpose we shall divide economic agents into two groups – consumers, who have no productive opportunities, and producers, whose sole concern is with production.[5] It is the consumers who are responsible for saving in the economy. The precise mechanism for saving is immaterial at this stage; it could result from the development of either financial markets or financial institutions. The important point is that the individual's budget constraint is broken.

Suppose therefore that consumers have the opportunity to save by lending or to dis-save by borrowing, and that they are faced with a fixed rate of interest, r, which is the same for borrowers and lenders and does not vary with the scale of their borrowing or lending. Their situation and choices open to them can be represented by Figure 3.5.

The point A represents the consumer's income, OY_1 and OY_2 in the two periods respectively and the line RR', which passes through A, represents his consumption opportunities, replacing the production possibility curve for the consumer. The slope of RR' is $(1+r)$, the rate at which consumption in one period can be exchanged for consumption in the other.[6] If $r = 0$, RR' is a 45° line; if the slope is greater (less) than 45°, r is positive (negative). The individual is able to shift from A to the point B on indifference curve I_2, where he consumes OC_1 in period 1 and lends the balance of his income for that period C_1Y_1. This enables him to consume OC_2 in period 2, using the second period income, OY_2, and the repayment with interest of

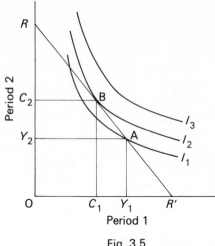

Fig. 3.5

the loan, $Y_2 C_2$. Thus the ability to borrow or lend relaxes the consumer's budget constraint and allows him to improve his position.

It is clear from Figure 3.5 that the amount of saving in period 1 (and correspondingly dis-saving in period 2) will depend upon the slope of the line RR', i.e. upon the rate of interest, r. At some rates of interest the consumer would choose to be a lender, while at others he might choose to borrow. Figure 3.6 enables us to investigate how lending and borrowing are likely to vary with the rate of interest, i.e. to examine the relation between saving and the rate of interest.

Suppose that, as before, the consumer's income is represented by the point A. If the interest rate is represented by the line $R_0 R'_0$, which is tangential to I_1 at A, he will neither save nor dis-save in period 1. With a higher rate of interest, shown by $R_1 R'_1$, the consumer would choose to save by moving to B on I_2; and with a lower rate, shown by $R_2 R'_2$, he would dis-save by moving to C on I_3.

In the vicinity of point A, the consumer's income in the two periods, there is no doubt that a rise in the rate of interest raises the level of saving or reduces dis-saving – there is a positive relation between saving and the rate of interest. But this positive relation does not necessarily continue indefinitely as the rate of interest increases. It is possible that a very high rate of interest would lead to a lower level of saving than prevailed at a somewhat lower rate, though a rate of interest higher than that shown by $R_0 R'_0$ could never lead to actual dis-saving.[7] Though this qualification must be borne in mind, the fact that a positive relation between saving and the rate of

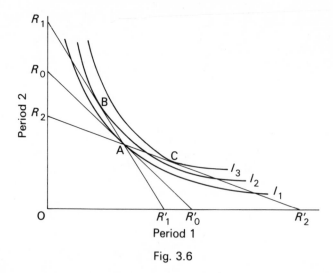

Fig. 3.6

interest must prevail over at least part of the range is the justification for drawing an upward-sloping saving schedule in Figure 3.1.

So far the theory does not allow us to conclude that opening financial markets where none existed previously would necessarily increase saving. At the same time as opportunities for saving become available so do opportunities for borrowing, and if the rate of interest turned out to be low it is theoretically possible that more consumers would avail themselves of the chance to borrow than would choose to save. Whether this is likely to happen in practice is a question which we reserve for later discussion.

A financial system comprises institutions as well as financial markets, and financial institutions have an additional effect on saving; they affect people's attitudes towards it. To many people present needs seem urgent, and those of the future are uncertain and remote. There may therefore be a tendency for people to discount future needs. For this reason institutional arrangements are often devised to ensure that people make some provision for their retirement, and savings institutions put considerable effort into persuading people of the advantages of having funds available in future. We can be confident that these efforts by the financial institutions to market saving will increase the level of saving that actually takes place.

The effect of changing attitudes towards saving can be illustrated by means of indifference curves between current and future consumption. In Figure 3.7 the indifference curves $I_1 - I_3$ reflect a bias in favour of present as against future consumption. If income in the

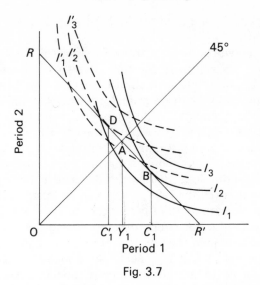

Fig. 3.7

two periods was equal a positive rate of interest would be needed to deter dis-saving. The dashed indifference curves $I_1' - I_3'$ show the effect of marketing efforts and other institutional arrangements which encourage saving. These indifference curves are flatter, because by heightening perceptions of future needs the additional period 2 consumption which is required in order to persuade people to cut their consumption in period 1 has been reduced. As before, RR' shows the savings opportunities which are available, and it can be seen easily that the level of saving for any given interest rate is increased. For example with the income shown at A and the interest rate represented by RR', in the absence of marketing the consumer would choose to move to B, with dis-saving of $Y_1 C_1$. But when the slope of the indifference curves has been changed by the marketing effort he chooses instead to move to D, giving saving of $C_1' Y_1$. The effect of the marketing effort is therefore to raise the level of saving at any rate of interest.

THE RATE OF INTEREST AND INVESTMENT

We turn now to the effects of making the facilities of the financial system available to producers. We imagine that the producer has a certain amount of resources available, and that these can be used to produce either consumption or investment goods. Investment goods produced in period 1 are used by the producer to make consumption goods in period 2.

The producer will now concentrate on maximizing the value of his production, regardless of the time-pattern of his own consumption needs. His consumption in the first period is not determined by his own production of consumption goods at that time, because he can borrow to supplement any deficiency or lend any surplus. Again, the consumption goods produced in the second period can either be used for his own consumption in that period or sold to pay off debts incurred in the first. Thus, while consumption is limited by the total value of his production, decisions concerning the allocation of productive resources in the two periods can be taken quite separately from decisions concerning the time-pattern of consumption.

The value attached to a unit of consumption goods depends on when it is produced, and the relative valuation of consumption goods produced in periods 1 and 2 respectively is measured by the rate of interest. The higher is the rate of interest the less output in period 2 is worth in terms of period 1 output. This is illustrated in Figure 3.8, in which the set of lines labelled RR' are lines of equal value, all having the slope $(1+r)$ so that the value OR on the period 2 axis is $(1+r)$ times OR' on the period 1. The further is the line RR' from the origin the greater is the value represented, so R_0R_0', R_1R_1' etc. are in ascending order of value.

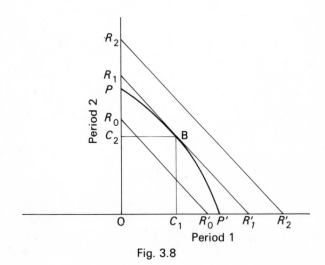

Fig. 3.8

In order to maximize the value of his output the producer will choose to produce OC_1 and OC_2 of consumption goods in periods 1 and 2 respectively, thus placing himself at B on *PP'* where it is tangential to R_1R_1', the highest attainable value line. Measuring investment in terms of consumption goods output forgone, investment is C_1P'. The yield on additional investment at B is just equal to the rate of interest.[8]

It is easy to see from Figure 3.8 how the level of investment will vary with the rate of interest. A fall in r, which implies that the set of *RR'* lines will be flatter, shifts the point B towards the period 2 axis and increases the level of investment. Conversely, a rise in the rate of interest will reduce investment, which is therefore an inverse function of the rate of interest (as indicated by the falling investment schedule in Figure 3.1).

We cannot yet say whether investment in the new situation will be higher or lower than it was in the rudimentary economy. Clearly, if producers had to provide for their own consumption needs there would be some who were unable to take full advantage of investment opportunities; these producers will invest more because the prevailing rate of interest will be lower than the rate of return at the margin of their investment previously. On the other hand, some producers will now invest less because projects which were previously marginal offer too low a return, and it pays them to produce consumption goods in period 1 instead. The net effect depends on how high the interest rate turns out to be. However, we can say that the average quality of the investment that takes place will rise. For it is the producers with opportunities to earn a rate of return higher than the rate of interest who will invest more, whereas those investing less will be those whose investments were comparatively low yielding.

The possibility of borrowing resources also extends the production opportunities open to the producer, who can augment his own resources for investment in the first period, with the loan to be repaid out of part of his period 2 production. This is of the utmost importance, because it means that the scale of investment is not limited to what the investor can find from his own resources, and large-scale investment offers a potentially much higher rate of return than many small scale projects.

This is illustrated in Figure 3.9, in which the production possibility curve *PP'* extends beyond the vertical axis (reflecting the possibility of borrowing) and exhibits economies of scale in the range *XZ*, i.e. in this range the marginal return to investment increases. If the producer was restricted to investing his own resources he

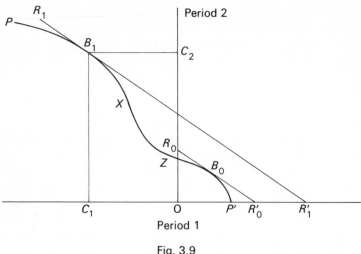

Fig. 3.9

would choose to move B_0, where the value of his output would be OR_0'. But by borrowing OC_1 for investment he can invest a total of C_1P' in period 1, to yield OC_2 of consumption goods in period 2, i.e. he can move to B_1 on PP' and take advantage of the economies of scale. This allows him to produce a higher value of output, OR_1'. Since many of the more attractive investment possibilities entail investment on a scale which greatly exceeds the investing company's own resources in any year, the financial system, which facilitates such investment, contributes greatly to its productivity.

INTERMEDIATION AND INVESTMENT

These effects, which result from the breaking of the budget constraints facing savers and investors, are known as *intermediation* effects.[9] They justify the slopes of the saving and investment schedules in Figure 3.1. These are now repeated in Figure 3.10, which illustrates the effects of intermediation on saving, investment and the rate of interest. The vertical line AB represents the levels of saving and investment in the absence of financial markets; these are of course equal. Saving and investment are shown as independent of the rate of interest, because in the absence of financial markets no uniform rate of interest exists – each economic agent has his own implied rate of interest at the margin of his own saving and investment (as illustrated in Figure 3.4), but there is no reason to suppose

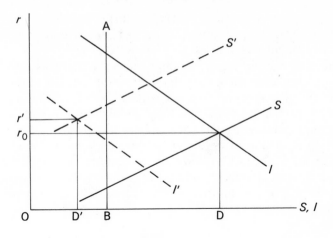

Fig. 3.10

that different agents will have the same implied rate. In contrast, when financial activity is possible, we can expect to have the customary upward-sloping saving schedule and downward-sloping investment schedule as shown. In Figure 3.10 S and I intersect at the equilibrium rate of interest, r_0, with saving and investment at OD. In this figure D falls to the right of B, indicating higher levels of saving and investment when intermediation is possible than in a rudimentary system.

This is much the most probable outcome. The provision of opportunities for saving and active marketing of savings facilities are likely to raise the level of saving and so push S out to the right. And the mobilization of saving to finance large scale investment raises the investment schedule. It is therefore unlikely that the introduction of a financial system would reduce saving and investment. But it is a theoretical possibility that cannot be ruled out altogether. In Figure 3.10 S' and I' have been drawn to intersect at a level of saving and investment OD', which is less than OB in the rudimentary case. The problem is that the opening of financial markets and institutions gives *consumers* as well as producers access to credit, so that the net supply of saving may actually be reduced. It is not a very likely occurrence, but it cannot be ruled out altogether. It would, for example, be quite rational for consumers to choose to borrow in excess of their current income if they expected incomes to be much larger in future – as might, perhaps, occur if an important natural resource was discovered in a small country. Nevertheless,

even in this case, the effect on future output would not necessarily
be adverse, because, as noted on p. 45, the average productivity
of the investment which did take place would rise.

Some countries, however, attempt to ensure that financial markets
do promote investment rather than consumption. Governments may
restrict consumers' access to the financial markets or ensure that the
cost of consumer borrowing is high. Similar discrimination against
certain types of investment, deemed by the government to be of a
comparatively low priority (e.g. investment in land or some buildings)
may also take place. This allows governments to obtain the advantages of improved opportunities for saving, whilst ensuring that a
very high proportion of that saving is directed towards productive
investment.

NOTES

1. We are even assuming the absence of a medium of exchange.
2. The reverse process, shifting consumption from period 2 to period 1, is more
   difficult, but can occur to some extent through the consumption of capital.
3. Which would imply that the additional consumption gained in period 2 was
   less than the amount given up in period 1.
4. This is the assumption of a diminishing marginal rate of substitution in
   consumption.
5. Consumer/producers may be regarded as taking consumption and production
   decisions separately.
6. Strictly speaking the slope of RR' is minus $(1+r)$.
7. An increase in the rate of interest has both income and substitution effects.
   It is possible that the income effect may lead the consumer to demand more
   consumption in period 1 and less in period 2, thereby discouraging saving.
   The substitution effect of an increase in the rate of interest will always tend
   to increase saving.
8. I.e. at B on PP', the additional period 2 output obtained by forgoing one unit
   of period 1 output is $(1+r)$.
9. See, for example, Basil J. Moore, *An Introduction to the Theory of Finance*,
   Chapter 1.

4 ASSET TRANSFORMATION

When we took a preliminary look at the financial system in Chapter 1 we noted that financial institutions and markets had the dual functions of transferring resources from savers to investors and of helping both these groups to obtain financial instruments with the characteristics they wanted.

Savers needs are in fact very varied. While some are prepared to put money away for a long time and to accept a certain degree of risk, the majority are most concerned with the safety of their savings and put a premium on liquidity – the ability to turn them into cash at short notice. Investors' requirements also cover a very wide range; for some it is long-term capital which is required, preferably without any obligation to repay if a project proves unsuccessful, while for others funds may be required for only a short period and can be repaid with a high degree of certainty. The needs of some savers and some investors do not therefore necessarily conflict, though even when no conflict exists the financial system has the task of bringing those with matching requirements together. However, taking saving as a whole there is a strong bias towards a preference for safety and liquidity, whereas on the investment side the principal need is for long-term finance which must frequently be exposed to a significant degree of risk.

In the absence of financial institutions and markets some compromise would have to be found. This would inevitably be unsatisfactory to both parties, and would be liable to reduce the levels of saving and investment in the economy. Moreover, the processes of bringing savers and investors together and agreeing terms would be costly, and this too would be likely to depress investment activity. Thus, in addition to their function of releasing savers and investors from budget constraints, which we discussed in the last chapter, the financial system also has to transform the risk-bearing liabilities of ultimate borrowers into safe assets for lenders, to transform long-maturity liabilities into liquid assets, and to reduce the costs incurred in the saving/investment process.

In this chapter we examine how these functions are carried out. We deal first with risk, and show how unnecessary risks can be avoided and those that remain can be borne by those savers most willing to take risk. Then we go on to maturity transformation and liquidity. Finally we consider the means employed to cut transactions costs and show how a reduction in these costs benefits savers and investors and raises the level of financial activity in the economy.

RISK TRANSFORMATION

Investment is an inherently risky activity, though the degree of risk depends upon the form the investment takes. The results of business activity are always unpredictable, and while businessmen may attempt to reduce risk, by such means as diversifying their activities, integrating with suppliers or customers, or entering into long-term contracts, they cannot eliminate risk altogether. The costs and benefits of investment by public authorities are equally uncertain. Constructing and equipping a new hospital may cost much more than anyone expected at the time the decision to build was taken; the running costs may turn out to be higher than anticipated; or the need and therefore usage may turn out to be less. Even investment in housing carries an element of risk; the area may decline, perhaps as a result of a recession in local industry, with a consequential fall in the value of property.

In every case the risk must be borne by someone. With public authority investment it is the taxpayer who bears the risk, because the government taps the savings market by issuing loans, and guarantees the saver against loss. With houses the risk is shared between the owner and the mortgagor, though the latter bears little risk unless the sum lent lies close to the market value of the property. In the case of business investment the risk is borne by the owners of the financial assets which form the firm's capital, but the capital is usually divided into debt and equity, and the risk is not borne equally by both parts. The debt component is relatively safe, often secured on some of the firm's assets or by 'covenants' inserted into loan agreements; these covenants usually give the lender the right to immediate repayment if the firm fails to carry out its obligations. The business risk – the variability of income or capital value associated with business activity

– is therefore concentrated on the firm's equity, to which the benefits of a good performance accrue or which absorbs the first slice of any loss.

This division of companies' liabilities into distinct categories with very different degrees of risk exposure is vitally important to the working of the financial system, because it permits savers and institutions who are averse to risk to specialize in low-risk financial instruments, whilst leaving other savers or institutions whose needs do not inhibit the holding of risky assets to specialize in the function of risk-bearing. It is paralleled by a distinction between *default* risk and *equity* risk.

Default risk is attached to debt: it is the risk that the borrower will default on his obligations, i.e. that he will fail to pay interest or to repay the loan itself when it is due. The probability of default is a measure of default risk and a safe asset is one for which this probability is zero, i.e. there is complete confidence that interest will be paid and capital repaid as agreed at the outset. The holders of debt instruments such as deposits or loans normally wish to ensure that the default risk is low (loans) or even negligible (deposits), and the charge for a loan will include a premium – fixed at the time the loan is granted – to compensate the lender for the risk of loss. Thus, while the rate of interest which a borrower must pay for a loan reflects the risk of loss contemplated at the time the loan is granted, it does not normally depend on how successful he turns out to be in using the funds profitably.

Equity risk derives from the uncertainty surrounding the income which will be earned by business assets. Because the income is uncertain the future value of the assets themselves cannot be predicted exactly, and neither can the remuneration which the holder of equity assets will receive. The return to the equity-holder is therefore related to the profitability of the enterprise in question. If the enterprise is successful equity assets will maintain or increase their value, whereas if it is a failure the value of the equity will be reduced or even lost altogether.

While the conceptual distinction between default risk for debt and variability of return for equity is useful, it is not in fact absolutely clear-cut in practice. Default does not necessarily imply total loss to the lender; it is really a question of varying amounts of loss with different probabilities. And very occasionally, when the risk entailed in a project seems too high for a straightforward loan, lenders may nevertheless agree to grant the loan, but on condition that they receive some additional income if the project is successful.[1]

DEFAULT RISK

Risk transformation is one important function of deposit-taking institutions like banks and building societies. The depositors who hold the institutions' liabilities must be able to regard them as absolutely safe. The institutions' loans, however, inevitably bear some default risk. Their ability to transform these risky assets into riskless liabilities depends on three things; the risk of loss on each loan, controlling their risks, providing sufficient capital of their own to absorb any unexpected losses.

Lenders go about the task of trying to ensure that the probability of any individual loan going into default is low in a number of ways. First, they consider the purpose of the loan, and whether they think it is legitimate. Legitimate purposes would include house purchase, investment by a firm in new plant and equipment or stocks, purchase of consumer durables, or the temporary finance of a peak in a consumer's spending. But to make a loan which was intended to enable a borrower to live beyond his means, or to allow a business to maintain its working capital during a period of continuing and persistent losses, would usually be regarded as unjustified. Secondly, the lender considers the borrower's income. In the case of a house mortgage or a consumer instalment loan, he wishes to be satisfied that the borrower has sufficient income to pay the interest and make capital payments on the agreed terms, without undue strain. In the case of a loan to a business, he will wish to be satisfied that the borrower has sufficient income to meet the terms of the loan, either from his other activities or from the income generated by assets purchased with the loan itself. In reaching a decision the lender will often rely heavily on his judgment of the borrower, rather than on the precise project for which the loan is required. Thirdly, the lender may look for security over assets. If the borrower should be unable to carry out his commitments under the loan agreement, the lender with a charge over marketable assets such as buildings or marketable securities may be able to recover his loan, albeit with some cost and delay. Alternatively, the security may in effect be provided by a firm's existing activities; if the firm is itself in a position to absorb losses, the loan may not be at risk. Finally, the lender may reduce the risk of loss on his loan by writing 'covenants' into the loan agreement, so that he is able to demand immediate repayment of the loan if there is a serious risk that the firm will be unable to carry out its obligations. Unless the lender is reasonably confident that he will get his money back he is unlikely to accede to a loan request.

The second method through which deposit-taking institutions limit the risk of loss is by pooling risks. Deposit-taking institutions try to make a large number of small loans rather than a small number of large ones, because, although this does not reduce the expected loss on their portfolio of loans overall, it does give considerably improved predictability and limits the *maximum* loss for which the institution has to allow. By making a large number of loans institutions can expect their actual loss experience to be very close to the average loss rate for that type of business, whereas if only a small number of loans were made the institution might have the misfortune to find that an unusually high proportion had gone sour.

The effect of spreading risks on the maximum loss which an institution need contemplate, for various sizes of loan portfolio, is illustrated in Table 4.1. It is assumed that the chance of default on any single loan is 1 in 100 (i.e. the probability of default, $p = 0.01$) and that the risks are *independent*, in the sense that the fact that one borrower defaults on a loan makes it neither more nor less likely that other borrowers will default too. The first two columns of the table show how the number and percentage of losses respectively which the institution might expect on average rise as the number of loans made by the institution increases from 10 to 10 000. But the institution may be unlucky and find that more borrowers default, so it has to guard against the possibility that more than 1 per cent of its loans will fail: with 1000 loans it might reasonably expect that on average ten would be lost, but if it was lucky it might lose only five and if it was unlucky it could lose fifteen or more – if it was exceptionally unlucky it might even experience, say, forty losses.

The institution can never entirely rule out the possibility that losses will be greater than it has allowed for. What it can do is decide

TABLE 4.1   LOAN LOSSES WHERE $p = 0.01$

Number of loans	Expected number (%) of losses	Maximum tolerable[1] number (%) of losses
10	0 (0)	1 (10)
100	1 (1)	4 (4)
1000	10 (1)	19 (1.9)
10000	100 (1)	126 (1.26)

[1] Probability of greater number < 0.005

on the risk it is prepared to take that losses will exceed the amount for which it has provided, and make allowance for losses accordingly. In Table 4.1 it has been assumed that the institution is prepared to accept a 1 in 200 chance that it will suffer losses greater than the maximum number for which it has allowed. The third column of the table shows how this maximum tolerable number of losses increases with the number of loans, and the final column expresses those losses as a percentage of loans granted.[2] It can be seen very clearly that with a small number of loans the maximum percentage loss with which the institution has to contend is substantially above the average level of 1 per cent – for example, 4 per cent if 100 loans are made – but as the number of loans increases the maximum tolerable loss moves steadily closer towards the average. By the time an institution had 10 000 loans in its portfolio it could rely on its loss experience being little worse than the average for that type of loan.

The conclusion, however, does depend critically on the institution's ability to control the level of risk on each loan successfully (to 1 per cent in this example) and on the default risks being independent. Achieving an adequate spread of risk is not merely a matter of making a large number of loans. Banks try to ensure that their loans are not concentrated too heavily in any single branch of economic activity or any single area of the country. For example, if the exchange rate is overvalued exporting industries as a whole may get into difficulties, and the probability of losses in that part of a bank's loan portfolio will rise. Similarly, if the economy of one part of the country goes through a difficult period, perhaps as a result of the failure of a major industry, loans to other enterprises which depend upon the prosperity of the area will also be threatened. Institutions also seek to restrict the maximum size of any single loan, because clearly the risk of one large loan is much greater than that of the equivalent number of small loans.

The expected default risk will normally be incorporated in the charge made for a loan. If a bank expects that on average 1 per cent of its loans to a particular category of borrower will be lost each year, then a charge of 1 per cent will be included in the rate of interest paid by such borrowers on loans. This loading for default risk will of course vary between categories of loans, corresponding to the different levels of loss anticipated.

While institutions can include a premium for the *expected* level of losses in the charges they make to borrowers, in the nature of things they cannot charge for unexpected losses. The protection for depositors against unpredicted losses lies in the capital and reserves (the equity) of the financial institution. Losses in excess of those predicted are born by the institution's own capital, and the liabilities to depositors are threatened only if losses are so high that all of the institution's capital is used up. In order to provide adequate protection to depositors the size and concentration of loans in an institution's portfolio is often related to the scale of its own capital and reserves. For example, banks would not regard it as safe to make loans amounting to more than 10 per cent of their own capital to any single borrower; and an excessive concentration of loans for one single activity, such as property development, could endanger depositors' funds.[3]

No matter how well an institution may spread its risk there remains a significant danger that it will experience unexpectedly heavy losses. Its average loss experience may rise because it fails to control its risks properly or, as is more likely, because of a change in the general level of losses associated with the kinds of business in which it is engaged. For example, bankruptcies in the economy are influenced by the general level of economic activity, and there is little that any single bank can do to protect itself entirely from the effects of economic fluctuations. Institutions with large and diversified portfolios are in fact much more vulnerable to fluctuations in loss experience for this kind of reason than they are to excessive losses due to the inherent uncertainty attached to individual loans.

The ability of financial institutions to transform risky loans into safe deposits depends then upon the three factors we have discussed. They need to *control* risk and incorporate an allowance for probable losses in the charge they make for loans; they must *spread* risk to guard against the possibility that loans to some customers or categories of customer will lead to unusually heavy losses; and they must ensure that their own *capital* is adequate to absorb any losses they may incur through a failure to control risk properly, adverse economic conditions, or concentration of lending in their portfolios.

EQUITY RISK

Financial institutions and markets also transform equity risk in the economy. The principal institutions which perform this function in the UK are the investment and unit trusts, which provide specialized fund management services, and the life assurance and pension funds, which manage very large asset portfolios corresponding to their liabilities to policyholders or members respectively. The key to transforming equity risk lies in diversification – the spreading of assets over a number of different holdings. Spreading ensures that there will be some degree of offsetting between losers and winners, so that the saver avoids the extremes and can reasonably expect his return to reflect the average performance of the kinds of investment made.

Suppose that a person invests £1000 in the ordinary shares of a firm. The value of the investment in a year's time, that is the price of the shares plus any dividends received, is uncertain. Let us call this v. The value, v, may have risen above £1000 or fallen below it. However, the investor will believe that some ranges of value are more likely than others, and we can draw a frequency distribution showing the probability or likelihood he attaches to v lying in certain ranges in a year's time. These probabilities reflect nothing more than the saver's guesses as to the future values, e.g. a probability of 0.4 that v will lie in a certain range implies that the saver thinks that there is a 40 per cent chance of this outcome.

Figure 4.1 illustrates one possible frequency distribution. For example, the probability that v will lie in the range £800–£1000 is shown as 0.25. With this frequency distribution the average value[4] of v would be £1098.

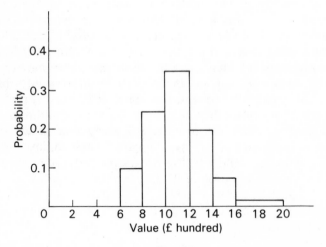

Fig. 4.1

Where the outcome of an investment is unpredictable, as it is in this example, the investment is clearly risky. To conform with everyday usage we shall say that the risk increases with the spread of the frequency distribution; a risky investment is one in which the possibility of an outcome either much greater or much less than the average is substantial. The most common measure of risk is in fact the *standard deviation* of the frequency distribution, a measure which increases as the spread widens.[5]

The frequency distribution of v is usually shown as a continuous curve, with the arithmetic mean, or *expected value*, written as μ and the standard deviation as σ, as illustrated in Figure 4.2.

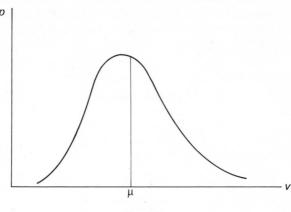

Fig. 4.2

Suppose now that instead of making one single investment of £1000 with expected value, μ and risk, σ, the saver makes n investments of £1000 each with expected values, $\mu_1 \ldots \mu_n$, and risk, $\sigma_1 \ldots \sigma_n$. Suppose further that the investments are *independent*, in the sense that the value of each one of them at the end of the year is entirely unaffected by the values of all the others. If we write the value of the whole portfolios as V, with expected value μ_p and standard deviation (risk) σ_p, it can be shown that

$$\mu_p = \mu_1 + \mu_2 + \ldots + \mu_n,$$

i.e. the expected value of the portfolio is the sum of the expected values of the n investments, and,

$$\sigma_p = \sqrt{(\sigma_1^2 + \sigma_2^2 \ldots + \sigma_n^2)}.$$

In the special case where the expected values and risks of the n investments are all the same, say μ and σ respectively, this reduces to

$$\mu_p = n\mu$$

$$\sigma_p = \sigma\sqrt{n}$$

i.e. the expected value of the portfolio increases in proportion to the number of elements in it, but the risk increases in proportion only to the square root of the number of investments.

Now let us use this example to examine how diversification reduces risk. Compare the risk *per £1000 invested* of investing a capital sum on the one hand in a single asset and on the other in equal amounts of n assets, each with the same risk σ. In the case of the single investment the risk will be σ as before, but if n investments are made the risk per £1000 falls to $\sigma/\sqrt{n}$ – that is the spread of the frequency distribution is reduced by a factor of $\sqrt{n}$.[6]

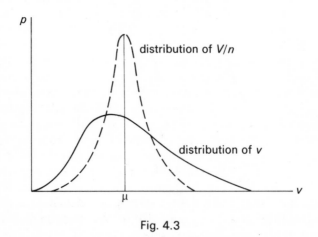

Fig. 4.3

Figure 4.3 illustrates the effect of diversification on the frequency distribution of the return to investment. The frequency distribution of v illustrates the distribution for each single investment of £1000, while that of V/n shows the corresponding distribution per £1000 of the entire portfolio. It can be seen that if all the individual investments have the same expected value μ, the distribution of V/n also has the expected value μ but that it is more concentrated than the distribution of v, and will also generally become more symmetric about μ than the individual distributions.[7] Thus diversification – the spreading of assets over a number of separate holdings – reduces the risk to which the holder is exposed.

The relation between the risk of a portfolio and the number of securities amongst which it is divided depends crucially on the assumption that the values of the individual securities are independent. In general this is unlikely to be the case; for example, during a boom share prices tend to rise together so that a high value of one investment is associated with high values of others. Interdependence of this kind, known as positive covariance, increases the risk of the portfolio as a whole.

On the other hand, the example which assumed that the risks of the individual securities were independent, understates the extent to which it may be possible to reduce risk through diversification. Risk can be reduced even further if the portfolio is divided between assets whose values tend to deviate in *opposite* directions from their expected values. For example, if two companies in some industry are in keen competition and each accounts for a substantial share of the market, an improvement in the profitability of one due to a gain in market share will be matched by reduced profitability for the other company. By holding shares in both companies the saver would be able to eliminate that part of the risk attached to variations in market share. When a gain in the value of one share is associated with a loss in the value of another, we say that there is *negative covariance*. Negative covariance within a portfolio reduces risk.[8]

Financial markets, which allow the equity of a company to be broken down into smaller lots, make diversification a practical possibility. They give both individuals and institutions the ability to divide their asset portfolios amongst a number of investments. However, the transactions costs involved in buying and selling securities militate against very small holdings and many savers have insufficient resources to obtain an adequate spread of investments themselves at a reasonable cost. This is one reason why financial institutions, which are able to diversify their own portfolios, can offer an attractive service.

THE PROVISION OF LIQUIDITY

Financial markets and institutions also make it possible to satisfy investors' needs for permanent or long-term capital and many savers' desires for a high degree of liquidity in their assets simultaneously. Since the financial institutions which transform maturities and provide savers with liquidity rely to some extent on the existence of good asset markets, we shall consider the ways in which the markets contribute to liquidity first.

When there is an active market for a financial asset a holder is able to obtain cash before the asset's maturity date, which may be some way off in the case of bonds, and indeed does not exist at all for irredeemable securities including ordinary shares. An active market, with many competing buyers and sellers, also means that the holder can rely on receiving a fair price at the time he sells. This will not in general be the same as the value of the asset at maturity (where applicable), but it is fair in the sense that the seller does not have to bargain from a position of weakness at the time he wishes to make the sale. The provision of liquidity – the ability to turn securities into cash at short notice – is one of the principal functions of organized financial markets.

Markets operate successfully when transactors have differing needs, a variety of motives for dealing, or differing views about the value of securities. It is such differences which generate trading activity and which make it likely that a seller of a security will be able to find a buyer without difficulty. For example, in the ordinary share market, in any period sales are likely to be made by executors for estates, who have to raise cash in order to pay capital transfer tax, and purchases will be made by pension funds, which are receiving an inflow of contributions to invest. In the interbank market one bank which has access to deposits but no immediate need for additional cash will lend to another with excess loan demand. In the gilt-edged market a pension fund, which prefers to hold long-dated securities, will sell stocks for which the remaining term is short, perhaps to a bank, which is anxious to increase the more liquid part of its portfolio. Or, returning to the share market, two institutional investors may hold differing opinions about the future profitability of a particular company, and the pessimist will sell the shares to the optimist.

Transactions in securities can and do take place outside organized markets, but the existence of an organized market which brings together a large number of potential transactors in securities is one means of providing liquidity and of making it easier for buyers and sellers to deal. For example, in the sterling money markets the brokers are in touch with a large number of institutions or other clients, some of whom may have spare funds whilst others are likely to be short of funds. By dealing through the broker each institution can make contact easily with a suitable counterpart, and it is the broker's range of contacts which makes it possible for the single client to place funds or obtain funds readily.

In some markets, such as the stock market, there are professional market-makers – economic agents who find the price at which buying and selling orders match or who are themselves prepared to buy or sell on request. In the German stock exchanges, for example, these market-makers simply record buying and selling orders and calculate the price at which they will be equal. In Britain, by contrast, the 'jobbers' on the Stock Exchange are prepared to buy or sell on request and hold a stock of the financial asset in question which they either add to or run down. Similarly, in the UK Treasury bill market, the Discount Houses, who are the market-makers, act as principals and hold a stock of bills. Dealers who are prepared to act as principals add to liquidity in the market because they enable sellers to make a sale without delay. In the absence of professional dealers a seller might find that there were no buyers forthcoming, and have to wait some time before a buyer could be found.

The main providers of liquidity amongst the financial institutions are the deposit-taking institutions like banks and building societies. They contribute to the liquidity of the financial system by issuing liabilities (deposits) with a maturity shorter than their assets. In order to do this they rely on; the law of averages, as it affects their depositors and borrowers, structured asset portfolios, including assets with varying degrees to liquidity, access to financial markets, in which some of these assets can be sold before maturity.

The application of the law of averages to default risk has already been discussed, and it was shown that by making a large number of loans an institution could avoid the risk that its experience would depart far from the general average. The same principle can be applied to the deposit-taking activities of clearing banks or building societies. They know that in any period some of their depositors will wish to encash their deposits, but they can be reasonably confident that at the same time others will wish to make new deposits with them. In the case of banks, while they must assume that some borrowers will wish to make greater use of their overdraft facilities, the demands of others are likely to fall. Institutions therefore need liquidity only to cover the *net* position. The *maximum* demand for cash against which the institution needs to guard is determined by the same considerations as before. A large number of depositors reduces the maximum percentage deposit loss which is likely, and independence between depositors also reduces deposit variability. Indeed, negative covariance may help to reduce the institution's liquidity requirements. For example, a clearing bank, which has both individuals and shops amongst its customers, knows that a reduction in the deposits in one group is likely to be partly offset by an increase in the deposits of the other.

Cash inflows and outflows will not match exactly; some variability in the cash demands by an institution's depositors remains. By holding a structured asset portfolio the institution ensures that it can honour its liabilities. The institution must keep a proportion of its assets in a liquid form, some highly liquid to deal with short-term variability in its cash needs, and some less so but which can be realized if there is a persistent need for cash – due, for example, to a steady deposit loss or a sustained rise in the demand for loans. The liquidity of the institution's portfolio ought to reflect the volatility and maturity structure of its liabilities. Where deposits are of short maturity and volatile the institution must maintain a high level of liquidity, and cannot afford to hold a significant proportion of long-maturity assets in its portfolio.

Maturity transformation by financial institutions depends ultimately on their continued access to markets, particularly markets for deposits. Institutions must be able to remain competitive in the (informal) market for deposits, for if they do not they are liable to suffer a persistent loss of deposits. For this reason many deposit-taking institutions lend at variable rates of interest with the rate set by means of a link to some standard rate, which in turn moves with deposit interest rates. Thus if the deposit rate becomes uncompetitive, the institution is able to raise both deposit and lending rates together, without the risk that its own profitability will be endangered by a narrowing of its margins. Such a link may be formal, as in the case of bank overdrafts quoted as base rate plus a fixed margin, or it may be a matter of practice, as with the building societies which generally change deposit and loan rates together. Institutions in other countries, such as the Savings and Loan Associations in the USA, have sometimes run into difficulties as a result of making long-term loans at fixed rates of interest, and finding subsequently that their deposit-rates were uncompeitive.

Continued access to the deposit market is of prime importance to those banks which borrow a high proportion of their deposits in this market. Their deposits are generally for fixed terms, and they rely on their ability to obtain new deposits in order to refinance loans when their existing deposits fall due. They depend therefore entirely on their ability to bid for funds by offering a competitive interest rate, and on the maintenance of their 'reputation' in financial circles. If even a shadow of doubt is cast over the soundness of a financial institution it is liable to find itself faced with a withdrawal of deposits and an inability to obtain new deposits in the market. This is what happened in Britain during the secondary banking crisis in 1974/5, when many institutions which otherwise appeared to be sound experienced considerable difficulty in renewing deposits and had to seek help from the Bank of England and the clearing banks.

Access to markets also helps the financial institutions to maintain a suitable degree of liquidity in their asset portfolios. Without such markets it might be difficult for them to find enough liquid financial instruments for their needs, and because they know that higher-yielding but somewhat longer-dated financial instruments can be sold if necessary, they are able to earn a higher yield on their asset portfolios. For example, 5-year gilt-edged securities held by the banks can be sold if need be in order to replenish their more liquid assets.

REDUCING TRANSACTIONS COSTS

Financial markets and institutions also assist the users of the system by reducing the transactions costs they face – the time and trouble as well as the actual expense of conducting business. They do this in a number of ways. First, they provide convenient places of business, to which savers with funds to lend and borrowers in search of money can go, thereby avoiding the need to seek out a suitable counterpart on each occasion. Secondly, the financial institutions provide standardized products, thereby cutting the information costs associated with scrutinizing individual financial instruments. Thirdly, they specialize and operate on a substantial scale, which enables them to acquire expertise and cut costs through the use of tested procedures and routines. Finally, within the markets there are supervisory committees with a responsibility for surveillance, whose job it is to maintain the quality of the financial instruments traded by means of centralized monitoring and to ensure that the market participants conform with accepted codes of behaviour. This frees the users of the markets from the need to collect the information and carry out the detailed analysis which would be required in order to make their own assessment.

The financial system in Britain relies on competition between financial institutions and within financial markets to keep down operating costs. It is competition that determines the margins between deposit and lending rates which banks can earn on their business and low cost competitors undercut their rivals in order to expand their share of the market. Institutions which have persistently higher costs than their competitors are likely to go out of business. In some instances, however, competition is muted as a result of agreements amongst the participants; the effect of such agreements on operating costs within the financial system is a subject to which we shall return later.

In Chapter 3 we made the simplifying assumption that the rate of interest facing borrowers and lenders was the same. In reality, however, the cost to a borrower is higher than the return received by the lender, because it is the gross cost (interest + expenses) which is relevant to the former and the net return (interest − expenses) which is relevant to the lender. Figure 4.4 illustrates the effect of transactions costs on financial activity.

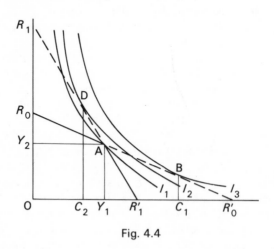

Fig. 4.4

As before let us suppose that an individual has income given by point A in the diagram, i.e. OY_1 in period 1 and OY_2 in period 2. However, now instead of being faced by a single rate of interest he receives the rate, r_0, represented by $R_0R'_0$ if he acts as a lender, but has to pay the rate, r_1, represented by $R_1R'_1$ if he is a borrower. The individual's opportunity line is therefore $R_0AR'_1$ in Figure 4.4, and with the indifference curves shown in the figure he would choose to remain at point A, neither borrowing nor lending. If the borrowing rate had been r_0 he would have chosen to move to point B and to borrow Y_1C_1, whereas if the lending rate had been r_1 he would have moved to D and lent C_2Y_1. Transactions costs, which open up a gap between borrowing and lending rates, therefore discourage financial activity. Clearly the closer r_0 and r_1 are together – i.e. the lower are transactions costs – the more likely it is that either borrowing or lending will take place.

By reducing the transactions costs faced by borrowers and lenders, the financial system cuts the gross cost of funds to borrowers and raises the net return to savers. On the normal assumptions about

savers' and investors' behaviour the lower cost to borrowers will raise
the level of investment and the rise in the return to savers will raise
the level of saving.

ASSET TRANSFORMATION AND THE LEVELS OF SAVING AND INVESTMENT

We shall conclude this chapter by analysing the effects of asset transformation on savings and investment and on the rate of interest in
the economy. There is no doubt that a reduction in transactions
costs raises investment, lowers the rate of interest paid by borrowers,
and raises the return which lenders receive. This is illustrated in
Figure 4.5.

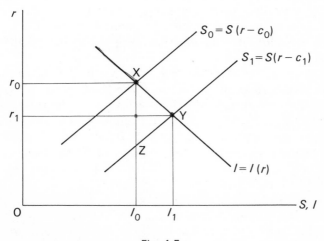

Fig. 4.5

It is necessary at this stage to distinguish between the rate of
interest paid by the borrower, which we shall continue to denote by
r, and that received by the lender, which we shall denote by $r - c$,
where c covers the operating and any other transaction costs incurred
by borrowers and lenders. In Figure 4.5 the investment schedule is
shown as a declining function of r, as before, and the saving schedule
is a rising function of $(r - c)$. In the initial position, in the absence of
financial institutions and markets, we suppose that transactions costs
amount to c_0, and the equilibrium is at point X, with investment
(equal to saving) OI_0 and the rate of interest at r_0. Now suppose that

the financial system reduces transactions costs to c_1, the difference between c_0 and c_1 being represented by XZ. The saving schedule therefore moves to S_1, and investment rises to OI_1 with the rate of interest paid by borrowers falling to r_1. As Figure 4.5 shows the reduction in the rate of interest from r_0 to r_1 is less than the reduction in transactions costs, XZ, so the net return to savers also increases.

The effects of risk and maturity transformation are less clear-cut. There is no doubt that they will increase borrowers' demands for funds. Firms which are able to match the maturity of their assets and liabilities and which have good access to equity capital can limit risks arising from the structure of their financing, and this makes it possible for them to contemplate embarking on more risky investment projects. This is illustrated in Figure 4.6. The position before asset transformation is available is shown by the schedules labelled I and S, giving a level of investment OI_0 and a rate of interest r_0. The effect of asset transformation on investment is to shift the I schedule to I' and this alone would raise investment to OI_1 and the rate of interest to r_1.

Unfortunately, however, we cannot deduce from *a priori* argument that asset transformation will increase the level of saving. The problem lies in the precautionary objective for saving, because improved liquidity and lower risk mean that the amount of wealth required to satisfy precautionary needs is reduced. It is therefore theoretically possible that asset transformation might reduce the level of saving.

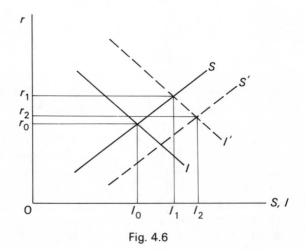

Fig. 4.6

However, there are two reasons why this is unlikely in practice. First, the improvement in the characteristics of the financial instruments available to savers must make saving more attractive, especially saving through the financial system as opposed to accumulating physical assets. Secondly, in the absence of suitable financial instruments people may choose not to save but instead employ other social arrangements to provide for their support. For example, it may be customary for people who are in need to fall back on family and friends, rather than to attempt to accumulate sufficient wealth to stand on their own feet. If these effects are dominant, the saving schedule will shift from S to some position such as S' in the diagram, investment will rise further to OI_2 and the rate of interest will fall to r_2 (which may even lie below r_0).[9] Thus in normal circumstances we can expect asset transformation to encourage both saving and investment and to raise the level of investment in the economy.

NOTES

1. In other words, they demand an element of equity return for taking on equity risk.
2. The number of losses has been calculated using the Poisson or Normal distribution, as appropriate.
3. And did in fact do so in the UK in the financial crisis of 1975.
4. I.e. the mid-points of the ranges weighted by their probabilities.
5. The standard deviation is the square root of the *variance* measured as $\Sigma f(v-\mu)^2$ where v and μ are the values and mean value of the share respectively and f is the probability attached to each value, v.
6. Of each £1000 of the portfolio, £1000/n goes in every asset. So the risk of each investment is σ/n, and with n such investments σ_p is equal to $(\sigma\sqrt{n})/n = \sigma/\sqrt{n}$.
7. If n is large the distribution of V/n takes on the shape of the *Normal* distribution.
8. The effects of covariance on risk can be illustrated in the following way. Suppose that a portfolio is divided between two shares X_1 and X_2 in the proportions a_1 and a_2 ($= 1-a_1$), with expected values μ_1 and μ_2 respectively. Suppose that the variances are σ_1^2 and σ_2^2 and the covariance (defined as $\Sigma f(v_1 - \mu_2)(v_2 - \mu_2)$, where f is the probability of v_1 and v_2 occurring together) is σ_{12}. It is convenient to write σ_{12} in terms of the correlation R_{12} between X_1 and X_2, since R_{12} lies between -1 and $+1$.

$$\sigma_{12} = R_{12}\,\sigma_1\,\sigma_2$$

If the total return on the portfolio is V, with mean μ_p, and variance σ_p^2,

$$\mu_p = a_1\mu_1 + a_2\mu_2$$

and

$$\sigma_p^2 = a_1^2 \sigma_1^2 + 2a_1 a_2 R_{12} \sigma_1 \sigma_2 + a_2^2 \sigma_2^2$$

If the values of the shares are independent $R_{12} = 0$ and this reduces to

$$\sigma_p^2 = a_1^2 \sigma_1^2 + a_2^2 \sigma_2^2$$

Its maximum occurs when the values of the shares are perfectly correlated (as, for example, with two shares in the same company), in which case $R_{12} = 1$ and

$$\sigma_{max}^2 = (a_1 \sigma_1 + a_2 \sigma_2)^2$$

If there is a perfect negative correlation ($R_{12} = -1$) the variance of V is at a minimum, and

$$\sigma_{min}^2 = (a_1 \sigma_1 - a_2 \sigma_2)^2$$

The general result is that the greater the negative covariance of v_1 and v_2 the lower is the variance of V.

Notice that the risk also depends on the values of a_1 and a_2, the proportions of the portfolio held in each share. For the special case of $R_{12} = -1$, the risk attached to V can be eliminated altogether if a_1 and a_2 are chosen so that $a_1/a_2 = \sigma_2/\sigma_1$.

In practice it is impossible to eliminate risk completely through diversification. Some part of the uncertainty connected with the value of equity depends on the performance of the economy of a country as a whole (or of the world economy for an international portfolio). General prosperity will affect the general level of equity values, as will changes in financial or political conditions. Uncertainty connected with the market as a whole is known as market risk, and cannot be diversified away. What diversification can eliminate is the risk attached to particular companies, namely the risk that they will perform well or badly relative to the market as a whole.

9. If the greater ease of satisfying the precautionary objective had the dominant effect, S would shift to the left, with the rate of interest rising and investment turning out to be at a level lower than OI_1 – conceivably even lower than OI_0.

5 INTEREST RATES

In this chapter we shall begin by looking at the factors which determine the general level of interest rates and then go on to explain some of the reasons why the interest rates on financial instruments differ – for example differences in risk, term to maturity, vulnerability to price level changes, and transactions costs. At the end of the chapter we shall discuss the relationship between interest rates on financial instruments and economic efficiency.

The function of the rate of interest r, in equating saving and investment, has already been noted. Figure 5.1 repeats part of Figure 3.1, which illustrates how r is determined by the intersection of an upward-sloping savings schedule and a downward-sloping investment schedule. A rise in the profitability of investment or a fall in the desire to save will shift the relevant schedule and raise the equilibrium rate of interest.

It is easy to illustrate this aspect of the determination of r in the context of particular financial institutions and markets. Suppose that building societies are faced with an increased demand for mortgages. Initially they may run down liquidity and possibly ration loans, but if the high demand persists they will eventually raise both deposit

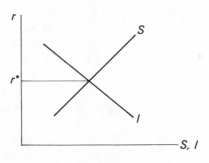

Fig. 5.1

and mortgage interest rates in order on the one hand to attract more saving, which will enable them to grant more loans, and on the other to curb demand for mortgages, thus bringing saving and investment back into balance. Though complicated by other factors, a similar process applies in the capital market. An inflow of saving will bid up the price of securities,[1] will allow firms to raise new finance more cheaply, and so will encourage them to draw more heavily on the capital market to finance investment.

In discussing the mechanism through which saving and investment are brought into balance we normally stress the part played by the rates of interest or prices of securities. In practice, other terms of credit, e.g. some form of qualitative rationing, may also be important. But changes in these terms are usually temporary – a response to a transient disequilibrium between the demand for funds and what is available – rather than permanent; whereas changes in the flows of saving or investment which last for a more extended period generally have their impact upon the price of funds.

THE INTEREST RATE AND THE MARKET FOR LOANABLE FUNDS

It is now time to broaden our analysis of interest rate determination to allow for *monetary* influences. Money has a distinctive role to play because, unlike other financial assets, changes in money holdings are often unplanned; they are not the consequence of conscious decisions. For example, if an employee is asked to work additional overtime his income, and hence his money balances, will be more than he expected. Or again, if a firm's sales fall below its expectations its revenue will be reduced and its money balances will be run down accordingly. Changes in economic agents' money balances do of course affect their future behaviour, but some time is likely to pass before they alter their expenditure or buy or sell other financial assets in order to return their money holdings to the normal level. In the short-run, therefore, money holdings will often be out of equilibrium, and it is quite possible for the supply of money and the demand for money – interpreted as what people had planned to hold – to be out of balance.

Consider then the market for *loanable funds*, consisting of all financial instruments other than money. For the present we shall ignore shifts between different categories of loanable funds, and look only at overall increases in supply or demand. If r stands for the rate of interest on financial instruments, like deposits or loans, r can be regarded as the price of loanable funds.[2]

The sources of supply and demand for loanable funds are as follows: for supply, saving, reductions in the demand for money, increases in the supply of money; for demand, investment, borrowing for consumption, increases in the demand for money.

Saving, which is the main source of supply of loanable funds, arises in all sectors of the economy and may take many forms. Personal saving, i.e. the excess of personal income over consumption spending, may consist, *inter alia*, of contributions to pension funds, the repayment of mortgage loans, deposits with building societies or banks, or the purchase of securities. Business saving comprises retained profits and, most important, depreciation charges; what is not reinvested in the business is usually held in a liquid form. The government too may contribute to saving in the economy by raising more in taxes than it needs for its own current expenditure; any surplus goes to offset part of the public sector's own investment.

The supply of loanable funds is augmented by any reduction in economic agents' desired money holdings in favour of other financial assets. For example, when someone shifts a deposit from a bank to a building society this raises the supply of loanable funds, because the bank does not lend less when the ownership of its deposits changes, but the building society can use the increase in its deposits to raise its lending. Any increase in the money supply, over and above that part of current saving which people want to hold as money, also adds to the supply of loanable funds; additional bank deposits are matched by increased lending or higher holdings of securities.

The investment, which creates the principal source of demand for loanable funds, is also to be found in all sectors of the economy. Persons require finance for housing, industrial companies to pay for factories, plant and equipment, and governments need money for many forms of capital spending, including hospitals, schools and roads to name only a few. Some investment is financed directly out of current saving, but most is financed by borrowing or a reduction in money holdings.

Consumers buying durable household goods, or even just borrowing to pay for a holiday, also contribute to the demand for loanable funds, as do public sector bodies with current account deficits to finance. Moreover, from time to time economic agents may choose to borrow simply in order to build up their money holdings – for example, firms making sure of their finance before embarking on an investment programme.

We can simplify the factors affecting the supply and demand for loanable funds by treating borrowing for consumption as an offset against saving[3] and regarding the increase in the demand for money as a net figure. Making the further simplifying assumption that current saving is not held in the form of money and defining

$$S = \text{saving}^4$$
$$I = \text{investment}^4$$
$$\Delta M = \text{increase in the supply of money}$$
$$\Delta H = \text{increase in the demand for money}$$

the equation for balance in the market for loanable funds is

$$S + \Delta M = I + \Delta H$$

Note that if $\Delta M = \Delta H$ this reduces to $S = I$, where both S and I are functions of r as before.

Now consider the effect of increasing the money supply. This adds to the saving available in the capital market, so that instead of S in Figure 5.1 we have $S + \Delta M$. The effect of incorporating the increase in the money supply is therefore to reduce the rate of interest in Figure 5.2 from r_0 to r_1.

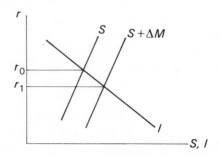

Fig. 5.2

To see how this comes about, suppose that instead of raising new funds through the stock market companies borrow from their banks, and the banks increase the money supply when they make these loans. Because companies are borrowing from the banks the pressure of demand in the securities markets will be reduced, the price of securities will rise, and the rate of interest on securities fall correspondingly.

A rise in the demand for money will have the opposite effect. It has to be added to investment demand, and for a given level of

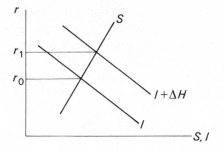

Fig. 5.3

saving, Figure 5.3 shows that the effect is to raise the rate of interest from r_0 to r_1.[5]

All the elements of demand and supply for loanable funds have been brought together in Figure 5.4. It is clear that the effect on the rate of interest of any shift in S, ΔM, I or ΔH will depend on the elasticities of *both* lines. The less elastic (steeper) is $S + \Delta M$ and the more elastic (flatter) is $I + \Delta H$ the greater will be the effect of any shift in I or ΔH on the equilibrium rate of interest.

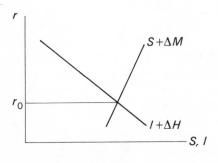

Fig. 5.4

The equilibrium situation illustrated in Figure 5.4 is only a short-run situation. Although the rate of interest may be in equilibrium, unless desired saving equals desired investment and the desired increase in money holdings matches the increase in the money supply, the economy as a whole will not be in equilibrium and the situation will be one of constant change. For example, if S is less than I and ΔM is greater than ΔH people will be receiving more income and building up larger money balances than they intended, with the result that they will alter their saving plans for the future.

The factors leading to changes in the demand for money have been the subject of much discussion. People need to hold more money to carry out their everyday affairs when their incomes rise; as noted above, firms may choose to build up their money balances in advance of major capital spending programmes; people may choose to hold more money as their wealth increases; and lastly, people may choose to alter their money balances as their confidence about the future waxes or wanes, and as a result of changing views about the future trend of security prices.

It is easy to accommodate a gradual increase or decline in the amount of money which people wish to hold within this framework of analysis. So long as the flows of saving and investment and monetary changes are of the same orders of magnitude, i.e. no single element is very much larger than the others within the period relevant for analysis, there is no difficulty. But sudden or substantial changes in the demand for money may temporarily outweigh other influences on interest rates. It is very unlikely that the supply of money will adjust to match a sharp change in demand completely, because rapid changes in the money supply often run counter to monetary policy, and they depend too upon the banks being willing to make considerable adjustments in the scale of their own assets and liabilities. In these circumstances monetary conditions become the principal short-run determinants of the interest rate, which must adjust to the extent needed to dissuade asset-holders from attempting to alter their money holdings further. However, it is in the nature of sharp changes in the demand for money that they are a response to temporary conditions, often reflecting economic or political uncertainty, and that with the passage of time a change in monetary conditions will be reversed. Thus in the longer term the demand and supply of money will alter together and it is the flows of saving and investment which are the more important determinants of interest rates.

THE STRUCTURE OF INTEREST RATES

Let us now drop the assumption of a single rate of interest, and consider why it is that the rates of interest or yields on financial instruments differ. Why do some borrowers pay more than others? Why do equity shares yield more than property? Why do both yield less than gilt-edged securities? Why are the yields on long-dated securities different from those on short-dated ones?

These are some of the questions which must now be answered. As our benchmark we shall take the risk-free rate of interest on government securities of the appropriate term; there is no default risk and the flow of income (in money terms) is certain. We begin, therefore, by considering the factors which influence the term structure of interest rates.

TERM

The interest rate on any category of security varies with its *term* or maturity. The normal situation is that long-term securities bear higher rates of interest than short-term, because of the bias of borrowers towards long-term liabilities and of lenders towards short. The higher rates of interest on long-term securities are needed to persuade either lenders or borrowers to depart from their preferred maturities and to provide a margin out of which those financial intermediaries which help to bridge the gap through maturity transformation are able to cover their costs. The differences in interest rates which are needed for this purpose are known as *liquidity premia*, and these may be expected to rise with the term of the security.

But the term structure is also affected by other important considerations, which result from time to time in short rates exceeding long – a situation which is at first sight perverse. When deciding whether to lend for long or short periods savers must take account not only of the interest they will earn initially but also of the interest rates which they expect to prevail in future. They can choose between making a single investment for a long period at a rate of interest fixed at the outset, or of making repeated short-term investments at whatever short rates prevail during that period. Ignoring liquidity premia, the rate of interest demanded by a long-term investor will therefore depend on what he would hope to earn from a series of short-term investments – his expected return by the end of the period from the two alternatives must be the same. It follows that the rate of interest on long-term securities must be some kind of average of the short rates which are expected to prevail in future. The links between long rates and expected future short rates are known as *expectations* effects.

It is expectations effects which explain why short rates are sometimes higher than long. If high short rates are thought to be temporary, so that people generally expect them to be lower in future, the average short rate during the period of a long-term loan will be less than the current short rate, and the difference may more than offset the effect of liquidity premia on the term structure of interest rates.[6]

DEFAULT RISK

The risk that a borrower may default on his obligations affects the rate of interest he must pay for a loan, which includes a 'loading' for risk. In many instances lenders distinguish a relatively small number of risk categories, and put potential borrowers into the category which they think appropriate. The loading in the interest rate the borrower is charged reflects the risk of loss for that category. Sometimes this classification is carried out on a formal basis – for example, in the USA there are bond-rating services, which classify companies into risk categories. Banks draw a distinction between 'blue chip' companies and those to which they attribute a higher risk. Instalment loans from banks generally incorporate a lower risk-loading than similar loans from finance houses, because the risk of default is generally lower for the customers of the former. Commercial bills which have been accepted, i.e. guaranteed, by a bank yield less than trade bills which have no similar guarantee. When loans are negotiated individually the risk-loading may be a factor in the negotiation; for example a company seeking a loan for an investment project may attempt to persuade its bank that it deserves to be placed in a more favourable risk class.

Note that default risk is by no means the only or most important factor influencing the margin by which the cost of loans exceeds the risk-free rate of interest. The loading must also take account of the administrative costs incurred by the lender, which, particularly for relatively small loans or loans involving extensive documentation, may substantially exceed the loading for risk.

EQUITY RISK

Before considering the way in which equity risk is incorporated in asset yields we must first consider how the yield on equity – a somewhat elusive concept – is measured.

The cost to a company of issuing equity shares is determined by the dividends it is expected to pay in future. If the dividend was expected to be constant, we could express the cost as the dividend divided by the net proceeds per share issued. But dividends are not usually expected to be constant, so some allowance must be made for anticipated changes in dividend payments.

Dividends may in fact be expected to change for several reasons. First, the company may be thought to have entered a period of unusual prosperity or unusual difficulty, which will affect its profitability and dividend payments. Secondly, most companies aim to retain part of their profits in order to develop their business, and to the extent that they are successful this can be expected to lead to gradually rising dividend payments. Thirdly, in a period of inflation the money values of the company's income, expenses and profits may be expected to rise broadly in line with the price level – an expectation that may of course be disappointed for extended periods – so inflationary expectations are also reflected in anticipated dividend payments.

There is no very good reason to expect dividends to change in a regular fashion from year to year, even though many companies do attempt to maintain some stability in their dividend payments, but fortunately it is possible to convert erratic changes in dividends into a mathematically equivalent constant annual rate of growth. If this rate is g and the dividend yield is d, the cost of equity capital to the company can be expressed as $(d+g)$.[7]

The cost to the company is the same as the return which the holders of equity shares expect to receive. To see this, consider the total return to a shareholder over a period of a year from a company whose dividend yield is d and for which the dividend is expected to grow by g from one year to the next. If the general level of interest rates is constant the rise in dividend will lead to a proportional increase in the price of the shares, so that in the course of the year the shareholder receives a dividend yield of d plus capital appreciation of g; and this rate of return continues so long as dividends grow and are expected to continue to grow at the rate g.

In general the equity yield $(d+g)$ will be higher than the risk-free rate of interest r, because the flow of income from equity shares is uncertain and asset holders demand some compensation for their exposure to risk.[8] The yield margin over the risk-free rate will reflect the intensity of risk-aversion amongst asset-holders in general – the greater their reluctance to accept risk the higher the margin must be.

The yield which asset-holders expect to earn on the shares of equally risky companies should in principle be the same; otherwise they would have an incentive to sell the shares of the lower-yielding companies and buy those of the higher, and this would alter the relative share prices until the yields were equal. This does not imply that *dividend* yields will be equal, because the expected growth of dividends varies from one company to another, and this is reflected in the dividend yields on their shares – a low dividend yield implies that the rate of growth of dividends is expected to be high.

High-risk companies, i.e. those for which expected profits in future are very uncertain, may need to pay more for equity capital than low-risk companies. However, the margin need not necessarily be large because the asset-holder with a large portfolio can eliminate the extra risk through diversification. Indeed, there is a possibility that very risky investments may appeal to the gambling instincts in some investors, and so attract funds more readily than safer investments for which the maximum likely return is lower; if this occurs the average yield on highly risky investments would be less than on safer holdings.[9]

It is important to note that only part of the risk associated with equity shares can be eliminated by diversification. A diversified portfolio will enable the investor to be confident that his assets will yield the same as the average of the market,[10] but they do not give him any protection against a decline in profitability as a whole, or against a fall in equity prices as a result of an increase in the general level of interest rates. Strictly speaking, therefore, it is the extent to which the yield on the shares of a particular company is expected to vary with general market movements which determines the risk attached to that share, and which is reflected in the risk loading in the yield demanded by asset holders.

INFLATION

We must now distinguish between *nominal* and *real* rates of interest. The nominal rate is the rate of interest expressed in money terms, whereas the real rate makes an adjustment for the effect of changes in the general price level. Suppose that a 1-year loan bears a rate of interest of 15 per cent, and that during the course of the year the general price level in the economy rises by 12 per cent so that the loan itself and the interest received is worth 12 per cent less at the end of the year than at the beginning. Then at the end of the year the lender has £115 per £100 lent, but in terms of the prices prevailing at the beginning of the year this is only £(115/1.12), i.e. £102.7. The real rate of interest is consequently only 2.7 per cent.

If the rate of inflation is low the relation between the nominal yield, i, the real yield, r, and the expected rate of inflation, $\dot{p}$, is:[11]

$$i = r + \dot{p}$$

As we have already said, expected inflation accounts for part of the difference between the dividend yield on equities and the yield on gilt-edged securities. Bonds are claims to nominal income flows, whereas ordinary shares and property are claims to flows of real income, because dividends and rent are expected to rise broadly in line with the price level in future. As a result, the expected yields on claims to real-income flows include a growth element for inflation.[12]

COST AND PROFITS

The rates of interest charged to borrowers and the cost to a company of raising equity capital must also include an allowance for transaction costs. These vary with the size and complexity of the transactions concerned. Transactions costs are usually subject to economies of scale – they rise less than in proportion to the size of transactions – so that the loading for transactions costs is larger for small loans, or small issues of equity capital, than it is for large. The transactions costs of raising new capital are sometimes charged as a separate fee, rather than being recovered in the form of a higher interest rate. But the loading for servicing costs, e.g. the cost of monitoring a loan and of collecting payments at the due dates specified in the loan agreement, are usually built into the interest rate charged. Differences in transactions costs are the principal reason why loans to the banks' retail customers bear higher rates of interest than wholesale loans.

The rate of interest charged for a loan by a financial intermediary will also include an element for profit, and the amount which the intermediary can hope to earn is influenced by the strength of competition which it faces. For example, in the market for wholesale bank loans there is a very large number of potential lenders, and competition is extremely keen. Borrowers are prepared to shop around and take funds from those lenders who offer them the most favourable terms. In the retail bank loan market competition is more restrained, because borrowers place more weight on the maintenance of the goodwill which goes with long-established relationships with their banks and are generally reluctant to shift from one bank to another as a result of a failure to negotiate a small reduction in interest rates. Indeed, the ability to obtain a loan at all, and the terms regarding repayment and security attached to it, are usually of much greater importance in the eyes of the borrower.

Costs and profit margins may be influenced by agreements between lenders, such as the recommended rates agreed by the Building

Societies Association, and government regulations may also affect transactions costs. Most restrictive agreements and regulations have the effect of raising transactions costs.

THE ALLOCATION OF FUNDS

Putting all these elements together, the rate charged for a loan of any term will be made up of the following components: risk-free rate for that term, plus loading for default risk, plus loading for servicing costs, plus loading for profit. Similarly, the dividend yield required for an issue of equity shares will include; real yield required on a risk-free perpetuity,[13] plus loading for equity risk, minus allowance for real growth of dividends. The rates charged for loans of differing terms reflect liquidity premia and expected future rates of interest, and nominal and real yields are linked by expectations of inflation.

Suppose now that competition within the financial system was sufficient to ensure that lenders were unable to earn excess profits, and suppose further that lenders were in a position to assess risks accurately. Then the price which borrowers had to pay for funds would reflect the going risk-free rate of interest for the appropriate term, the costs incurred in connection with their loans, and an appropriate loading for risk. The allocation of funds would be 'efficient' in the sense that each borrower had to pay a price which reflected the going rate for funds in general and the specific costs and risk associated with his own business. The same would apply to equity capital.

If firms chose to raise money for all projects which were able to earn at least enough to meet the financing costs, and did not go ahead with lower-yielding projects, this efficiency in the supply of funds would feed through into an efficient allocation of investment. By finding the rate of interest which equated saving and investment in the economy, and charging in addition for specific risks and costs, the financial system would price funds according to their opportunity costs. It would then be left to the potential borrowers to determine the allocation of resources amongst competing investment projects, in the light of their own estimates of the likely returns.

Funds, in other words, would go to the highest bidders. If there was an increase in demand for mortgages by potential house-owners they would be prepared to pay more for mortgages, so building societies would raise their deposit and mortgage rates, putting upward pressure on interest rates generally. Funds would be attracted from, say, the banks, some of whose borrowers would be unwilling to pay the higher rates of interest. Or again, improved industrial investment prospects might encourage firms to raise additional equity capital, and this too would result in funds being drawn away from alternative uses.

How closely the British financial system approximates to this ideal has been a matter of considerable debate, and we shall consider the matter more fully in Chapter 15. At this stage, however, there are a number of points to note. That differences in the strength of competition, and consequently of costs and profitability, of different segments of the market can detract from efficiency is obvious. But while such differences do occur in practice to some extent in Britain, they are unlikely to be factors of major importance. More significant, perhaps, are questions to do with the assessment of risk. It has often been asserted that financial institutions in Britain lack the competence to assess risk properly, and are consequently unduly conservative in their lending practices. Moreover, it is said, the long-term institutions place too much emphasis on current dividends and on the outlook for companies in the short-term. If these allegations are true they would imply that the system did not allocate resources efficiently, but would be biased against projects which were risky or which yielded their return only gradually and over a long period.

Questions have also been raised over the extent to which rates of interest do in fact balance saving and investment in the economy. It is suggested that the general level of interest rates might be inappropriate to prevailing economic conditions. This could be caused by a faulty monetary policy, a malfunctioning of the capital market, or other structural deficiencies in the economy. Whatever the cause, interest rates which were too low would be associated with more investment than was desirable, and excessively high interest rates would curb investment unnecessarily. However efficient the allocation of the investment that did take place, the allocation of resources as a whole would be out of balance.

Finally, this concept of efficiency itself may require qualification. Is profitability, or the return to the private economic agent, the right criterion for deciding whether or not investment should take place? It is sometimes argued that other criteria are also relevant. For example, a proposal to set up a business in an area with heavy unemployment might be justified, even if the profitability measured in conventional terms on the capital invested was lower than could be obtained on alternative projects elsewhere. This is one instance where social returns and private returns may diverge, and it can be argued that efficient allocation would reflect the former rather than the latter. How best to take account of such divergence is another matter to which we shall return later.

NOTES

1. Which implies that the rate of interest falls (see Chapter 1).
2. By aggregating all categories of financial instruments in this way we implicitly assume that *relative* rates of interest are constant.
3. This treatment corresponds to the national accounts statisticians' concept of saving.
4. S and I must be defined consistently. Thus if I is gross investment S must include depreciation.
5. In Figure 5.3 ΔH, the increase in the demand for money, has been treated as independent of the rate of interest. In practice the demand for money is normally somewhat interest-elastic, and this has the effect of making the $(I + \Delta H)$ line more elastic (flatter).
6. At the time of writing, sterling CDs yielded $16\frac{1}{2}$ per cent, and long-dated gilt-edged securities yielded 13 per cent, reflecting the view that short rates were likely to be substantially lower in the next 20 years than they were then.
7. The dividend yield is (dividend)/(share price). The transactions costs of issuing the shares have been ignored.
8. The position may be reversed in periods of inflation when the uncertainty attached to inflation may make 'risk-free' assets expressed in nominal terms seem riskier than equity shares.
9. There is some evidence of this phenomenon in the USA.
10. Or better if he is successful in selecting companies whose performance is better than the market as a whole expects.
11. Strictly $(1+i) = (1+r)(1+\dot{p})$.
12. At the time of writing the dividend yield on ordinary shares was approximately 6 per cent on average, while long-dated gilt-edged securities yielded around 13 per cent. If we suppose that the dividend yield includes a loading of 2 per cent for equity risk and that the real growth of dividends is expected to average 1 per cent per annum in future, then the risk-free real yield would be given by (6 per cent + 1 per cent − 2 per cent) = 5 per cent. The implied allowance for inflation would thus be (13 per cent − 5 per cent) = 8 per cent.
13. A perpetuity is an undated security, i.e. one which promises a guaranteed annual payment in perpetuity.

PART III THE USERS OF THE SYSTEM

In this Part the behaviour of the users of the financial system is examined in greater depth. The financial facilities required by different categories of user are a product of their economic activities. The following chapters therefore distinguish between the four major user sectors of the economy – personal, industrial and commercial companies, public and overseas – and consider the behaviour of each in turn.

Saving and investment by the personal sector are discussed in the next chapter. The personal sector is the most important source of saving in the economy; the reasons why people save, how much they save, and the forms in which they choose to hold their savings are considered. The quality of borrowing facilities is also of great concern to the personal sector, especially the availability of funds for house ownership and for buying consumer durables.

For industrial and commercial companies, which are the subject of Chapter 7, it is the ability to raise finance which matters most. The factors which influence balance sheet structure and their need for equity and debt finance are considered, as are the sources from which companies obtain their funds. The use which they make of the financial system to hold liquid balances and for other purposes is also examined, and particular attention is paid to some of the special financial problems faced by small companies.

The largest borrower from the financial system in recent years has been the public sector, whose financing is considered in Chapter 8. The contributions of the central government, local authorities and public corporations to the public sector's external borrowing are studied and the sources from which the public sector raises finance are reviewed. The effects of public sector borrowing on the supply of finance for other borrowers are also considered.

The 'overseas sector' brings together all the changes in assets and liabilities involving transactions between UK and overseas residents. Many of these transactions are considered elsewhere, but the sector as a whole is examined briefly in Chapter 9. Close financial linkages with other countries mean that in some circumstances flows of capital into or out of the UK play a significant part in balancing saving with investment.

6 PERSONAL SAVING AND INVESTMENT

The personal sector is the chief source of saving in the UK capital market. As noted in Chapter 2 personal sector saving amounted to some 8½ per cent of GDP in 1976–80. During this period the personal sector built up its holdings of financial assets by about 11 per cent of GDP per year on average, and these savings were made available to borrowers through the financial system. The personal sector also undertakes a significant volume of investment, 3 per cent of GDP in 1976–80. Most of the capital and some of the consumption spending is financed by borrowing, and the sector's liabilities increased by about 4½ per cent of GDP per year in the same period.

The personal sector's bias towards holding assets which are safe and have a high degree of liquidity helps to explain why maturity transformation by the financial system is necessary. In Chapter 1 we took a preliminary look at the reasons why people save and the ways in which their motives influence their choice of financial assets. Our task in this chapter is to examine these matters in greater depth, in order to account both for the personal sector's asset holdings and for the flows of funds which they supply to and draw from the financial system.

PERSONAL SECTOR WEALTH

The 'personal' sector in the UK includes not only households and individuals, as might be expected, but also the business activities of sole traders and partnerships, such as farms, retail shops and independent professional men and women, and private non-profit-making bodies such as charities, trade unions and clubs. However, individuals and households account for about 90 per cent of personal sector wealth, and while the factors which influence the behaviour of the other components are often different from those affecting private persons, with few exceptions the figures give a reasonably accurate picture of household behaviour.

Table 6.1 shows the personal sector's assets and liabilities at the end of 1979. Net wealth, i.e. the difference between the sector's assets and liabilities, amounted to about £540 billion, roughly four times personal disposable income (PDI) in 1979.[1] Physical assets comprised 71 per cent of net wealth, financial assets 42 per cent, and borrowing 13 per cent.

Land and buildings made up over 75 per cent of the sector's physical assets, with dwellings alone amounting to nearly 65 per cent. Consumer durables – household furnishings and equipment – amounted to a little under 20 per cent, and the rest, about 5 per cent, consisted of stocks, vehicles, plant and equipment. Most of the latter, and no doubt considerable proportions of the 'other' land and buildings, are held by the non-household components of the sector.

At the end of 1979 the personal sector's holdings of financial assets were worth a little under one-and-three-quarter times its disposable income. The most liquid categories – notes and coin, deposits with banks and other financial institutions, and national savings – accounted for over 40 per cent of the total. Direct holdings of securities and loans, whether to the government, UK companies or overseas bodies, amounted to about 20 per cent, but were less than indirect holdings of these assets through unit trusts, life assurance and pension funds, which amounted to about 30 per cent of total financial assets. Most of the balance consisted of trade and other debtors – assets held in connection with business activities. Over 25 per cent of the bank deposits and about 8 per cent of the securities and loans are held by the non-household components.

Most of the sector's liabilities are incurred in order to finance the purchase of physical assets, and at the end of 1979 liabilities amounted to a little under 20 per cent of the value of physical assets. Much the most important form of liability was loans for house purchase, equal also to nearly 20 per cent of the value of dwellings. Bank loans and instalment debt, which comprised nearly a quarter of all liabilities, are used mainly for the purchase of consumer durables, stock and vehicles. About half of the bank loans relate to business activities, as does part of the creditors item.

MOTIVES FOR SAVING

A person's wealth represents the accumulation of his own saving

TABLE 6.1   BALANCE SHEET OF THE PERSONAL
SECTOR, END 1979

	(£ billion)
Physical assets	
Dwellings	243.1
Other land and buildings	49.0
Consumer durables	68.9
Stocks, vehicles, equipment	21.2
	382.1
Financial assets	
Notes and coin	8.0
Bank deposits	30.8
OFI deposits	48.0
National Savings	12.4
Central and local government securities and loans	13.3
Company securities	31.4
Overseas securities	1.8
Unit trust units	2.5
Equity in life assurance and pension funds	68.2
Trade and other debtors	8.0
Other	5.5
	230.1
Liabilities	
Bank loans and advances	11.9
Instalment debt	4.4
Loans for house purchase	45.0
Creditors and accounts payable	5.9
Other	3.2
	70.4
Net wealth	541.8

Source: Financial Statistics, February 1981, Table C

over the years together with any gifts or bequests he may have received. People save for a variety of motives. First, a certain amount of short-term saving takes place to meet seasonal or other peaks in spending, for example summer holidays, Christmas presents, consumer durables, or simply anything which demands a substantial cash outlay at one time. This kind of saving is really nothing more than short-run cash-flow management – a building up or running down of money-holdings in order to iron out fluctuations in income and spending. The financial assets held in this connection are generally cash or deposits.

Secondly, people save out of a sense of precaution; they aim to build up a nest egg for emergencies. They might, for example, wish to guard against the misfortune of losing their jobs or having to accept short-time working for an extended period, during which their income would be much less than they had been accustomed to. Or they might want to hold a reserve in case, quite unexpectedly, their house or car had to undergo expensive repairs. Savings held for precautionary reasons often also take the form of deposits, but other liquid assets such as national savings or even short-dated securities all fill the bill.

Thirdly, people save for their old age or to ensure that, if they die young, their dependants are looked after. These motives for saving are extremely important, and are the fundamental reason for the strength of life assurance and pension funds in Britain. But there are other ways of achieving the same objectives. Ordinary shares and fixed interest securities, designed to preserve the value of capital and provide a satisfactory income after retirement, are often held for this purpose; a substantial proportion of the building societies' deposits are held by people saving for retirement; whilst others choose to save by purchasing their own home or investing in their own business.

Concern to provide for old age or dependants shades into a straightforward desire to accumulate capital. People enjoy the ownership of wealth, for the security it gives and for the opportunities it provides, without necessarily wishing either to spend the income derived from their wealth themselves or, indeed, to sell the assets at some stage to finance their own consumption. Capital accumulation normally takes the form of business assets, marketable securities of all kinds, houses, and, to a more limited extent, deposits. In the past, the desire to build up a thriving private business has been a particularly powerful motive for saving.

Finally, people will save in order to provide for their own comfort and pleasure. They accumulate wealth in the form of houses, motor cars, or consumer durables, not because they hope to derive any money income from them, or even to avoid expenditure of other kinds, but because they enjoy living in a well-furnished, spacious house or having the freedom and convenience which a car provides.

THEORIES OF SAVING

Enumerating the motives for saving helps us to understand why people save and gives some guidance on the form that saving will take. But it tells us very little about *how much* people will choose to save or how their saving will be affected by factors such as interest rates, income or wealth. These matters are the central concern of theories of saving.

Table 6.2 shows personal saving as a percentage of PDI in recent years. While the precise figures must be taken with a pinch of salt – the error margin in estimates of saving derived from national accounts statistics is large – they indicate that personal saving was on a plateau, averaging about 9 per cent of PDI, at the beginning of the 1970s, but that it rose sharply in 1973 and 1974, since when it has averaged over 12 per cent of PDI. A sharp rise in the personal savings ratio was a common phenomenon in many countries in the mid-

TABLE 6.2   PERSONAL SAVING AS A PERCENTAGE OF PERSONAL DISPOSABLE INCOME, 1970–80

	(%)
1970	9.3
1971	7.6
1972	9.7
1973	11.7
1974	13.5
1975	12.7
1976	11.9
1977	10.8
1978	12.7
1979	14.1
1980	15.3

Source: Financial Statistics, April 1981, Table 10.1

seventies – one which took economists by surprise – and since then attempts have been made to develop the theory of saving to account satisfactorily for what occurred.

The rise in personal saving seemed to run counter to Keynesian theory, which stressed the link between personal saving and current income. If income rose, saving would rise too, but more than in proportion to income, whereas if income fell saving would suffer a disproportionate cut. In times of prosperity people would be slow to adjust their spending habits to their higher levels of income, whereas when times were bad they would draw on the precautionary balances they had accumulated earlier. This Keynesian approach provides insights into the ways in which changes in personal saving are likely to be induced by fluctuations in economic activity; but it proved less satisfactory in suggesting how personal saving would react to other shocks to the economic system.

More recent theories of saving put greater stress on long-run income concepts, and link saving to personal wealth rather than to current income. An individual's standard of living is determined not only by his current income, but also by his wealth and the income which he expects to earn in the future. For a typical person, the time-pattern of income during his life-span will not coincide with the time-pattern of his consumption; saving in some periods balanced by dis-saving in others permits him to match his consumption with his needs.[2] This approach encompasses several of the motives for saving discussed earlier, e.g. saving to meet seasonal peaks in consumption, saving by young couples to buy or furnish houses, and saving for retirement. Moreover, since the amounts required for all these purposes reflect a person's standard of living and are linked to long-run income, this approach suggests that an individual's desired holdings of financial assets should move broadly in line with the trend of income. The notion of a desired wealth–income ratio can also be extended to liquid saving held for precautionary reasons.

The effect of the rate of interest on the level of saving has already been discussed in Chapter 3. Two potentially contrary effects were noted. On the one hand a rise in interest rates made saving more attractive, because it increased the saver's command over resources in the future; there was a positive substitution effect. On the other hand, because interest rates were higher it was possible to provide for known or estimated future needs with a lower level of saving; there was a negative income effect. The substitution effect may sometimes be rather weak because, as the discussion of motives has shown, much of saving does not depend on the carrot of a real return. The possibility of a negative income effect is much more than a theoretical curiosity, and may in fact be quite important in practice. For example, when a pension scheme provides pensions which are related to the members' final salaries, the size of the fund which has to be accumulated and the level of contributions are reduced by increases in the rate of interest.

Whatever the direction of the effect of changes in the rate of interest on total saving, there can be no doubt that relative interest rates have pronounced effects upon the composition of saving. One example is the effect of inflation on real rates of return. If as a result of inflation, people expect the real return on financial savings to be negative, so that these savings lose in real value, they have a clear incentive to hold physical assets, e.g. houses, which retain their real value rather than financial assets, such as deposits. Another is the effect of changes in the relative rates of interest on interest-bearing bank and building society deposits, which strongly influence the flows of personal saving into the respective types of institution.

Since the early 1970s the UK has suffered from a high, but fluctuating, rate of inflation, generally low growth of real income, considerable uncertainty in the economic environment, and yields on financial assets which have often turned out to be negative in real terms. Together these factors account for the rise in the savings ratio, with inflation probably the main cause.

Inflation has eroded the real wealth of the personal sector, particularly that part which is held in the form of liquid assets. Table 6.3 shows that the ratio of personal-sector liquid-asset holdings to PDI was virtually static at a little under 85 per cent until the end of 1973. Then it fell very quickly during 1974 and 1975, two years with exceptionally high rates of inflation – retail prices rose by 16 and 24 per cent respectively. In a period of inflation a high level of saving in the form of liquid assets is needed simply to keep the ratio to PDI constant, let alone to move it back to its previous level. For example, if people held liquid assets amounting to 70 per cent of PDI and if inflation ran at 10 per cent, they would have to save 7 per cent of their income in order to prevent a fall in the ratio of liquid assets to PDI. From 1970 to 1973 retail price inflation averaged only about 8 per cent per year, and if the suggestion that households' needs for transactions and precautionary balances are related to their incomes is valid, the much higher rates of inflation subsequently are sufficient to explain the growth of liquid saving.

Inflation in recent years has also been associated with low real returns on saving, and this has led to increased saving through

TABLE 6.3   PERSONAL SECTOR LIQUID ASSETS AS
A PERCENTAGE OF PERSONAL DISPOSABLE
INCOME, 1970-80

	(%)
1970	83.2
1971	84.7
1972	84.2
1973	83.6
1974	79.4
1975	71.9
1976	69.1
1977	69.8
1978	68.4
1979	67.9
1980	67.6

Source: Financial Statistics, September 1979, Table 10.3, and April 1981, Tables 10.1 and 10.4

pension funds. As noted above, lower expected yields imply that higher contributions to pension funds from current wages and salaries, which count as part of personal saving, are needed; in addition employers have been compelled to make additional payments to pension funds, to top them up in order to reduce deficiencies which have arisen as a result of the failure of assets accumulated earlier to earn as much as had been hoped.

Finally, the generally low level of economic growth may also have influenced personal saving. If it had been purely a cyclical downturn Keynesian theory would have suggested that personal saving should fall. But in fact we seem to be faced with a less buoyant economy in the medium-term, and the low growth of real income has been associated with rising unemployment and uncertain economic conditions. These may well have encouraged people to be wary of taking on new spending commitments and have caused them instead to build up the level of their savings.

CHOICE OF ASSETS

Some of the major differences between financial assets are by now familiar – for example differences with respect to liquidity, yield, and capital-certainty in nominal or real terms. Other characteristics of particular assets are also very important to their holders, e.g. bank deposits are a convenient means of making payments, as well as a home for savings; building society deposits may give their owner priority if there is a queue for mortgages in future; and people may choose to embark upon a contractual savings arrangement because they value the discipline to save which this imposes upon them. In deciding how their wealth will be divided amongst the physical and financial assets available to them, savers have to evaluate the characteristics of the assets in relation to their own needs.

It is convenient to divide the factors which influence the personal saver's evaluation of the alternative financial assets into three categories: structural factors, legislative factors, market factors. The structural factors relate to the motives for saving which have been discussed already. Everyone has some need of precautionary balances, but the amount required depends very much on the risks to which people are exposed. The National Health Service and other social security benefits are important structural factors which greatly reduce the need for precautionary balances. So is the State Retirement Pensions scheme, which make it unnecessary for individuals to provide so fully for themselves. Taking a broader perspective, a country's record of economic and political stability influences the ways in which people choose to save. In countries which have experienced very rapid inflation, in which those who held long-term assets have experienced a serious erosion of their wealth, or which have suffered from serious political instability, people generally seek the freedom of manoeuvre which liquidity endows and have a very strong preference for short-term assets such as bank deposits. Structural factors, then, reflect a country's history and its general social arrangements.

Some of these arrangements are embodied in legislation, others are more deeply rooted in custom or convention. But in addition, there are legislative factors, which are not necessarily such permanent features of the economy, which also influence saving behaviour. The system of occupational pension schemes in Britain, with their associated tax arrangements is one example; these provide a very strong incentive for saving in this form, since contributions are a charge on gross income, the earnings of the funds are accumulated tax-free, a proportion of the accumulated fund can be paid as a capital sum at retirement, and the pension payments themselves are taxed as earned income. The private individual who attempts to build up his own personal saving for retirement has none of these advantages.

Life assurance too is encouraged through tax incentives, under which the government pays to the insurance company a sum equal to 15 per cent of the gross premiums. Although for some individuals the rate of tax on the insurance company's investment income exceeds the tax they would have had to pay themselves, there is usually a net tax advantage to saving through this medium. The tax arrangements therefore help to account for the strength of both these forms of long-term contractual saving in the UK.

Tax or subsidy arrangements also favour mortgage borrowing for house purchase. The taxpayer is permitted to charge interest on the first £25 000 of a mortgage against his gross income before tax; at the current standard rate of tax this reduces the effective cost of the mortgage by 30 per cent of the interest payment, and the reduction in cost is even greater for people whose marginal rates of tax are over 30 per cent.[3] This tax concession has encouraged many people to save in the form of housing, rather than to increase their holdings of financial assets. The administrative arrangements for collecting income tax on deposit interest also gives building societies a competitive advantage in the market for savings.[4] Legislative factors like these can in principle be changed fairly easily – but there is no doubt that while they remain in force they have a considerable influence on the pattern of personal saving.

The last group of factors affecting personal saving behaviour are market factors, notably the relative yields offered by different savings media. In choosing between two deposit-taking institutions, the saver will frequently choose that which offers the higher yield, or in deciding with which life assurance company he should take out a policy he will look at the prospective returns offered. Other important market factors are the availability of branches, advertising and other means of selling the services of financial institutions. Market factors have their main impact on the saver's choice amongst *similar* financial instruments.

Market factors have an important bearing on the allocation of saving in the short-run. If the demand for owner-occupied housing is high, whilst industrial demand for external finance is low, the rate of interest on building society deposits will rise relative to that paid by banks, and an above-average proportion of personal saving will flow to the former. Again, by offering high rates of interest on national savings and gilt-edged securities, the government is able to attract funds away from deposit-taking institutions. But in the long term the structural and legislative factors are the more fundamental. Whether interest rates are high or low, money continues to flow into life assurance and pension funds, and while the amount varies with economic conditions, the average level is determined by structural and legislative considerations. The experience of inflation and the tax advantages for owner-occupied housing combine to ensure that building societies, the financial institutions which specialize in the provision of housing finance, will face a continued high demand for funds. The structural and legislative factors are themselves determinants of the relative interest rates and other aspects of competition between institutions which prevail in the market for savings.

PERSONAL BORROWING

Personal borrowing is usually connected with the purchase of physical assets, though there is some borrowing for consumption, mainly by means of bank overdrafts or through the use of credit cards, and some for the purchase of financial assets or land. Dwellings are the predominant physical asset for which individuals borrow, but cars and many consumer durables are also often financed through hire purchase of personal instalment loans. Business assets financed by borrowing include not only tangible assets, such as the farmer's barn, but also intangible assets, such as the lawyer's share in a partnership.

Home ownership is usually financed with the help of a mortgage loan; in recent years between 85 and 90 per cent of new dwellings have involved a building-society mortgage, and the purchasers of most existing houses also utilize mortgage finance. The maximum amount a purchaser can borrow is governed by the value of the property on which the loan is secured, by the purchaser's income, which determines how much he can afford for interest and capital repayments, and by the term of the mortgage. Loans on modern houses may be for periods of up to 30 years, but shorter periods are normal for older houses, and most lenders expect a loan to be repaid before the borrower retires. Borrowers usually arrange to make level monthly or quarterly payments of capital and interest combined, which may, however, be varied if interest rates change, so in the early years of a mortgage relatively little capital is repaid. When a house is sold the balance of the mortgage loan is repaid in full; the house-owner who is moving from one house to another negotiates a new loan for the house he is buying.

With mortgage loans so prevalent it is surprising at first sight to find that loans for house purchase amount to less than 20 per cent of the value of dwellings (see Table 6.1). There are two main reasons: rising house prices have meant that owners have built up their equity in their house much faster than the capital repayments on their loans would suggest; and many older people who originally financed their home with the help of a loan have repaid in full.

The provision of mortgage finance to the personal sector on reasonable terms is one of the most important functions of the financial system in Britain today. Without it, personal sector investment in housing would collapse. The high nominal interest rates associated with inflation have, in fact, caused severe difficulties in the housing market in recent years, a subject to which we return in Chapter 16.

Credit facilities for the purchase of consumer durable goods[5] – provided by banks, finance companies or the retailers themselves – help consumers in two ways. They enable people to obtain the use of goods earlier than if they had to save the whole purchase price before the goods were acquired; and by creating a contractual obligation to repay the loan by instalments, and in amounts which the lender seeks to ensure are reasonable in relation to the consumer's income, they provide a discipline which discourages the consumer from spending his money on the spur of the moment in other, less beneficial ways. Consumer instalment loans are normally at a fixed rate of interest, often expressed as a percentage of the initial sum borrowed.[6]

The personal sector also makes use of borrowing facilities for many other purposes, including bridging loans when people buy a new house before selling their old one, and loans to finance the fixed and working capital needed by traders and professional people, the payment of large tax bills before other assets can be realized, and everyday needs to tide people over until the next pay cheque is due. Much of this borrowing takes the form of a bank overdraft, technically repayable on demand and in practice reviewed at regular intervals, with interest charged at a rate which varies with the general market level.

The liabilities of the personal sector are all debts; the interest and repayment terms are settled at the outset – though the rate of interest may be variable. The maturity of the debts is related to the assets acquired – long-term mortgages for house purchase, short or medium-term loans for house improvements or the purchase of consumer durables or cars, and generally short-term credit for other purposes.

TABLE 6.4   SOURCES AND USES OF FUNDS OF THE
PERSONAL SECTOR, 1976-80

					(£ billion)
	1976	1977	1978	1979	1980
Sources of Funds					
Saving etc.[1]		8	14.2	18.3	23.6[2]
Loans for house purchase	3.9	4.3	5.4	6.4	6.9
Other borrowing	1.1	1.7	2.4	4.0	3.3
Total sources	14.2	15.8	21.9	28.7	33.7
Uses of Funds					
Physical investment					
Dwellings	2.1	2.6	3.2	3.9 ⎫	7.3
Other fixed assets	1.4	1.7	2.0	2.3 ⎬	
Stocks	0.1	0.4	0.2	0.5	−0.4[2]
Total physical investment	3.6	4.7	5.5	6.7	7.0
Financial assets					
Deposits[3] etc.	5.2	7.6	9.2	13.6	14.8
National Savings etc.	0.6	1.3	1.5	1.1	1.4
Other general government debt	2.0	0.8	0.1	2.5	2.3
Company securities[4]	−1.5	−1.8	−1.2	−2.1	−2.0
Life assurance and pension funds	5.6	6.1	7.3	9.3	10.7
Total financial assets	11.9	14.0	17.0	24.4	27.1
Unidentified etc.	−1.2	−2.9	−0.6	−2.4	−0.4
Total uses	14.2	15.8	21.9	28.7	33.7

Sources: Blue Book, 1980, Table 4.2; *Financial Statistics*, April 1981, Tables 1.1 and 1.9;
       Economic Trends, April 1981
   [1] Saving, after adjusting for stock appreciation, taxes on capital and capital transfers
   [2] Partly estimated
   [3] Including notes and coin
   [4] Including purchases of unit trust units

PERSONAL SECTOR FINANCING

The financial transactions of the personal sector in recent years are shown in Table 6.4. Personal sector saving accounted for about two-thirds of the total sources of funds, with the balance being loans for house purchase and other borrowing. Just under 25 per cent of the funds available were invested in physical assets, with over 75 per cent in financial assets. This is in striking contrast with the balance sheet proportions (Table 6.1) of over 60 per cent physical to under 40 per cent financial assets. Inflation is again the main explanation for this discrepancy; the value in money terms of physical assets increases in a period of inflation, whereas the financial assets category includes a high proportion with fixed nominal values, some assets whose nominal values have fallen, and others whose value has failed to keep pace with inflation.

Investment in dwellings makes up over half of the sector's physical investment, and, as mentioned above, is highly dependent upon the availability of mortgage loans. It is noticeable that the loans for house purchase substantially exceed investment in new dwellings. When existing houses are sold their owners are able to realize part or all of their capital, with the mortgage loan taken on by the new purchaser providing the funds.

Turning to financial assets, it can be seen that cash, deposits and national savings have accounted for 60 per cent of financial asset acquisitions, with life assurance and pension funds amounting to just over 40 per cent. The rise in saving in the last decade has been associated with a relative increase in the importance of saving through deposit-taking institutions; 20 years ago the division between deposits and long-term contractual saving was much more even. Purchases of national savings and other general government debt (gilt-edged securities and local authority loans) are sensitive to interest rates (and other terms) and have varied substantially from year to year, reflecting the strength with which the government has competed for funds from personal savers.

For many years now the personal sector has made net sales of company securities. This is probably largely a consequence of the incidence of capital transfer tax, the changing arrangements in society for maintenance during retirement, and the tax concessions available for saving through institutional channels. Capital transfer tax is levied when capital is transferred from one person to another, either during the donor's lifetime or after his death. Since substantial capital sums are frequently involved, payment of this tax usually entails the sale of securities. Once tax has been paid the recipients of bequests may also choose to hold their wealth in other forms, stimulated perhaps by the tax concessions available. The same goes for people who realize substantial capital sums from the sale of property or of private business interests. Moreover, whereas in the past many people of moderate means chose to purchase securities as a means of saving for retirement most are now covered by occupational pension schemes or have access to pension arrangements provided by life assurance companies – alternatives which have substantial attendant tax advantages. New purchasers of securities are not, therefore, coming forward from within the personal sector in sufficient numbers to acquire the securities sold for the reasons indicated. The value of the net sales of company securities is affected by security prices generally, because the timing of realizations is not generally dictated by prevailing prices, and the value of estates passing at death is a major determinant. Similar arguments apply to sales of existing housing, and help to account for the excess of loans for house purchase over investment in dwellings.

The flows of saving through life assurance and pension funds have been on a rising trend in recent years; from approximately 3 per cent of GDP 20 years ago they now amount to about 5 per cent. The contribution to long-term saving in the economy is of the highest importance. Though they were always strong, this sustained inflow of funds coupled with the diminished importance of direct personal sector holdings of company securities, has created a situation in which the life assurance and pension funds now dominate the supply of funds in the long-term capital market. The implications are discussed in Chapter 12.

Other borrowing – bank borrowing, other instalment lending and trade credit – has risen to a high level in recent years. A substantial proportion represents finance for business activities, whose requirements have increased steadily in a period of inflation.

NOTES

1. Personal income less direct taxes, national insurance, etc. contributions and transfers abroad.
2. This notion is already familiar from our discussion of saving in Chapter 3.
3. Equivalent subsidy arrangements are available for those mortgagees with insufficient taxable income.

4. Where legislative factors favour a particular category of borrower or finance for a specific purpose, there is said to be a *privileged circuit*.
5. The purchase of consumer durable goods is treated as consumption rather than investment in the national income accounts, though holdings are treated as physical assets in the personal sector's balance sheet.
6. I.e. a *flat* rate – which is a little over half of the true rate of interest charged on the balance of the loan outstanding.

7 COMPANY FINANCIAL BEHAVIOUR

Industrial and commercial companies control about a quarter of the nation's physical assets, and, as we saw in Chapter 2, almost half of the investment in the economy takes place in the company sector.[1] Companies also make an important contribution to saving, much of it reflecting depreciation charges on their assets, and a substantial proportion of investment is financed from their own resources. But a considerable part depends upon external financing – long-term or short-term debt, the issue of new ordinary shares, government grants, or assets leased and property rented from other sectors. Companies are therefore numbered amongst the most important users of the financial system. In this chapter we shall examine in more detail their financing needs and the ways in which these are met.

THE COMPANY SECTOR'S BALANCE SHEET

There are no very up-to-date figures of the balance sheet of the UK company sector as a whole, but Table 7.1 gives a balance sheet summary for companies in manufacturing and distribution in 1977. At that time the balance sheet total for these companies amounted to just over £100 billion.[2]

Amongst the assets, fixed assets formed the largest proportion. These consist mainly of tangible assets such as buildings, plant and equipment, but also include an element of 'goodwill', representing the premium over the value of tangible assets which companies sometimes pay when purchasing another company. In a period of inflation the accounting value of fixed assets almost certainly under-estimates their true value, since companies revalue their assets to take account of inflation only infrequently. The second largest component in assets is stocks and work in progress, which together accounted for nearly 30 per cent of the total. Debtors – representing goods delivered for which payment has not yet been received – amounted

TABLE 7.1   UK COMPANIES IN MANUFACTURING AND DISTRIBUTION:
BALANCE SHEET SUMMARY, 1977

(£ billion)

Liabilities		Assets	
Shareholders' interest	41.5	Fixed assets	37.5
Minority interests	2.0	Stock, etc.	29.5
Long-term loans	9.5	Debtors	24.3
Bank loans	10.1	Trade investments	4.5
Other short-term loans	2.4	Liquid assets	6.4
Creditors etc.	29.7		
Deferred tax	7.2		
Total	102.3	Total	102.3

Source: Business Monitor MA3, eleventh issue, Table 1

to nearly a quarter, and the other items – trade investments, which comprise minority holdings in other companies, and liquid assets, consisting of bank deposits and other liquid financial instruments – were also quite significant. Within the total, fixed assets and trade investments – the companies' long-term assets – accounted for only about 40 per cent, with the balance – working capital[3] – around 60 per cent. Both elements, of course, require appropriate financing, but the working capital is turned over more frequently and can be compressed or expanded in the light of prevailing financial conditions.

A company's financing comes in many forms. First there is share capital – the *ordinary shares* which give their holders a right to dividends which the company pays out of its profits, the size of the dividend (if any) reflecting the company's profitability, and sometimes also *preferred shares* which give their holders the right to a fixed dividend out of post-tax profits, which must be paid before the ordinary shareholders receive anything. Then there are *long-term loans*. Most commonly loan capital consists of *debentures* or *unsecured loan stocks*, which are distinguished by the fact that the former are secured by some means on assets of the company. There are many variants on these basic themes, for example participating preference shares where the return is geared in some way to profitability, and convertible debentures, which carry a fixed rate of interest but which also give the holder the option of converting into ordinary shares on some future date at a predetermined price.

Share capital and long-term loans are generally regarded as the permanent capital of the company. In 1977 they comprised just over half the liabilities of UK companies. Share capital alone, including minority interests of outside shareholders in subsidiary companies, accounted for over 40 per cent, with long-term loans, which are mostly at fixed rates of interest, running at under 10 per cent.

Companies' other liabilities consist of *bank and other short-term loans, creditors*, and *deferred tax*. Many bank loans are in fact medium-term loans, often connected with the finance of specific investment projects. But the greater part is relatively short-term, at least in the sense that facilities have to be reviewed and possibly renegotiated at fairly frequent (e.g. annual) intervals. Most are also at variable rates of interest, i.e. the rate is linked to the bank's base rate, which it may change periodically, or to some other market rate. Bank loans and other short-term loans were slightly larger than long-term loans in 1977 (and would be considerably larger by 1981).

Just as debtors bulk large on the assets side of companies' balance sheets, so, at nearly 30 per cent of the total, creditors form an important component of their liabilities. These represent wages and salaries which have accrued for work done but for which payment has not yet been made, raw materials and other supplies purchased but not yet paid for, and tax liabilities due in the near future. Liabilities to creditors are in fact often offset against debtors, with only the net position shown; the figures reveal that manufacturing and distribution companies were net borrowers under this heading in 1977.

The final element on the liabilities side of the balance sheet is deferred tax, which amounted to about 7 per cent of the total. This is an important element, which results mainly from the accelerated depreciation provisions in the tax law, under which companies may charge depreciation at a higher rate in calculating their taxable income than is in fact warranted by the loss of value of the assets through usage or the passage of time, and from the tax treatment of stocks in recent years, when companies have been permitted to make a deduction from their income in respect of part of the increase in the value of their stocks – an arrangement which was introduced to take account of the effects of inflation on stock values. Although deferred tax may in principle have to be paid sometime in the future, in practice it is unlikely to be paid by a company which continues in business.

The costs and obligations attached to the different components of companies' liabilities vary. Deferred tax and some parts of the money due to creditors cost the company nothing, at least until bills fall due for payment; beyond that date, the cost of credit may be high because discounts for prompt payment may have to be forgone. Short-term debt from banks or other sources is generally cheaper than long-term borrowing, though this position may be reversed if short-term interest rates are temporarily high (see Chapter 5 above). Properly treated, the cost of equity capital is the expected return to the company's shareholders, and, once an allowance for putative higher dividends in future is included, exceeds the cost of debt.

In terms of the other obligations which liabilities impose upon a company, the ranking is approximately reversed. Equity may in principle be the most expensive form of capital, but there is no obligation to repay equity or even to pay dividends on it. There is a clear obligation to repay long-term loans at specified times, and similar arrangements frequently apply to short- and medium-term borrowing. Failure to make the stipulated payments will result in sanctions on the company, ranging from inability to obtain further credit to the appointment of a receiver or liquidator. The penalties for failure to pay creditors at the appointed time may also be large. Wage and salary payments cannot easily be delayed; there is more leeway with tax payments, though an interest penalty may be incurred; and excessive delay in paying suppliers may result in further supplies being withheld.

GEARING

The principal financial decision a firm has to take concerns the division of its liabilities between equity and debt. The aim of the firm's owners is to maximize the rate of return on the equity capital, subject to taking an acceptable degree of risk. As we shall see, this risk depends on the firm's 'gearing', reflecting the relative proportions of debt and equity.

We shall define *Primary Gearing* as the ratio of debt to equity in a firm's balance sheet. Thus, if D = debt and E = equity

$$\text{Gearing} = D/E,$$

the debt/equity ratio.

Now let us examine how the *expected* return on equity varies with a firm's gearing. Suppose that a firm expects to earn profits at a rate

p on all of its assets, however financed, and that the rate of interest paid on debt is i. Then the equity return ER is given by

$$ER = \frac{p(E + D) - Di}{E}$$

$$= p + D/E (p - i)$$

So long as $p > i$, the expected return on equity rises with D/E; but conversely, if $i > p$ (i.e. the expected rate of return is less than the cost of debt), high gearing reduces the return to equity. Normally a firm will not embark upon an investment project unless it expects that p will be greater than i, so that the expected return on equity generally increase with the firm's gearing.

But so does the risk to which the equity holder is exposed. The rate of profit which the firm will earn on its assets is uncertain, and the likelihood that it will differ from the hoped-for level has to be reckoned with. In Chapter 4 we measured risk by the standard deviation of the frequency distribution of the rate of return, and we shall continue to adopt this measure here. Suppose that p is variable, that its frequency distribution has standard deviation σ_p, and that the rate of interest which the firm pays on its debt, i, is a firm commitment. Then the risk attached to the equity return, ER, is given by[4]

$$\sigma_{ER} = (1 + D/E) \sigma_p$$

which rises with the debt/equity ratio.

The effect of gearing on equity return and risk can be illustrated by means of numerical examples. Table 7.2 shows for different levels of profitability how the equity return varies with a company's primary gearing. The rate of interest on debt, i, has been taken as 10 per cent throughout, and debt/equity ratios ranging from 0.5 to 3.0 are illustrated. If the rate of profit on the company's assets is also 10 per cent, then ER is 10 per cent, irrespective of the debt/equity ratio. If p fell to 5 per cent the ER would remain positive so long as the debt/equity ratio did not exceed 1.0, but with higher gearing the company would make losses; and if profitability fell to nil ER would be negative if there was any debt to service at all. When p rises above 10 per cent the effect on ER is magnified and, as the table shows, high gearing can be associated with very high rates of return. By reading across the rows of the table it can be seen clearly that the dispersion of the rate of return on equity capital increases the higher is the company's gearing.

TABLE 7.2   THE EFFECT OF PRIMARY GEARING ON THE EQUITY
RETURN (i = 10 per cent)

Debt/equity ratio	Equity return (ER) (%)				
	p = nil	p = 5%	p = 10%	p = 15%	p = 20%
0.5	−5	2.5	10	17.5	25
1.0	−10	nil	10	20	30
2.0	−20	−5	10	25	40
3.0	−30	−10	10	30	50

Another way of looking at this question is to consider a company's
Income Gearing, the proportion of its profits which are absorbed by
interest payments on debt. This depends both on its debt/equity
ratio and on the relationship between profitability and the rate of
interest charged on loans. Table 7.3 shows how income gearing varies
for a company which earns 15 per cent on its assets, for debt/equity
ratios ranging from 0.5 to 3.0 and for rates of interest from 5 to 20
per cent.[5] Provided that the rate of interest lies well below the return
on assets, income gearing remains low, even for high debt/equity
ratios. But if the charge for debt approaches the rate of return on
assets even moderately geared companies (primary gearing) find that
a high proportion of their income is absorbed by interest.

Table 7.4 provides a further illustration of the dangers faced by
highly geared companies. As has already been mentioned, short-term

TABLE 7.3   PRIMARY GEARING AND INCOME GEARING:
THE EFFECTS OF VARYING THE RATE OF INTEREST
(p = 15 per cent)

Debt/equity ratio	Income gearing (%)			
	i = 5%	i = 10%	i = 15%	i = 20%
0.5	11.1	22.2	33.3	44.4
1.0	16.7	33.3	50.0	66.7
2.0	22.2	44.4	66.7	88.9
3.0	25.0	50.0	75.0	100.0

TABLE 7.4 THE EFFECT OF PRIMARY GEARING
ON THE EQUITY RETURN WHEN PROFITS (p) FALL
FROM 15 TO 5 PER CENT AND THE COST OF
BORROWING (i) RISES FROM 10 TO 15 PER CENT

Debt/equity ratio	Equity return (ER) (%)	
	$p = 15\%, i = 10\%$	$p = 5\%, i = 15\%$
0.5	17.5	nil
1.0	20	−5
2.0	25	−15
3.0	30	−25

debt is frequently at variable rates of interest, and if a company is
unfortunate it may well find itself hit simultaneously by a fall in
profitability and a rise in the interest payable on its borrowings.
Suppose that in normal circumstances a company expects to earn
15 per cent on its assets, and to pay 10 per cent as before on its
debt. The first column of Table 7.4 shows how the equity return
rises with the company's gearing in these conditions – as gearing rises
from 0.5 to 3.0, ER rises from 17.5 to 30 per cent. But now suppose
that there is a credit squeeze and profitability falls to 5 per cent,
while the rate of interest on debt rises to 15 per cent. In these conditions, with gearing of 0.5, the company just breaks even after paying
interest, and with higher gearing ER is negative. Indeed, with a debt/
equity ratio of 3.0, the company's losses (after interest) would
amount to as much as a quarter of its equity capital in one year.

The effect of gearing on the risk a company faces is very familiar
to lenders, and influences both the rate of interest they charge for
loans and their willingness to make loans at all. It will be recalled
that lenders attempt to limit their exposure to risk and try to keep
default risk to a low level. In looking for protection against possible
losses they have regard to; the profitability of the borrower, the
strength of the borrower's balance sheet, the possibility of taking
security on specific assets.

In order to obtain a loan a borrower has to be able to show that
there is a high probability that he will earn sufficient profit to cover
the interest payments and that his business will generate sufficient
cash to cover scheduled debt repayments. Lenders – particularly
long-term lenders – will generally expect a considerable margin to

spare to provide a cushion if things go wrong. High primary gearing eats into this margin. In deciding how much it is safe to lend, a lender will also look at the volatility of profits. As Tables 7.2 and 7.4 show, when profits are volatile high gearing can easily lead to losses.

A balance sheet is said to be strong if it exhibits a low debt/equity ratio. The higher the proportion of equity in its liabilities the greater the losses a company can withstand without its viability being called in question. Equity takes the first slice of loss, so that the stronger the balance sheet the less likely it is that a lender will be unable to recover his loan.

Lenders are also influenced by the nature of a company's business and the assets it employs. If there is a high proportion of fixed assets, the lenders may take security on these assets (or a floating charge over assets) to reduce the probability of loss. Such security gives the lender a prior claim on the company's assets if it is wound up. But security is generally regarded as an added insurance against loss, rather than as sufficient justification for making a loan, and even if security is available lenders are unlikely to be willing to accept high gearing unless profits are expected to be stable.

Because default risk increases with the borrower's gearing, companies must expect to pay more for loans if their gearing rises. Unless they are able to increase their equity base companies therefore face a rising cost of debt as their borrowing expands. This is illustrated in Figure 7.1, which shows how the rate of interest rises with the debt/equity ratio. It is not necessarily only the marginal borrowing that will cost more, because a higher debt/equity ratio makes all of a company's debt riskier. After some point, shown as X_3 in Figure 7.1, the risk will become too high for lenders to entertain further loan

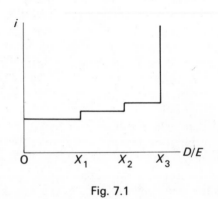

Fig. 7.1

requests. This point is, of course, dependent on the nature of the business.

The rising cost of debt capital compels us to modify our earlier conclusion that the equity return would vary positively with the level of primary gearing. That conclusion was reached on the assumption that the cost of debt would be constant. With a rising cost of debt, equity return will in fact reach a peak and then diminish, as is illustrated in Figure 7.2. As a company's gearing rises it moves from one risk class to another, and this has a sharp effect on ER, at X_1 and X_2 in the figure. Gearing cannot rise beyond X_3 because lenders are unwilling to provide more debt at that stage, but the maximum ER actually occurs before this, when the debt/equity ratio is at X_2 in Figure 7.2.

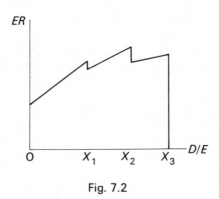

Fig. 7.2

A firm which aimed to maximize the return on its equity capital, subject to an acceptable degree of risk, would aim to prevent its gearing rising above X_2. In fact it would almost certainly stop well short of this level, partly in order to reduce its own exposure to risk and partly because the firm is concerned with the *total* cost of finance and the cost of equity finance may also increase as the equity return becomes riskier. Investors, as noted previously, have to be compensated for exposure to risk, and the higher is a company's gearing the greater the extent to which its profitability will be affected by swings in economic activity generally.

Highly geared firms are very vulnerable in bad times, not just because they make a loss on their equity capital if total profits fall and/or interest rates rise, but because companies may face further severe difficulties in the aftermath of poor profits, difficulties which may easily threaten their future independence.

A loss reduces a firm's equity base, and if it continues to employ the same capital as before its debt/equity ratio automatically rises. For example, if a firm with a debt/equity ratio of 1.0 makes a loss amounting to 20 per cent of its equity capital (or 10 per cent of assets) in some year, and if in order to continue in business its balance sheet total remains unchanged, the loss itself raises the debt/equity ratio to 1.5 : 1 (60 : 40 instead of 50 : 50). The burden of interest payments rises because there is more debt and less equity, and because, in view of its higher gearing and recent loss experience, the cost of new or renegotiated debt is likely to rise. It may not be easy for a company to avoid these difficulties by raising new equity capital, because investors will usually exact a high price for supplying new equity at a time that a firm is making losses.

All this assumes that lenders will be willing to increase their loans, albeit with a higher interest rate attached. In fact, if a company is making losses and its gearing is rising, lenders may be extremely reluctant to increase loans, or even to renew loans as they mature. As a result, the firm may have to contract by cutting stocks or selling parts of its business – actions which have had to be taken by many firms in recent years. If losses continue, or if the difficulty of retrenchment is too great, the company may be compelled to seek a takeover by another company with a stronger equity base or go out of business altogether. In either event the equity-holders are likely to suffer a sharp diminution in the value of their assets, and the more senior managers may well lose their jobs.

The result is that most firms aim to keep their debt/equity ratios well below the maximum levels which lenders are likely to tolerate. By so doing they hope to be able to weather a storm without suffering permanent damage to their business and with their freedom of action intact.

EQUITY FINANCE

A company's equity is its true risk capital. It is equity which enables companies to take the risks which are inherent in business, and it is the availability of equity which allows companies to embark upon investment programmes which increase their risk exposure. Spare equity, reflected in a level of gearing which is lower than the maximum which lenders think reasonable, is the key to additional borrowing, and companies which have strong balance sheets and reasonable profits seldom have difficulty in borrowing.

In principle, the cost of equity capital to a company is the cost of the dividends it is expected to pay in future. As we saw in Chapter 5 this cost is measured by the dividend yield plus the expected annual rate of growth of dividends.[6] This theoretical cost of equity is likely to exceed the cost of debt, partly because of the risk premium which savers demand for exposure to equity risk, and partly because UK companies are permitted to pay interest out of pre-tax profits whereas dividends are paid out of post-tax profits.

In choosing between debt and equity capital, however, companies may also be concerned with the implications for their net cash flow of raising finance by either means, and the expected cash flow cost of equity may well be less than the cost of debt. The cash flow cost of equity is the profits needed to pay dividends at whatever rate is planned in the short-run; in the case of external finance this is the planned dividend (grossed up for tax) divided by the share price. In a period of inflation when the nominal rate of interest on debt includes a substantial component to compensate lenders for the loss in real value of their capital, the initial cash flow cost of equity may be considerably lower than that of debt.

In principle, companies should treat retained profits as having the same cost as external equity issues, but in practice company directors do not always see retentions in this light: they do not have to justify the use of internal funds to providers of finance, and when internal funds are available they may be more inclined to take risks or invest in relatively marginal projects.

It is important also to remember that the *committed* cost of equity is zero. There is no obligation on the company to pay dividends, and indeed, unless there are sufficient profits available, the company is not entitled to pay dividends to its shareholders. Small or rapidly growing companies often find this feature of equity particularly attractive, because it enables them to retain a very high proportion of their profits and employ them in further expansion of their business.

Large companies in the UK normally raise new equity capital by means of a rights issue to their shareholders, but small companies without a Stock Exchange quotation and larger companies in special circumstances may place shares with one or more financial institutions. (See pp. 120–3 below, and Chapter 12.)

DEBT FINANCE

Debt finance is attractive to companies because it allows them to increase the scale of their business at a defined cost without giving up either a share of the profits or control of the enterprise. It is also the case that debt is often more readily available than equity, and for some firms the only practical source of increased equity capital is retained profits.

A distinction is often drawn between short-term and long-term debt, and the ratio of short to long-term debt in a company's liabilities is known as its *secondary gearing.* Low secondary gearing is one indication of strength in a company, because long-term does not need to be renegotiated frequently, and the company can consequently take steps to renew its long-term capital at times of its own choosing. A company which has a high proportion of short-term debt in its liabilities is exposed to interest-rate fluctuations and runs the risk of finding the supply of funds reduced or cut off at a critical time.

Long-term loans are usually raised by issuing securities in the capital market, though the possibility of direct negotiation with one or more long-term institutions or, in the case of small companies, with a specialist institution cannot be ruled out. The banking system is the dominant source of short-term loan finance.

Long-term loans generally have a life of 20–30 years, are repaid at maturity[7] and carry a fixed rate of interest. Long-term debt is particularly well suited to companies' needs for several reasons. First, it reflects the lives of many of a company's fixed assets, so that the cash generated by these assets as profit or depreciation charges can be used to service the debt. Secondly, long-term debt is usually regarded as part of the company's permanent capital, because so long as the company remains profitable it can expect to be able to refinance the debt at or around maturity. It is therefore suitable as a source of finance for both the company's fixed capital assets and the working capital which the company requires permanently. Thirdly, the rate of interest on long-term debt is usually fixed, so that the company is not at risk from swings in interest rates.

However, the supply of long-term debt to a company is not unlimited, because it needs to be able to provide adequate security to the lenders. It would be unreasonable to expect lenders to rely on profitability projections for 20 years ahead, so some alternative form of security is required. This may either be security over assets which are expected to retain their value, or covenants which form part of the loan agreements, specifying for example the maximum level of primary gearing which the company will be permitted to take on, and giving the lender the right to immediate repayment if the covenant is breached.

The most common form of short-term loan is the bank overdraft, under which firms are permitted to borrow up to an agreed limit, with interest charged only on the amount borrowed at any time. Commercial bills provide another important short-term instrument. In essence they are promises by companies to pay stated sums on an appointed day, usually three months ahead. These bills are often guaranteed ('accepted') by banks and sold ('discounted') for something less than their face value to provide the firms with cash immediately. The discount reflects prevailing short-term rates of interest.

Short-term loans are best suited to short-term needs. The archetypal short-term bank loan is an overdraft to cover the seasonal maximum in a firm's working capital. Loans of this kind are 'self-liquidating', because at the seasonal trough no part of the loan should be outstanding. Overdrafts and other short-term loans may also be used to meet a firm's financial needs due to fluctuations in profits or in investment spending. Although lenders do not usually intend their loans to be used for this purpose, some short-term loans do in practice form part of the permanent capital of a business.

Short-term loans are generally less attractive to firms than long-term because the firm cannot rely on the continued availability of the capital. Bank overdrafts, for example, are subject to regular renegotiation and review. Moreover, short-term loans are usually at variable rates of interest, with the consequence that if it is unlucky the firm may find itself paying much more than it had anticipated.

Nowadays firms also make considerable use of term loans from banks, and, to a lesser extent, finance houses. These range from ordinary instalment loans, with a fixed rate of interest and a regular repayment schedule, to custom-designed forms of medium-term project finance, in which a bank makes a loan to finance a particular investment project, and the term of the loan and the repayment schedule are linked to the expected cash flow. For example, all capital and interest payments may be deferred until after the project has begun to produce an income, with repayment over a fairly short period of years thereafter. Project loans of up to 7 years are not uncommon, and may extend to 10. Most medium-term project finance is at variable rates of interest. Banks also provide firms (or their overseas customers) with medium-term loans to finance exports of major capital goods, for which credit extending over a period of years is required. Such loans bear a fixed rate of interest, which is below the normal market level – the subsidy being provided by the government – and the credit risk is insured with the Export Credits Guarantee Department (see Chapter 13).

On average firms must expect long-term funding to cost slightly more than short, reflecting the existence of liquidity premia in the market. Nevertheless, long-term loans have in the past generally been preferred for their other attributes. However, in recent years firms have avoided taking on new long-term debt because long-term interest rates have seemed too high. If interest rates should fall in future a firm which had borrowed for a long period at a high fixed rate of interest would find itself saddled with a heavy interest burden for many years. To avoid this possibility firms have instead had recourse to medium-term and short-term loans from the banks at variable rates of interest. From the point of view of the firm these forms are inferior substitutes for long-term debt because they leave it exposed to unexpected increases in interest rates and entail more frequent renegotiation.

PROVISION OF FINANCE BY OTHER MEANS

In addition to building up equity capital from retained profits or raising new equity or debt in the financial markets, industrial and commercial companies make use of two other major sources of finance – the government and off-balance-sheet finance.

We have already drawn attention to the importance of deferred tax in companies' balance sheets (p. 103). By permitting companies to write off 100 per cent of new investment in plant and machinery and 50 per cent of investment in buildings in the first year the government forgoes a substantial amount of tax revenue, which remains in the hands of companies to help to finance their investment. The government also gives grants towards the cost of investment under the Industry Act, 1972. Regional development grants amounting to over £400 million (against qualifying capital expenditure of £2.4 billion) were paid under Section 7 of the Act in the year to 31 March 1979, and selective grants may also be made for regional and industrial assistance under both Sections 7 and 8. These grants often take the form of interest-relief grants, to reduce the cost of loan finance over a period of years, rather than outright cash payments shortly after the investment has taken place.

Rather than raise finance to purchase buildings and equipment themselves firms often choose to rent or lease instead. Rental of factories, offices and warehouses is a long-established practice which makes much less demand on a company's capital than direct ownership, and the rental payment can be regarded as a substitute for interest on debt and remuneration to the providers of equity capital. In a period of inflation it may in fact be a particularly attractive means of obtaining capital assets, because rental agreements will usually make much lower demands on a company's cash flow than interest payments on debt. This is because rental agreements contain escalation clauses, so that the rent is reviewed and altered in line with general market levels periodically and can therefore approximate to the real rate of interest; whereas in a period of inflation nominal interest rates on fixed-interest debt are at much higher levels.

Leasing of plant and equipment may also be advantageous, often for tax reasons. Although companies are permitted to write off the whole of the cost of plant and equipment against profits in the year in which the equipment is purchased, they do not receive any tax rebate if their capital allowances exceed their taxable profits. 'Tax exhaustion' is common amongst companies with large investment programmes or which are suffering from poor profitability. Leasing enables these companies to obtain the benefit of the capital allowances, since the terms of the leases reflect the fact that the lessors have sufficient taxable profits to absorb the available allowances.

SOURCES AND USES OF FUNDS

Our discusson so far has concentrated upon companies' balance sheets and in particular on the structure of liabilities which companies find appropriate for their business. We turn now to examine their sources and uses of funds, which highlight the purposes for which companies have required *additional* funds in recent years and the sources from which these funds have been obtained. Table 7.5 shows figures for successive 5-year periods, beginning in 1958, and for the most recent years. The 5-year averages bring out the trends in company financing, though there have, of course, been quite substantial year to year variations.

Since financing requirements derive ultimately from the uses to which companies put their funds, it is convenient to begin with uses, of which fixed investment is the most important. It can be divided between replacement and investment for expansion. The former does not involve a change in the scale of the business, and while it does entail new investment in fixed capital there is no concomitant increase in working capital requirements. In principle replacement investment should be financed out of depreciation allowances on existing equipment, either built up in previous years or derived from

TABLE 7.5   SOURCES AND USES OF FUNDS OF INDUSTRIAL AND COMMERCIAL COMPANIES, 1958–80

	Per cent of total sources/uses						
	1958–62	1963–67	1968–72	1973–77	1978	1979	1980
Uses							
Gross domestic fixed capital formation	58	61	53	57	62	59	80
Value of physical increase in stocks and work in progress	7	9	4	4	4	10	−19
Acquisition of financial assets:							
i liquid assets	4	4	13	15	15	4	20
ii cash purchases of subsidiaries and trade investments	8	8	6	5	4	5	5
iii investment overseas	7	6	5	6	9	17	13
iv export and other credit given	2	3	2	6	6	8	4
v other identified assets	—	1	2	4	1	1	−1
Unidentified (residual)	14	8	15	3	−1	−3	−2
Total uses	100	100	100	100	100	100	100
Sources							
Undistributed income	72	67	52	49	67	63	54
of which: depreciation	(28)	(30)	(28)	(34)	(40)	(41)	(60)[1]
Capital transfers (net)	—	2	8	3	2	1	2
Bank borrowing	10	12	19	24	15	22	37
UK capital issues: ordinary shares	11 }	3	3	—	—	—	5
debentures and preference shares	}	9	4	5	4	4	2
Other loans and mortgages	4	3	4	3	2	3	4
Import and other credit received	—	—	3	5	3	7	—
Overseas	3	4	6	11	7	—	−3
Total sources	100	100	100	100	100	100	100
(£ billion – annual averages)	(2.9)	(3.8)	(6.2)	(12.4)	(19.0)	(22.1)	(18.1)

Source: See footnote 8

[1] Estimated

current operations. Unless replacement investment involves significant changes in products or processes it does not materially affect the risks a company faces. On the other hand, investment for expansion is always risky, the degree of risk depending on business conditions and upon the novelty of the product or process. A firm's ability to take these risks depends on its financial strength. This is partly a question of current profitability on its other activities, since profits derived elsewhere can be used to cover debt servicing costs and possibly initial losses on new activities, and partly on the strength of its balance sheet, which affects the extent to which the company is vulnerable to misfortune. Investment for expansion is by no means confined to the fixed capital involved, since expansion will inevitably entail some increase in working capital as well.

There has been no very pronounced trend in the share of fixed investment in companies' uses of funds in the last 20 years. Investment in stocks appears to have declined – the high figure for 1979 and low figure for 1980 reflect involuntary stock-building in the former followed by destocking in the latter.

In recent years investment in fixed assets and stocks in the UK has amounted to between 60 and 70 per cent of industrial and commercial companies' total uses of funds. The balance, 30–40 per cent, has been devoted to investment in financial assets (including investment abroad).

As the value of a company's business increases its need for liquid assets grows. In part these are held for ordinary transactions purposes, such as the payment of wages and salaries and the bills for purchases of raw materials and other supplies. In part they are held for precautionary purposes, in case expenditure should run ahead of revenue: liquid assets can be regarded as an alternative to unused bank overdraft facilities in satisfying this need, an alternative which has the advantage of allowing the company greater discretion and flexibility. Again, part of liquid asset holdings will have been built up by companies in advance of known spending commitments. By their very nature the increase in liquid asset holdings can be expected to absorb a higher proportion of companies' funds in good years than in bad, since it is at such times that companies can afford to build them up. However, an unusually rapid increase in liquid assets was a feature of the period beginning in the late 1960s. This can be attributed to the high level of inflation which raised the *nominal* value of companies' business and imposed considerable financing requirements on them. The fluctuations in this item from 1978 to 1980 mirror those in stockbuilding – involuntary stockbuilding takes place partly at the expense of liquidity, and destocking enables firms to rebuild liquid assets.

Companies which wish to expand frequently choose to do so through a takeover or merger with another company. Takeovers and mergers occur for many reasons, including *inter alia* desires to enter related lines of business and attempts to strengthen market positions by gaining control of important suppliers or customers. Sometimes takeovers are financed by the issue of new shares, with the takeover 'raider' gaining control by offering the 'victim's' owners shares in its own company in place of those they held previously. In such cases no additional funds are required. But in others the raider pays cash for the shares of the victim company, and finance has to be obtained for this purpose. As Table 7.5 shows, cash required for the purchase of subsidiaries and trade investments has typically been a significant element in companies' total uses of funds, though it was lower in the 1970s than in the previous decade.

Investment overseas is treated statistically as the acquisition of a financial asset, though it often involves the purchase of fixed assets and stocks abroad. This too has been an important use of funds for UK companies, because a number of large multinational companies are based in the UK and many other companies have overseas subsidiaries. The figures in Table 7.5 exclude investment which was financed from profits earned and retained abroad, but even after this exclusion the figure in the most recent years amounted to well over 10 per cent of total uses of funds. Until the abolition of exchange control in 1979, the bulk of this investment was financed by overseas or foreign currency borrowing, but companies are now free to finance this investment by whatever means they choose.

In comparison with the balance sheet total for creditors in Table 7.1 the figure for export and other credit given is remarkably small. The low level is misleading. It reflects the fact that most trade credit goes unrecorded in the company financing statistics.

The bottom row of the uses of funds represents the discrepancy between independent estimates of sources and uses. In some periods it has been too large for comfort, indicating either that certain important uses were under-recorded, or alternatively that the sources of funds were over-stated.

Turning now to the sources of funds it is clear that companies' undistributed incomes form much the most important source. This category which includes retained profits, depreciation charges, and additions to tax reserves, is known as *internal* finance. However, the contribution of internal finance to total source of funds was on a downward trend during most of the last 20 years, though recently there has been some recovery. At the same time as internal finance as a whole was diminishing in importance the share of depreciation was rising. In principle this is available for replacement rather than expansion, although the opportunity to employ new technology may be taken. The implication of the fall in internal finance, coupled with the rise in depreciation, is that the contribution of internal finance to the *growth* of companies' equity has been declining.[9]

Capital transfers consist of government grants for investment. Their significance as a source of funds has varied substantially over the last 20 years, though even when their aggregate contribution to financing has been small they may well have been a key factor in promoting investment in some instances. The high level of capital transfers in 1968–72 reflects the use of investment grants, rather than accelerated depreciation allowances, as a means of stimulating investment in that period. In later periods the lower level of grants was matched by a reduction in tax payments.[10]

Over the entire period bank borrowing has been a significant source of *external* funds for UK companies, but it has become increasingly important in recent years. This again is a consequence of inflation. Not only has inflation increased firms' working capital needs; but, as already mentioned, it has caused them to avoid raising long-term debt capital at high nominal interest rates, and to turn instead to the banks for short and (increasingly) medium-term finance at variable rates of interest.

UK capital issues have shown the opposite trend. In the decade from 1958 to 1967 capital issues provided about 40 per cent of companies' external finance, but thanks to high long-term interest rates there have been virtually no new issues of long-term loans since 1972, so this element in companies' sources of funds has been less important recently. Although new issues of ordinary shares have averaged only about 4 per cent of companies' total sources of funds, this understates their significance for industry's equity base. New issues provide *additional* equity, in the same way as that part of undistributed income which does not consist of depreciation allowances contributes to equity.[11] Thus, for example, in the period 1973–77 new issues of ordinary shares which amount to 5 per cent of sources of funds should be compared with new equity from internal sources amounting to 15 per cent (49 per cent minus 34 per cent), i.e. external sources provided some 25 per cent of the additional equity capital in this period.

Other loans and mortgages are a comparatively small category,

which includes loans by long-term institutions for property development, mortgage or other loans made directly by financial institutions
to industrial and commercial customers, and loans by the government to help to support companies in difficulties. Import and other
credit received is the counterpart amongst sources of funds of export
and other credit given from the uses.

Just as UK companies employ funds in investing abroad, so foreign
companies with operations in the UK contribute to the financing of
their activities here. The substantial growth in this source of funds
up to 1973–77 was due mainly to inward investment in connection
with North Sea oil exploration and development. Now that most
further investment can be financed from profits earned from fields
which have entered production (included in undistributed income)
this source of funds has fallen away sharply.

It is important to recognize that the composition of external
financing of industrial and commercial companies has much more to
do with demand than with supply conditions. Most of those seeking
funds are able to choose between alternatives available in the market,
provided they are willing to pay the going price. Thus the decline in
industrial debentures and corresponding rise in bank loans does not
reflect any *constriction* in the supply of the former – it is a result of
reluctance by firms to pay the going rates of interest (which are
linked to rates on gilt-edged stocks). Similarly, the decline in finance
from abroad reflects a reduced need for such funds rather than any
shortage of supply to UK companies.

SMALL FIRMS

The purposes for which small firms require finance differ comparatively little from those of large firms. An analysis of the accounts of
a sample of small companies carried out for the Wilson Committee[12]
showed that the balance sheets of small firms contained a lower
proportion of physical assets than those of large firms, suggesting
that on average small firms were less capital-intensive, with correspondingly high components of trade debtors and creditors. The
smallest group of firms – those with capital employed of less than
£250 000 in 1975 – were also more liquid than large firms, though
firms in the next size group – up to £4 million at that time – relied
quite heavily on bank borrowing. However, even if the composition
of assets of large and small firms does not differ greatly, from the
point of view of external suppliers of finance, lending or investment

in small firms is appreciably riskier. Small firms typically have much more limited management resources – they are usually dependent upon at most a handful of key individuals – and since they also tend to be less diversified than their larger competitors, their fortunes are more closely linked to those of particular industries.

Small firms' access to external finance is generally much more restricted than that of their larger competitors. For equity capital many small firms depend largely on their own resources – the profits they are able to retain or funds which they can obtain from relatives or close friends. For debt they rely heavily on the clearing banks, and to a lesser extent on the finance houses. Since the ability to borrow depends ultimately on an adequate supply of risk capital many small firms find that their growth is limited by their ability to generate internal funds.

The lack of external equity investment in small firms has a variety of causes, stemming both from the attitudes of the owners themselves and the needs of outside investors. Many small businessmen are extremely reluctant to give up equity in their firms; they fear that outside equity shareholders might eventually try to take control, and, with their own personal standard of living at risk, they feel that the rewards of success should also be theirs. Moreover, potential investors may demand terms which seem to the owner to put much too low a valuation on his company. From the point of view of the outside shareholder, however, the terms may be quite reasonable. Equity investment in small firms entails considerable costs of investigation before investments are made, and comparatively high administrative costs to monitor investments thereafter. Some of these costs may be avoided by the private investor who is familiar with a company's business, but any such investor has to recognize that a minority shareholding in a small company generally has very poor marketability, and that he is likely to be in a weak position if he wishes to sell.

These problems are of long standing, and were identified by the Macmillan Committee[13] which reported in 1931. The Committee pointed out that there was a gap, christened the 'Macmillan Gap', in the capital market provision for companies which were too small to make issues on the stock market. Since that time a number of institutions have been created to help to fill this gap, of which the most important is the Industrial and Commercial Finance Corporation (ICFC),[14] which was set up in 1946 and provides both long-term loan and equity capital to smaller companies. It views its holdings of equity as permanent. In addition, there are a number of Development Capital Companies, including some subsidiaries of the clearing banks, which are active in making equity investments in the more promising small companies. The Development Capital Companies do not usually regard themselves as permanent holders of equity, hoping instead to sell their holding if the company obtains a Stock Exchange listing subsequently. Some investment trusts are also active investors in small companies, and regard themselves as long-term holders.

Small companies depend on the clearing banks for most of their loan finance. The banks claim to be willing to provide as much finance as is reasonable, at a cost which reflects the cost of funds to them, the risk of loss, and the administrative costs inherent in retail lending. To control the risk of loss they take what security they can get. They recognize that small firms are likely to experience difficulty in raising external equity capital on acceptable terms and so, they claim, are prepared to tolerate higher levels of gearing than would be appropriate for larger companies. In their view, overcharging or an unrealistic attitude to risk on the part of any bank would lead to a loss of business to its competitors – they rely on competition to ensure that terms are fair.

Since the assessment of much of the risk in lending to small companies is not susceptible to precise calculation, it is hardly surprising to find that some of the banks' customers contest these claims. It is not so much the charge for loans that is at issue. Rather it is asserted that the banks are niggardly in their lending and oppressive in their demands for security. Competition between a small number of like-minded (and allegedly over-cautious) bankers does nothing to ensure that the proper needs of small firms are served.

Facts in this area are hard to come by. Some customers are certainly over-optimistic about their prospects of success, and few have full cognizance of the low risk of loss which is appropriate for institutions like banks. Quite often finance houses, which are able to support a higher level of risk, have been prepared to provide finance for the purchase of particular items of plant and equipment when banks would not extend their facilities further. But on the other side, bankers' attitudes to risk vary, and the threat of taking business to a competitor may not be powerful when assessment of risk has to be based partly on a business relationship built up over many years.

The Wilson Committee[15] felt that there was sufficient doubt about the adequacy of the supply of loan finance to small firms to warrant the setting up of an experimental loan-guarantee scheme, under which the banks would be able to off-load onto a guarantor part of the credit risk involved in loans to small companies, and the government have sponsored a scheme which began operating in June 1981. Arrangements of a similar kind exist in many other countries. The Committee also felt that improvements in the supply of equity capital were desirable and, apart from suggesting that there should be improvements in the market for unlisted securities, proposed the creation of a new kind of investment trust, Small Firm Investment Companies. Individuals who invested in these companies would be eligible for a certain amount of tax relief, and this would help to increase the supply of equity finance for the small company sector. No action on this recommendation has yet been taken (early 1981), though it has gained the support of the Confederation of British Industry. Instead the government have extended the possibility for individuals who invest directly in small firms to obtain tax relief on their investment.

IS INDUSTRY STARVED OF FUNDS?

It has often been suggested that the low level of industrial investment in the UK reflects deficiencies in the capital market, and that industry in Britain has been starved of funds for investment. We shall return to this question in Chapter 17. In the meantime we should draw attention to one of the main pieces of evidence adduced to support this assertion – the fact that capital gearing in Britain is low by international standards.

TABLE 7.6   INTERNATIONAL COMPARISON
OF CAPITAL GEARING,[1] 1976

	(%)
UK	53
USA	53
Japan	359
Germany	89
France·	152
Italy	301
Sweden	192

Source: Wilson Committee Report, Table 39
  [1] Capital gearing is the ratio of long and short-term debt to shareholders' interest

Table 7.6 shows that in 1976 capital gearing in the UK was closely comparable to that in the USA; it was somewhat lower than in Germany, and considerably lower than in the other countries shown. The spread of gearing levels is somewhat exaggerated due to differences in measurement – for example, trade creditors are included in the figures for debt for Japan – but the fact that gearing in Britain is lower than in many other countries is not disputed.

There are several possible reasons for this phenomenon. Those who argue that industry has been starved of funds suggest that it is because bankers and other financiers in the UK are more conservative than their counterparts in other countries, and limit gearing to a comparatively low level. The opposing view is that the low level of gearing in the UK and the USA reflects the fact that firms have good access to equity capital and that deficiencies in the capital markets in other countries compel firms to make more use of borrowed funds. In Japan, for example, external equity finance has often been difficult to obtain, and there is no doubt that of the countries listed the equity markets of the UK and USA are the strongest.

The evidence given by industry to the Wilson Committee suggested that large and medium sized firms did not regard the supply of finance as a constraint on investment. The principal reasons for our comparatively low investment were a lack of attractive investment opportunities coupled with poor profitability of existing operations. However, this evidence is scarcely conclusive. It should not blind us to the fact that firms may have found the cost of external financing too high, and so curtailed their investment programmes; or that their own views of the risks attached to further borrowing were coloured by their perceptions of what lenders would be likely to accept.

NOTES

1. Including financial companies and institutions.
2. The valuation of assets is taken from the companies' accounts, and no additional valuation adjustment for inflation has been made.
3. The term *working capital* is being interpreted to include the gross value of the relevant assets.
4. $ER = p(1 + D/E) - (D/E)i$.

   Since i is a constant it follows that

   $$\sigma_{ER} = (1 + D/E)\,\sigma_p.$$

5. Income gearing (%) = $\dfrac{Di}{(D+E)p} \times 100$

   Thus, for example, if $i = 5\%$ and $D/E = 0.5$

   $$\frac{D}{D+E} = \frac{1}{3}$$

   and

   income gearing (%) = $\dfrac{1}{3} \times \dfrac{5}{15} \times 100 = 11.1\%$.

6. All grossed up for tax.
7. Though repayment by instalments is possible, and a sinking fund is sometimes accumulated to provide the funds required for repayment at maturity.
8. Figures for 1958-77 are taken from *Wilson Committee Report*, Table 34. 1978-80 are from *Financial Statistics*, April 1981 and *Economic Trends*, April 1981.
9. Note that the figures for undistributed income and for the value of the physical increase in stock and work in progress in Table 7.5 are net of stock appreciation. Depreciation is at replacement cost.
10. The effect is to raise the 'additions to tax reserves' component of undistributed income.
11. Assuming that additions to tax reserves can be regarded as equity capital.
12. M. T. Jones, 'An Analysis of the Accounts of Small Companies', *Committee to Review the Functioning of Financial Institutions*, Studies of Small Firms' Financing (Research Report No. 3).
13. *Committee on Finance and Industry*, Report, Cmd 3897.
14. For further discussion, see Chapter 13.
15. Interim Report, *The Financing of Small Firms*, Cmd 7503.

8 PUBLIC SECTOR INVESTMENT AND FINANCING

The finance of the public sector is a topic whose breadth extends far beyond the matters which concern us here. Our examination of public sector financing in this chapter will therefore be restricted to ascertaining how the activities of the public sector, as generators and users of funds, fit into the pattern of investment and financing in the economy, and how the government and other public sector organizations affect the financial system. Public sector financial institutions, which form part of the system itself, will be considered in Chapter 13.

The public sector consists of the central government, local authorities and public corporations – that is the nationalized industries and certain other public sector bodies such as New Town Corporations and the National Enterprise Board. Although these components are quite distinct, and we shall give some consideration to the behaviour of each broad component individually, for many purposes it makes sense to treat the public sector as a whole. In formulating its financial policy the government takes account of the overall impact of the public sector's operations on financial markets, and an increase in the financing needs of one part of the sector may have to be accompanied by contraction elsewhere. The capital spending of all components are reviewed by the Treasury and other government departments, and are subject ultimately to a high degree of central influence and control. There are strong financial links within the public sector, the surpluses generated in some areas are channelled directly to other public sector users, and the bulk of the sector's external financing needs are raised centrally. The overall position of the sector determines the supply of certain categories of security, notably gilt-edged securities, and the public sector's demands on the capital market have implications for the level of interest rates and monetary growth.

The centralized consideration and control of public sector financing stands in sharp contrast with the dispersed decision-taking of the personal and company sectors. In these sectors economic agents take their own decisions in the light of the prices and terms prevailing in the financial markets. There is no overall control of saving or borrowing, and it is the changes in the market which maintain balance between them. For the public sector, however, there is a conscious attempt to ensure that the overall level of borrowing does not impose excessive strains on the capital market, which could be relieved only by driving up interest rates and contracting the supply of credit for other borrowers. On the other tack, when private demand for funds has been weak public sector borrowing has been deliberately increased in order to absorb saving which might otherwise have been excessive.

The relatively slight contribution to saving in the UK made by the public sector in recent years has already been brought out in Table 2.6. On average, public sector saving amounted to just over 1 per cent of GDP in 1978–80. On the other hand, the public sector has consistently played a much larger part in the nation's capital investment, with a figure of nearly 6 per cent of GDP in 1978–80. Public sector investment has in fact fallen in recent years as a consequence of government efforts to reduce the public sector's financial deficit – it averaged over 8 per cent of GDP in the 5 years 1973–77.

No complete balance sheet of the public sector's assets and liabilities is available, but Table 8.1 gives figures of the sector's liabilities to other sectors in March 1980. Of the total of £116 billion just under 80 per cent comprised sterling or foreign-currency debt of the central government. Over 15 per cent was local authority debt, with the balance the liabilities of public corporations. These figures, however, greatly understate the importance of local authorities and public corporations as holders of public sector assets, because 45 per cent of local authority debt and over 80 per cent of the public corporations' debt is owed to the central government. As might be expected, most of the debt is in sterling, but about $7\frac{1}{2}$ per cent is denominated in foreign currencies; most of this was issued as a means of obtaining foreign exchange to support the gold and foreign exchange reserves in the years from 1974 to 1978, though part of the central government component has been outstanding for much longer.

The sector and currency composition of the debt already gives one indication of the centralized nature of government finance. While most of the foreign-currency borrowing was by public corporations and local authorities, this took place under a guarantee against exchange loss from the central government, and was in effect a

TABLE 8.1   LIABILITIES[1] OF THE PUBLIC SECTOR,
31 MARCH 1980

	(£ billion)
Central government	
Sterling debt	87.4
Foreign currency debt	3.9
Local authorities	
Sterling debt	18.4
Foreign currency debt	0.2
Public corporations	
Sterling debt	1.7
Foreign currency debt	4.4
Total	
Sterling debt	107.5
Foreign currency debt	8.6
Total debt	116.1

Source: Financial Statistics, February 1981, Table 8
[1] Public sector debt held outside the public sector

substitute for borrowing from the central government itself. Equally, the comparatively low levels of total debt of local authorities and public corporations outstanding are indicative of their dependence upon the central government to raise finance on their behalf.

Public sector debt makes up a considerable part of the total primary securities issued by UK borrowers.[1] But, in spite of very large public sector borrowing requirements, it has been declining as a proportion of GDP in recent years: public sector debt (at market values) held outside the public sector amounted to 95 per cent of GDP in 1969 but had fallen to only 65 per cent of GDP 10 years later. This substantial reduction is a consequence of inflation; GDP in current prices has risen much faster than the total debt outstanding.

LOCAL AUTHORITIES AND PUBLIC CORPORATIONS

The capital expenditure and borrowing for each of the sub-sectors of the public sector are shown in Table 8.2. Local authorities and

TABLE 8.2 CAPITAL EXPENDITURE AND BORROWING OF CENTRAL GOVERNMENT, LOCAL AUTHORITIES AND PUBLIC CORPORATIONS, 1973–80

(£ billion)

	Central Government				Local Authorities				Public Corporations				Public Sector			
	1973–77 average	1978	1979	1980	1973–77 average	1978	1979	1980	1973–77 average	1978	1979	1980	1973–77 average	1978	1979	1980
Capital expenditure and grants (net of capital receipts)	1.6	2.5	2.5	3.1	3.5	3.3	3.5	3.7	3.8	4.8	5.8	7.0	8.9	10.7	11.8	13.9
Net lending and purchases of securities	2.8	2.1	3.5	4.2	0.3	0.0	0.3	0.5	0.3	0.6	0.4	0.2	1.2	0.5	0.4	0.3
Less Current account surplus	0.3	2.7	1.7	2.7	−1.3	−1.6	−1.5	−1.3	−2.1	−3.8	−3.7	−4.2	−3.0	−2.6	−3.5	−2.8
Other sources (net)	0.4	1.0	2.7	1.1	−0.2	−0.6	0.1	0.2	0.0	−0.3	1.1	−0.4	0.2	−0.2	3.9	1.0
Borrowing requirement (of which, from central government)	5.1	8.4	10.4	11.2	2.4 (1.1)	1.0 (0.4)	2.3 (0.6)	3.1 (1.2)	2.0 (1.1)	1.1 (1.8)	3.7 (3.3)	2.6 (3.4)	7.2	8.3	12.6	12.3

Source: Financial Statistics, April 1981, Tables 2.5, 3.7, 4.2 and 5.2

public corporations will be considered first, because both obtain a considerable proportion of their capital funds directly from the central government, and their operations therefore have important implications for central government finance. The table shows that capital expenditure and grants by local authorities has been running at about £3.5 billion per year recently. About half of this expenditure relates to housing, with the balance going towards the other important activities carried out by local authorities – for example road building, education and environmental services. Most of this expenditure has to be financed by borrowing, though local authorities receive grants from the central government to cover part of the cost of some projects, and they in turn make capital grants to the private sector for purposes such as house improvement or repair. Local authorities also make loans to the private sector, mainly in connection with house purchase. The capital spending programmes of local authorities are subject to fairly detailed scrutiny by central government departments, and their borrowing activities require Treasury consent. While short-term borrowing in anticipation of revenue receipts is permitted, the extent of such borrowing is also subject to central control.

Table 8.2 shows that local authorities are generally able to finance a considerable part of their capital spending out of the current account surplus on their operations. (This is computed before making any allowance for depreciation on their assets.) The item labelled 'other sources (net)' consists mainly of rate payments received in advance, and a statistical discrepancy which is sometimes fairly large. The balance of their funding has to be obtained externally, and for this purpose the local authorities draw both upon the central government and upon the financial markets generally.

The bulk of the borrowing from the central government comes from the Public Works Loan Board (PWLB), which is funded through the National Loans Fund (NLF).[2] Each authority has a quota which it may draw down from the PWLB, and the interest rates charged are linked to the current rate on long-term government debt.

Table 8.2 shows that local authorities currently obtain well under half of their finance from the central government. The balance is raised in the market, either as short-term loans, mortgages, or by issuing listed securities. Around 20 per cent of the total borrowing of local authorities is 'temporary debt', i.e. is for an initial maturity of less than 1 year, with the balance being 'longer-term debt'. Both temporary and longer-term debt are attractive to a wide range of potential holders, including banks, other financial institutions, companies (in the case of temporary debt), and the personal sector. At the end of March 1980 over three-quarters of local authority debt was within 5 years of maturity.

Public corporations represent the bulk of the 'enterprise' activities of the public sector. In 1980–81 their total capital expenditure amounted to £5.6 billion, including £0.8 billion for the Coal industry, £1.5 billion for Electricity, and £1.4 billion for the Post Office and Telecommunications. Like private sector enterprises public corporations also require funds for overseas investment and for the purchase of securities, though the sums required have been relatively small in recent years.

Part of the public corporations' capital spending is financed out of their undistributed income. The ability to contribute to their own financing varies very substantially between the more profitable and the loss-making corporations. For example in 1980–81 Electricity contributed £1.2 billion from internal sources, Gas £1.1 billion, and the Post Office and Telecommunications £1.5 billion. The largest borrowers were all loss-makers – Coal borrowed £0.8 billion, Steel £1.1 billion and the Railways £0.8 billion.[3]

Capital expenditure of the public corporations is controlled through a mixture of target rates of return on capital employed, specified for most of the corporations, and cash limits. The investment programme of each public corporation is intended to earn at least the target rate of return overall, but in addition to that the corporation is given an external financing limit, so that if its current profitability falls below expectations it may be compelled to reduce its capital spending correspondingly. In practice, when a corporation's profitability has fallen very substantially below what was hoped for, the government has been compelled to raise its cash limit.

As Table 8.2 shows most of the external financing of the public corporations is obtained from the central government, through the NLF. The surpluses earned by the more profitable corporations, whose profits exceed their own investment requirements, are paid into this fund, and the borrowing needs of other corporations are met from it. Instead of borrowing directly from the NLF, the public corporations have at times borrowed foreign exchange, which they have then sold to the government, mostly in order to bolster the gold- and foreign-exchange reserves. This foreign-currency borrowing is now being repaid, with the consequence that in both 1978 and 1980 borrowing from the central government exceeded the public corporations' own needs. The public corporations also make some use of borrowing facilities on preferential terms from bodies such as the European Investment Bank. The main domestic source of finance for public corporations, other than the central government, is the banks, which make advances to the corporations in the normal way.

CENTRAL GOVERNMENT AND THE PSBR

The financial needs of the central government reflect its own capital expenditure, grants made and net lending to other bodies in the public and private sectors, its own surplus or deficit arising from current operations, and any shortfall resulting from delays in receipts or payments.

The central government is directly responsible for a considerable amount of capital expenditure – £2.0 billion in 1980 – of which the most important elements are expenditure on roads and on the National Health Service. But it also contributes to expenditure in other sectors through capital grants – £2.3 billion in 1980 – to help to finance such activities as building by universities and colleges, housing associations, and regional and other investment grants in the private sector, together with capital grants to local authorities and public corporations. However, only part of this leads to borrowing, because the central government is the recipient of certain taxes on capital – mainly capital transfer tax and capital gains tax – amounting to over £1 billion in 1980 – which can legitimately be set against its own capital expenditure.

We have already seen that much of the borrowing by local authorities and public corporations is channelled through the NLF and therefore adds to the central government's financing needs. These items account for the bulk of the central government's net lending, but in addition there are smaller amounts involving transactions with the private and overseas sectors, and the central government also sometimes needs funds to purchase private sector securities or obtains funds by selling securities it owns. Overall the net lending and purchases of securities item amounted to £4.2 billion in 1980.[4]

In recent years the central government has run a deficit on its current account – that is its current expenditure has exceeded its receipts from taxes and other charges – which has to be financed by borrowing in the financial markets. The current deficit first emerged in 1975, since when the accounts of the central government have remained consistently in deficit.

The final, important element giving rise to central-government borrowing is the delay before the government receives the tax revenue due to it. Taxes accrue at the time that income is earned or (in the case of VAT) spending takes place, but the government does not receive the money until some time later. When, due to inflation, income and spending rise rapidly, the sum outstanding may increase considerably.[5]

Adding across the three components of the public sector in Table 8.2 and eliminating intra-sector transactions, gives the figures for the public sector as a whole. Thus in 1980 capital expenditure and grants amounted to £13.9 billion, net lending and purchases of securities outside of the public sector came to £0.3 billion, the current account surplus of the public sector as a whole was £2.8 billion, and a further £1.0 billion was added to the public sector's needs by the delays in receiving payments. Altogether then, the Public Sector Borrowing Requirement (PSBR) amounted to £12.3 billion, or $5\frac{1}{2}$ per cent of GDP. This compares with an average of about 7 per cent of GDP in the period 1973–77.

FINANCING THE PSBR

Before turning to look at how the PSBR is financed a further complication must be considered. The government holds the nation's gold and foreign exchange reserves, and purchases or sales of reserves affect the amount which the government has to borrow; the sale of an asset, foreign exchange, is an alternative to borrowing and the purchase of an asset entails an increase in the amount borrowed. However, transactions of this kind do not necessarily change the government's *domestic* borrowing in sterling. The level of the foreign exchange reserves is also affected by government borrowing denominated in foreign currencies, either directly from overseas residents or through the UK banking system; borrowing of this kind was important in the mid-1970s, and there have been substantial repayments subsequently. In addition, when overseas residents buy government securities, they themselves provide the finance for the corresponding increase in the foreign exchange reserves, so there is no direct impact on domestic borrowing.

The net effect of all these transactions is known as the government's requirement for 'external finance'. Table 8.3 shows that in some years, for example 1978, external finance made a contribution to the financing of the PSBR, so that the net effect was to reduce the government's domestic borrowing requirement, whereas in

TABLE 8.3   FINANCE OF THE PSBR, 1973–80: ANALYSIS BY SECTOR

(£ billion)

	PSBR	External finance	Total domestic *of which*	Banks[1]	OFI	Industrial and commercial companies	Personal sector
1973–77							
average	7.2	0.4	6.8	1.1	3.2	0.5	2.0
1978	8.3	1.0	7.4	0.1	4.2	0.8	2.3
1979	12.6	−0.6	13.2	1.5	7.0	0.6	4.1
1980	129.3	0.0	12.3	2.4	5.5	0.4	4.0

Source: Financial Statistics, April 1981, Table 2.6
    [1] Sterling borrowing

others, such as 1979, external factors increased the government's domestic borrowing requirement.

Table 8.3 shows the sources from which the public sector raised its finance in recent years. In view of the large financial surplus of the personal sector it is hardly surprising to find that the principal sources have been direct lending by the personal sector and funds channelled from that sector through other financial institutions. Industrial and commercial companies make a relatively small contribution (through their holdings of notes and coin and certain other short-term financial instruments), while the contribution of the banks has fluctuated from year to year, but has in any event represented only a relatively small proportion of the total.

Table 8.4 shows how the finance provided by the non-bank private sector has been divided between different types of financial instrument. The contribution made by holdings of notes and coin – non-interest-bearing government debt – is striking, and in a period of inflation when people's holdings of currency are steadily rising, this is a source on which governments are able to rely. The category, national savings etc., includes certificates of tax deposits which companies and persons can buy and hold until tax payments fall due. In an effort to attract funds from the personal and company sectors the government in recent years has tried to ensure that national savings and these tax instruments offer attractive terms to savers, and the importance of these financial instruments for government financing has been on the increase. Treasury bills etc. reflect not only

TABLE 8.4   NET ACQUISITION OF PUBLIC SECTOR LIABILITIES
BY THE NON-BANK PRIVATE SECTOR, 1973–80

(£ billion)

	Total	Notes and coin	National savings etc.	Treasury bills etc.	Gilt-edged stocks	Other
1973–77						
average	5.8	0.7	0.6	0.1	3.5	0.9
1978	7.2	1.2	1.8	−0.5	5.1	−0.3
1979	11.7	0.8	1.2	−0.2	8.8	1.0
1980	10.0	0.7	1.7	−0.5	7.7	0.4

Source: Financial Statistics, April 1981, Table 2.6

the non-bank private sector's holdings of these bills, but also, as an offsetting item, Bank of England holdings of commercial bills. By and large the non-bank private sector holds treasury bills only if the rate of interest on these bills exceeds what they can earn from holding bank deposits, and the fluctuations on this item have been connected with the way in which the government has implemented monetary policy.

Gilt-edged stocks form much the most important element in public sector finance, with the OFIs representing the dominant source of demand. For example, in 1980 OFIs bought £5.3 billion of gilt-edged stocks. But in recent years the personal sector has also been a significant source of demand for these securities. The high level of the PSBR in recent years has compelled the government to carry out a very substantial programme of new issues of gilt-edged securities, on terms which were likely to be attractive to the financial institutions as well as other private sector investors.

The 'other' category consists mainly of liabilities issued by local authorities. The extent to which they have relied upon the non-bank private sector has also been influenced by monetary conditions generally. When monetary policy has been restrictive, conditions have sometimes led to local authorities borrowing directly from this sector rather than indirectly through the banks. From the point of view of the lender, short-term loans to local authorities are good substitutes for interest-bearing bank deposits or certificates of deposit, and the choice between them rests upon the relative rates of interest offered.

THE PSBR AND THE CAPITAL MARKET

The implications of a high PSBR for the working of the economy are extremely controversial. On the one hand some people see the PSBR as the principal cause of the high rate of inflation and low rate of economic activity in the UK. On the other, it is often asserted that a high PSBR is an inevitable consequence of inflation, which gives rise to a combination of a high level of private saving and low private investment, thereby generating surplus saving which has to be absorbed by the public sector. However, whatever view is taken on this issue, there is no dispute that the size of the PSBR has important consequences for the capital market and for the conduct of monetary policy. A high PSBR means that the flow of private saving in the economy has to be directed to the public sector rather than being returned to other borrowers in the private sector; and a policy of controlling the rate of growth of the money supply implies that the bulk of the finance must be found from outside the banking sector, with implications for the interest rates and other terms which the government has to offer on its securities.

There have been considerable changes in the size and composition of the PSBR during the last 25 years. To see what has happened it is helpful to distinguish the saving, investment and financial surplus/deficit of the public sector itself from its net lending operations, i.e. loans to other sectors net of repayments and sales of public sector assets. Table 8.5 shows the former for the public sector as a whole and for its component parts since 1958. During the 15-year period 1958–72 saving averaged 5.7 per cent of GDP and investment 7.5 per cent of GDP. Although the financial deficit of the public sector as a whole was by no means insignificant, it averaged under 2 per cent of GDP, and the saving generated within the public sector was sufficient to finance about 75 per cent of public sector investment. The situation since 1973 has been quite different, as Table 8.5 demonstrates. In the 8-year period 1973–80 saving has amounted to only 2 per cent of GDP, while investment has averaged over 7 per cent of GDP in this period, although it has been on a downward trend. Thus the financial deficit amounted to over 5 per cent of GDP and public sector saving was sufficient to finance under 30 per cent of public sector investment.[6]

TABLE 8.5   SAVING AND INVESTMENT IN THE PUBLIC SECTOR, 1958-80

(Per cent of GDP at market prices)

	Public sector	Central government	Local authorities	Public corporations
Saving				
1958-62	4.3	2.3	0.9	1.1
1963-67	5.4	2.5	1.1	1.8
1968-72	7.3	4.3	1.3	1.7
1973-77	2.5	−0.8	1.3	2.0
1978	1.0	−2.4	1.0	2.4
1979	1.3	−1.4	0.8	1.9
1980	0.8	−1.8	0.6	2.0
Investment				
1958-62	6.6	0.9	2.5	3.2
1963-67	8.1	0.9	3.4	3.8
1968-72	7.9	1.1	3.6	3.2
1973-77	8.1	1.1	3.4	3.6
1978	5.9	0.8	2.1	3.0
1979	5.6	0.8	1.9	3.0
1980	5.8	0.9	1.7	3.2
Financial surplus/deficit				
1958-62	−2.3	1.4	−1.6	−2.1
1963-67	−2.8	1.5	−2.3	−2.0
1968-72	−0.6	3.2	−2.3	−1.5
1973-77	−5.6	−1.9	−2.1	−1.6
1978	−4.9	−3.2	−1.1	−0.6
1979	−4.4	−2.2	−1.1	−1.1
1980	−5.0	−2.6	−1.1	−1.3

Source: Wilson Committee Report, Table 12; *Financial Statistics*, April 1981, Table 1.1; *Economic Trends*, April 1981

Table 8.5 also shows that the fall in saving has been concentrated in the central government part of the public sector; indeed, after dropping in 1974 and 1975, saving by public corporations has been appreciably higher since 1975 than in earlier years. Before that the central government had a surplus on its current account, which was sufficient to finance not only its own investment but also to make a considerable contribution towards funding the capital requirements of the local authorities and public corporations. In contrast, since 1975 the central government has had to borrow in order to finance current expenditure as well as for capital purposes. Table 8.5 also shows that the recent downward trend in capital expenditure has affected all the components of the public sector.

It is not possible to say what is the 'correct' level of saving or investment by the public sector. So far as saving is concerned, it is a question of what level of saving in the economy as a whole is thought to be desirable. A high level of saving by the public sector helps to make it possible to achieve a high level of saving overall. Looked at in this way it seems plausible to suggest that the present level of public sector saving is too low. We saw in Table 2.5 that the level of saving in the UK was low by the standards of other industrial countries, and the continual complaints about the low level of investment in the UK suggest that a higher level of saving is required.

The level of investment which is appropriate for the public sector is partly a matter of political choice, as to which activities will be carried out within the public sector, and partly a matter of the returns which society can expect to receive from different types of investment. For example, a country like Britain in which a high proportion of utilities are in public ownership and in which the public sector is an important provider of dwellings must expect to have a higher level of public sector investment than countries in which the private sector plays a larger part in these activities. Public sector investment for income-yielding purposes is no more burdensome to society than equivalent investment by the private investor. It is more difficult to judge the correct level of investment for purposes which do not yield a direct income flow, for example, investment in the National Health Service which raises the standard of living rather than yield a flow of marketable services; but the principle that such investment should be judged and justified by its prospective return to society stands.

Public sector saving and investment have effects on the rate of interest which are identical with those of saving and investment by the private sector. We saw in Chapter 5 how investment tended to raise and saving to lower the rate of interest, and it follows that the balance between investment and saving in the public sector has implications for the rates of interest prevailing in financial markets generally. The high level of the public sector financial deficit in recent years must therefore have tended to raise the rates of interest payable by private sector borrowers.[7] To the extent that private sector investment is sensitive to the rate of interest this will have had the effect of discouraging some private investment.

The effects of net lending by the public sector, which as we have seen is sometimes an important contributor to the overall PSBR, are very different. In large part loans by the public sector act as a substitute for private sector finance. While some public sector lending facilitates private sector activity which might otherwise not take place – e.g. loans by the Export Credits Guarantee Department have helped to facilitate exports, and loans to housing associations have encouraged investment in dwellings by this means – the important characteristic is much less the fact that finance is provided than that the rate of interest is subsidized or other terms are eased.[8] That part of net lending which reflects the delay before taxes are received is of little consequence for economic activity; any acceleration of payments would lead only to relatively unimportant changes in the liquid balances held or short-term borrowing of the private sector.

NOTES

1. At 31 December 1980 public sector securities accounted for 45 per cent (by market value) of the UK sterling securities listed on the Stock Exchange.
2. This is a government fund which acts as a central source for loans within the public sector.
3. The figures are from *The Government's Expenditure Plans 1981–82 to 1983–84*, Cmnd 8175, HMSO 1981, Table 3.5.
4. This figure was inflated as a result of industrial action which delayed the receipt of money due to one of the major public corporations.
5. The very high figure for 1979, when items of this kind added £2.9 billion to borrowing by central government, was also affected by the sharp increase in VAT rates in that year.
6. These figures understate the true deterioration in public sector saving. If saving is measured net of depreciation at replacement cost, it appears that the public sector as a whole was dis-saving at a rate of about 1 per cent of GDP per year.
7. Though there is no doubt that the most important reason for the high nominal rates of interest has been the rate of inflation.
8. The effects of subsidies are discussed in Chapter 15.

9 THE OVERSEAS SECTOR AND THE UK FINANCIAL SYSTEM

The British economy has many links with other countries. Trade represents a significant proportion of economic activity, capital is able to flow in and out (with less or greater freedom according to the stringency of exchange control), and London is the most important centre in the International Banking System. We have already seen several examples of ways in which these links affect financial behaviour: UK companies need funds to invest abroad, foreign-controlled companies in this country obtain financing from their parents, and government financing is complicated by the management of the foreign exchange reserves. Other forms of capital transaction may also be extremely important. Portfolio investment abroad by financial institutions, the purchase of securities in the UK financial markets by overseas residents, and other short-term capital movements through the banking system are all examples. Most of the transactions involving the overseas sector entail the purchase or sale of foreign exchange at some stage, and their effect on the UK economy is intimately connected with the government's policy in the foreign exchange market. The main categories of transaction are summarized in Table 9.1.

CURRENT ACCOUNT TRANSACTIONS

The balance of payments surplus on current account measures the difference between what the UK receives by selling goods and services abroad and what it pays for imports of goods and services. The surplus therefore shows the net amount of finance that UK residents have available to acquire foreign assets, and this will be reflected in an increase in the foreign exchange reserves, a reduction in liabilities to foreigners, or the purchase of some other overseas assets.[1] Table 9.1 shows that in the period 1973–77 and again in 1979 the current account of the balance of payments was in deficit, with a small

TABLE 9.1   FINANCIAL TRANSACTIONS WITH OTHER COUNTRIES, 1973–80

				(£ billion)
	1973–77 average	1978	1979	1980
Current account balance	−1.5	0.7	−1.6	2.7
Direct investment				
Outward	−1.5	−2.6	−4.4	−2.7
Inward	1.6	2.4	2.2	1.7
Portfolio investment				
Outward	−0.3	−1.9	−2.2	−4.3
Inward	0.8	0.2	1.8	2.4
Bank deposits and other short-term items				
Outward	−10.0	−21.0	−30.2	−32.9
Inward	11.0	19.1	33.3	33.6
Other	0.4	1.7	2.4	0.2
Reserves etc.	0.5	−1.3	1.4	0.7

Source: Financial Statistics, April 1981, Table 1.11

surplus in 1978 and a much larger surplus in 1980. The size of the current account surplus or deficit is the result of many factors which influence the economy, including prevailing financial conditions and the exchange rates for sterling against other currencies. We cannot go further into these but simply note the implications of the surplus or deficit for changes in financial assets and liabilities.

CAPITAL TRANSACTIONS

Three categories of capital transaction are distinguished in Table 9.1: direct investment by companies, portfolio investment, and changes in holdings of bank deposits and other short-term items. Direct investment by companies is determined principally by the prospective profitability of investment at home and abroad, and by exchange controls which may have inhibited outward investment before 1979 – the recent rapid growth may partly be due to a back-log of investment which had been discouraged previously. Inward direct investment since the mid-1970s has included very substantial financing for North Sea oil exploration and development, though this is now declining because profits earned on existing fields provide a growing proportion of the further finance required. Quite apart from the use of retained profits foreign investment does not necessarily involve international capital flows, because part of the finance can often be raised locally. Capital flows for direct investment are therefore influenced, not only by profit opportunities, but also by the relative costs of raising finance at home and abroad.

Part of portfolio investment is similar in character. Industrial and commercial enterprises may choose to expand their overseas activities by buying existing companies, rather than developing new firms or building up their existing overseas operations. But portfolio investment also reflects the activities of financial investors, who often wish to hold diversified asset portfolios, spreading their risks across countries as well as amongst different kinds of security. Further, from time to time the prospects in particular markets may seem more attractive than those in the UK, leading to substantial capital outflows for portfolio investment. Until exchange controls were abolished in the autumn of 1979 UK financial institutions were unable to use domestic funds for overseas investment on any scale, but since then overseas portfolio investment has grown very rapidly.[2] For similar reasons of portfolio management foreign investors want to hold UK securities, and there is frequently an inflow into UK equities and, when conditions seem favourable, gilt-edged securities – for example, in 1979 and 1980 overseas investors purchased £1.2 billion and £1.5 billion of gilts respectively.

The scale of the entries for bank deposits and other short-term items in Table 9.1 reflects the dominance of London in the International Banking System. Banks in London take deposits from all over the world in a variety of currencies, of which the US dollar is still much the most important, and relend these funds to other borrowers. Most of this activity has little effect on the UK financial system – the funds pass through without influencing financial conditions here – but some of the overseas deposits are in sterling and may be used by the banks to hold domestic assets, or the banks themselves may sell foreign exchange in order to acquire sterling to lend to UK customers. The difference between the outward investment (lending) and inward investment (deposit-taking) therefore represents the extent to which UK borrowers have drawn on international sources of funds through the banking system. On average this amounted to £1 billion per year from 1973–77, there was a net outflow of nearly £2 billion in 1978; in 1979 the UK obtained over £3 billion in this way, and in 1980 there was a more modest inflow of under £1 billion.

Inflows and outflows through the banking system are sensitive to the short-term interest rates prevailing in the UK and in other countries, to the exchange rate for sterling, and to changes in the exchange rate which are expected to take place in future. Foreign investors are unlikely to increase their holdings of sterling bank deposits if UK interest rates are low or if sterling is expected to depreciate sharply. The size of the net inflow or outflow into sterling through the banking system is also influenced by the government's exchange-rate policy. We shall return to this in a moment, but at this point we note that in the absence of exchange-market intervention (i.e. with the foreign exchange reserves held constant) any shortage of funds in the UK will lead to an increase in interest rates which is likely to attract funds from overseas. Thus the current account deficit in the balance of payments in 1979 combined with the substantial net outflow for direct and portfolio investment abroad, created the need for funds which was met to a considerable degree by borrowing through the banking system. In 1980, however, the current account surplus was sufficient to finance the net outflow of long-term capital.

The 'other' item in Table 9.1 is mainly a statistical discrepancy. There is no way of telling how far this discrepancy reflects errors in the estimates of trading items, such as imports and exports, and how far it is due to errors in the estimates of capital transactions.

RESERVES

The net effect of all these transactions is a change in the gold and foreign exchange reserves.[3] This appears at the bottom of Table 9.1, which shows that on average the reserves gained £0.5 billion per year from 1973–77, there was a fall in the reserves in 1978, but the reserves rose again in 1979 and 1980.

EXCHANGE RATE POLICY

Any surplus or shortage of saving in the economy is reflected in its balance of payments. In Chapter 2 we noted that the balance of payments surplus on current account equals the excess of *domestic* saving over *domestic* investment, and in this chapter we have observed how outward direct and portfolio investment creates an additional need for funds while the corresponding inward investment supplements domestic saving. Balance between the demand and supply of funds may be achieved by varying interest rates and other conditions in financial markets, by drawing in additional funds from abroad or releasing surplus funds for lending overseas through the banking system, or through a change in the gold and foreign exchange reserves. The contribution made by each of these methods to maintaining balance depends on the government's exchange rate policy.

At one extreme, a country which adheres to a fixed exchange rate – where the government is committed to buying or selling its own currency to hold the exchange rate constant – has no control over short-term capital flows through the banking system. Whether depositors choose to deposit funds at home or abroad will depend on the prevailing levels of interest rates; if there is a surplus of saving at home, interest rates will tend to fall, and depositors will buy foreign exchange to place funds overseas. Again, if domestic opportunities for investment improve and sufficient domestic savings are not forthcoming, interest rates will rise and funds will be attracted from other countries. For Britain, with its sophisticated banking system, a very small difference between domestic and overseas rates of interest would be sufficient to shift a substantial volume of funds between sterling and foreign-currency deposits, if there was no possibility of the exchange rate changing. The result is that, with a fixed exchange rate, the rate of interest could not depart far from international levels. Any attempt by the government to hold the rate of interest well above the prevailing international level would result in a massive inflow into sterling, associated with a build-up of the foreign exchange reserves, while if interest rates were set too low the reserves would be steadily depleted.

At the other extreme a country which follows a flexible exchange-rate policy, refraining altogether from official intervention in the foreign exchange market, has much greater scope for interest rate variation. A shortage of saving at home will be reflected in high interest rates (to bring saving and investment into balance) and the economy will be insulated from any tendency to relieve the shortage through a capital inflow from abroad. In the case of Britain, for example, foreign investors attracted by the high rate of interest on sterling deposits will find that the exchange rate appreciates, until the possibility of an exchange loss is sufficient to counterbalance the advantage of the higher rate of interest. A flexible exchange rate regime results therefore in the balance between domestic saving and investment being reflected fully in domestic financial conditions (which may also, of course, be influenced by monetary policy), without any contribution from short-term international capital movements.

The real world lies somewhere between these two extremes. Countries which follow a fixed exchange-rate policy normally fix parities for the exchange rates of their currency relative to other countries and allow the actual exchange rates to fluctuate within relatively narrow bands around the exchange parities. If conditions change fundamentally the country remains free to alter the par values. Thus there is a real possibility, in both the short and long terms, that the exchange rate will rise or fall, and this means that domestic interest rates can differ to a limited extent from the prevailing international level.

At the other extreme, few countries feel able to follow a freely flexible exchange rate policy for more than a short period, because governments cannot in practice be wholly indifferent to the level of the exchange rate, which has important implications for income, employment and prices. High interest rates which lead to a substantial appreciation of the exchange rate, may damage a country's industry, and while this may be tolerable for a short period it cannot be permitted to go on indefinitely. A low interest rate, leading to depreciation of the exchange rate, may give an undesirable impulse to inflation. In consequence, governments are frequently under pressure to follow monetary policies which keep the exchange rate within an acceptable band, and to moderate rises or falls through exchange market intervention. This means that short-term international capital movements may still play some part in equating the supply with the demand for funds, and that interest rates and domestic financial conditions do not bear the entire burden of balancing saving and investment in the economy.

NOTES

1. In the case of a deficit in the current account of the balance of payments there has to be a corresponding fall in reserves, increase in liabilities or sale of assets.
2. Previously overseas portfolio investment by financial institutions had to be financed by foreign currency loans or by the purchase of foreign exchange from other investors who were selling overseas assets.

3. The reserves are also affected by other official financing items and by revaluations due to changes in the value of gold and in the foreign exchange value of sterling.

PART IV UK FINANCIAL INSTITUTIONS AND MARKETS

Borrowers and lenders, the users of the financial system, depend upon the facilities and services provided by financial institutions and markets. The activities of the institutions, the nature of the organized markets, and the factors which govern their behaviour in the UK form the subject-matter of this Part.

Chapter 10 deals with the main *deposit-taking institutions*. A distinction is drawn between retail deposit-taking institutions, which generally set the terms on which they are prepared to accept deposits or make loans and then satisfy the demand forthcoming at these terms, and wholesale institutions which deal in large sums and rely on access to the sterling money markets. The differing modes of operation are examined, and applied to the major categories of deposit-taking institutions – commercial banks, savings banks and building societies – in Britain. The contributions made by these institutions to meeting the needs of borrowers and lenders are also considered and criticisms of some of their practices discussed.

The *investing institutions* – principally the life assurance and pension funds which are important participants in the channelling of new saving to borrowers, but also the general insurance funds, investment and unit trusts which manage a significant volume of existing savings – are discussed in Chapter 11. The connection between the structure of their liabilities and the characteristics of their assets is stressed. Particular attention is paid to the structural and legislative influences on the nature and scale of their activities. The contributions of the investing institutions to the financial system and the reasons for the strength of life assurance and funded occupational pensions schemes in the UK are examined.

Some of the deposit-taking institutions and all of the investing institutions make use of the *organized financial markets*, the securities markets and the sterling money markets, which are discussed in Chapter 12. Some of these markets are, of course, also used directly by borrowers and lenders from the personal, company and public sectors. The functions and organization of the markets are described, and some of the implications for the securities markets of the growing dominance of financial institutions are considered.

Most financial systems include a number of *special credit institutions*, to fill gaps or carry out specific functions. The UK is no exception, though these institutions are much less prominent than in some other countries. The main UK special credit institutions and their functions are discussed in Chapter 13.

Chapter 14 deals with *regulation* in the financial system. The principles underlying prudential controls on financial institutions, and the main techniques employed in the UK, are discussed first. Then the combination of statutory and non-statutory controls in the securities markets is considered. Finally, there is a short discussion of economic controls which affect the behaviour of financial institutions.

10 DEPOSIT-TAKING INSTITUTIONS

The principal deposit-taking institutions in the UK are the commercial banks, with sterling deposits (from non-banks) of some £70 billion, the savings banks, whose deposits amount to about £10 billion, and the building societies with deposits (or 'shares') of nearly £50 billion at the end of 1980. Other types of institution, such as the finance houses and the discount market, also obtain part of their funds as deposits from the public, but the bulk of their resources are raised in other ways. We shall concentrate mainly on the commercial and savings banks and the building societies, but shall consider these other institutions briefly at the end of the chapter.

The liabilities of the different categories of deposit-taking institution are similar in many important respects. Deposits have a fixed money value, for all the major institutions the risk of loss is negligible, and they are either repayable on demand or after some agreed period. The institutions pay interest on most of their deposits, the rate varying with the term of the deposit, and in the cases where no interest is paid, such as current account deposits with most commercial banks, the depositor receives the benefit of other services provided by the institution. The result is that deposits of a similar term are regarded as close substitutes by the public.

The deposit-taking activities of these institutions can be divided usefully between the retail and wholesale markets.[1] Some of the banks operate in both markets, but most institutions specialize in one or other. Participation in the retail market generally entails operating through a network of branches, where deposits (up to some maximum sum) are accepted on standard terms. Established connections between customers and particular branches help to provide a stable deposit base and give rise to considerable inertia in the system, though differences between institutions in the terms they offer for deposits can nevertheless eventually lead to substantial movements of funds. By contrast, operating in the market for wholesale deposits (above some minimum sum) is usually a head office function, involving the use of brokers or direct telephone contact with large customers, though some large deposits may also be collected through branches. The interest rates paid for wholesale deposits are negotiated individually, and the amount of deposits taken by any institution is very sensitive to the terms it offers.

There are much greater differences between the deposit-taking institutions on the assets side of their balance sheets. Building societies specialize in making loans for house purchase – retail business carried out through a branch network. The savings banks have traditionally held their funds in public sector securities, either provided directly by the central government or purchased in organized securities markets. In recent years, however, the Trustee Savings Banks have begun to engage in lending to private-sector customers. The assets of the commercial banks are much more varied, including loans of all sizes to persons and firms, and investment in securities, mainly those of the public sector. Some of the commercial banks specialize in particular types of activity, such as corporate lending, whereas others are much more wide-ranging.

Apart from deposit-taking and lending many of these institutions provide other services, of which the most important is the provision of payments facilities.

The deposit-taking institutions hold assets for which the risk of loss is low, and they take care to spread their risks in the ways discussed in Chapter 4. They also avoid holding any substantial part of their assets in long-dated securities, whose value might fall sharply if interest rates rose. Their capital to deposits ratios are generally low, reflecting the nature of their assets.[2] For example, at the end of 1979 the ratio of free capital to deposits for the London clearing banks was 4.5 per cent, while for the building societies the average ratio of reserves to deposits was 3.5 per cent.

Although these financial institutions differ in their legal constitution – commercial banks are companies, Trustee Savings Banks are unincorporated societies and building societies are mutual organizations – all need to maintain an adequate ratio of capital and reserves and depend on their ability to earn a return on their assets which is sufficient to cover their costs. The difference between the rate of interest earned on assets and the rate paid on deposits is known as their margin. Out of this margin they have to pay their operating costs (less any charges for services provided). For an expanding institution the margin also has to be wide enough to allow the institution to add to its own capital and reserves since otherwise, in the absence of injections of new capital from outside, the capital to deposits ratio would gradually decline. For example, if building societies grow by 10 per cent per year their margin would have to include 0.35 per cent in addition to operating costs to enable them to maintain their reserve ratios.

Deposit-taking institutions have to manage their assets to make quite sure that they will always be in a position to repay deposits when they fall due and to honour loan commitments. The methods employed for this purpose vary. Those institutions which specialize in attracting retail deposits and making loans on standard terms generally hold a stock of liquid assets, which can be increased or run down as necessary. But institutions which negotiate the terms of large deposits individually rely less on holding a variable stock of liquid assets, because they have much greater control in the short-run over the size of their deposits, and can usually obtain the funds they need by altering the terms they offer.

RETAIL DEPOSIT-TAKING AND LENDING

Retail deposit-taking institutions like building societies or the clearing banks, which collect deposits through branch networks, normally publish the standard rates of interest they pay for deposits of different maturities. Their retail lending is also generally on standard terms for particular categories of loans (e.g. car purchase loans or house mortgages), or on terms which, though not published, are common knowledge amongst potential borrowers. The competitive strength of any particular institution reflects the size and location of its branch network, the interest rates that it pays on deposits and charges for loans, the quality of its management, and the range and convenience of the services it provides.

Liquid assets act as a buffer in these institutions' portfolios, reflecting and absorbing the effects of deposit and loan inflows and outflows. This is illustrated in Figure 10.1, which shows a tank containing liquid assets. The inflows of new deposits and loan repayments (including interest) tend to raise the level of liquid assets in the tank but at the same time the level is being reduced through outflows due to deposit withdrawals and new loans. The inflow from loan repayments is more or less fixed, determined by the loans made in previous periods, but the inflows and outflows of deposits and the outflow into new loans can be influenced by turning the relevant taps, i.e. by altering deposit interest rates and the rates of interest and other terms attached to new lending. Since the other character-

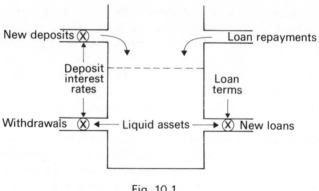

Fig. 10.1

istics of deposits and loans differ little between institutions, any institution (or category of institution) which alters its interest rates can expect the volume of its deposits and loans to change.

Financial institutions are often reluctant to change interest rates very frequently, mainly in order to avoid inconveniencing their customers but also for other administrative reasons. Each institution has some target level of liquidity, which depends on the volatility it normally experiences in its cash inflows and outflows, and which allows a considerable safety margin in case conditions should become unusually difficult. It aims to set its interest rates at levels which keep its inflows and outflows of funds in balance in the long run. Purely erratic or seasonal movements are likely to be reversed quite quickly, but an institution may also be prepared to tolerate a sustained rise or fall in liquidity for some time, with quite substantial departures from the target level. Whether it does so will depend on how long the institution expects the trend in liquid assets to last. Normally it will alter its interest rates only if the level of liquidity in the tank has altered significantly or if a substantial further change is expected. Deposit and loan rates are usually altered together in order to retain the necessary interest rate margin. The result is that an increased deposit inflow resulting from a rise in interest rates would also be associated with a reduced outflow for new loans as loans became more expensive.

Since the institutions know that any substantial change in relative interest rates will lead to a sustained deposit inflow or outflow, they usually alter their own rates quickly in response to sharp changes elsewhere, so that relative interest rates do not change by much. Thus the signal for a change in interest rates is either a substantial change in competing rates, thought likely to persist for some time, or an abnormally high or low level of liquid assets, combined with the expectation that they will rise or fall further.

WHOLESALE DEPOSIT-TAKING INSTITUTIONS

This model of a retail deposit-taking institution does not apply very well to banks in Britain today. Before the development of the sterling money markets it provided a reasonably good description of the clearing banks' behaviour, but most banks are now involved to a greater or lesser degree in wholesale business, and therefore operate in a somewhat different fashion. Rather than dealing with depositors and borrowers on standard terms, they bid for large deposits in organized markets and the terms for loans are negotiated individually. Both the rate paid for deposits and the rate charged for loans vary flexibly with the going rates for deposits and loans respectively, and loan rates are often expressed as a percentage margin over the cost of deposits.

Competition between wholesale deposit-taking institutions centres on the lending side of their business. Loan business is obtained by making contact with potential clients, identifying their needs, and providing loan facilities and other services in a form which is convenient for them. Large loans are often syndicated (divided up) amongst several banks. The bank leading the syndicate makes contact with the customer and is responsible for negotiating the terms of the loan and managing it subsequently. Other banks are invited by the lead bank to participate in the lending. Invitations to participate in syndicates depend on a bank's contacts with other banks and on the prospect that it will also act as a lead bank and be able to offer comparable lending opportunities to others. The margins banks are able to earn on loans depend on the strength of competition for lending business at the time; margins tend to narrow when competition is particularly fierce. Access to deposits depends on the institution's reputation – if the safety of deposits is for any reason called in question the supply may dry up completely – on its size and on its willingness to pay competitive interest rates.

Wholesale deposit-taking institutions provide for the safety of their deposits in much the same way as retail institutions. They control and spread their risks, avoid loans which are unduly large in relation to their capital and reserves, and ensure that their own capital is sufficient to absorb any losses. But the techniques they employ to provide liquidity are different. First, they hold *structured* asset portfolios in which the flow of loan repayments and maturities is relatively smooth and predictable. Secondly, they structure the maturity pattern of their deposits in order to avoid excessive reliance on very short-term funds. In some cases they actually match the maturity of particular loans and deposits, though since maturity transformation is an important function for banks, and one which enables them to earn a reasonable margin on their loans, the average maturity of their loans is generally considerably greater than that of their deposits. Thirdly, they hold a substantial part of their assets in 'market loans' – loans to other banks, local authorities, and others which are repayable within a short period, and certificates of deposit which can be sold if necessary. Finally, they rely on their ability to obtain new deposits so long as they are willing to bid a competitive rate: continued access to an organized market for deposits is the foundation stone of their mode of operation. Compared with retail institutions the wholesale institutions thus place much less emphasis on varying the liquid asset holdings as a means of maintaining the balance between total assets and liabilities. Instead, since they are able to alter interest rates flexibly, they depend on turning the taps to ensure that inflows and outflows of funds remain in balance.

The wholesale deposit-taking institutions are part of the sterling money markets (see Chapter 12). Nowadays lenders with large sums at their disposal generally seek to obtain as high a rate of interest as possible on their money (consistent with avoiding any risk of loss), and the organized sterling money markets provide them with this facility.

COMMERCIAL BANKS

At the end of 1980 there were over 350 commercial banks in the UK. Only about a third were UK-owned, the majority being subsidiaries or branches of foreign banks. The total liabilities in sterling and foreign currencies amounted to around £300 billion, of which roughly one-third was denominated in sterling. However, this total overstates the banks' liabilities to the public, because the banks engage in a considerable amount of deposit-taking and lending amongst themselves. Excluding inter-bank transactions of this kind brings their total liabilities down to some £220 billion.

Much of the foreign currency business reflects London's position as an international financial centre, and many of the foreign banks are present in London for this reason; foreign banks account for about 80 per cent of the foreign-currency deposits. But some of these banks are also active in certain forms of domestic lending, particularly large-scale corporate lending in the UK, and UK banks also play an active part in the international business. We shall not be concerned here with foreign currency depositing and lending for its own sake, since these activities do not impinge directly on the rest of the UK financial system. But participation in international financial markets provides UK banks with the ability to tap funds from abroad (in sterling as well as in foreign currencies) if there is a shortage of finance domestically, or to channel funds abroad when there is a surplus. The scope for movements of funds between sterling and other currencies is, of course, affected by exchange-rate policy.

The principal retail banks in England and Wales are the six London clearing banks, of which the big four (Barclays, Lloyds, Midland, and National Westminster) are the most important, the three Scottish clearing banks (Bank of Scotland, Clydesdale, and Royal Bank of Scotland), and the Northern Bank and Ulster Bank in Northern Ireland. The clearing banks carry out the bulk of the nation's cash distribution and money transmission activities.[3] They therefore occupy a central place in the system, the provision of an efficient payments mechanism being one of the most basic and essential functions of any financial system. The clearing banks also undertake most of the retail deposit and lending business in the economy. Current account deposits – those held primarily for immediate payments purposes – do not generally bear interest, though the clearing banks calculate an implicit interest payment which is set off against charges which would otherwise be levied for payments services. Retail savings or deposit accounts are interest-bearing and are usually repayable nominally at 7 days' notice, but in practice funds can be transferred to current accounts without notice and used for immediate payment. Retail lending by the clearing banks includes overdrafts and instalment loans to persons, bridging finance and some long-term mortgages for house purchase, and overdraft and term loans for small businesses. Through their branches the clearing banks are also in a good position to provide advice and other financial services.

With very few exceptions the non-clearing banks confine their deposit-taking and lending activities to wholesale transactions, and, in addition to their retail activities, the clearing banks are also heavily involved in this segment of the market. Deposits are taken for a variety of terms, though most have comparatively short maturities –

at the time the Wilson Committee reported about three-quarters of the wholesale deposits had a maturity of less than 3 months and only 5 per cent were for periods in excess of 1 year. The banks also attract funds by issuing negotiable Certificates of Deposit, which represent term liabilities for the banks but which can be sold before maturity to provide cash for their holders.

Wholesale lending to corporate customers generally takes the form of term loans, often syndicated amongst several banks if the loan is large. The terms range from 2 to about 7 years, with a small number extending to 12 years or even longer. The banks also help their corporate customers to obtain short-term finance by 'accepting', i.e. guaranteeing,[4] commercial bills, the most common maturity being three months, which they then either take into their own port-folios or sell on behalf of their clients. Some of the banks (the 'merchant banks') are corporate finance specialists, supplying advice on company financial policy, assisting with raising new funds in the capital market, and advising in takeover or merger negotiations. Many of the banks also provide investment management services to other financial institutions (e.g. pension funds, unit trusts) and wealthy private individuals.

Table 10.1 shows the sterling assets and liabilities of banks in the UK in December 1980. It is not possible to distinguish statistically between retail and wholesale activities, because, as noted above, the major retail banks are also heavily involved in wholesale business, and shortages or surpluses of funds arising from their retail activities are often accommodated through the wholesale deposit market. The table shows that sterling notes and deposits totalled just over £90 billion, of which around 30 per cent consisted of sight deposits (mainly non-interest-bearing) and notes, with the balance comprising interest-bearing time deposits and certificates of deposit. The clearing banks (London, Scottish, and Irish) accounted for approximately 55 per cent of the deposit total but for just over 70 per cent of the sight deposits and notes. Items in suspense and transmission (£3.6 billion) result from the time taken to clear payments through the money transmission system – funds debited from one account are not usually credited to another immediately – and capital and other funds (£13.6 billion) represented about $12\frac{1}{2}$ per cent of total liabilities.

About £40 billion of the banks' funds (nearly 45 per cent of depositors' funds) were held in a variety of short-term assets, some of which were required to satisfy the mandatory reserve asset ratios prescribed at the time by the Bank of England, but the bulk of which

TABLE 10.1   BANKS IN THE UK, STERLING ASSETS AND
LIABILITIES, DECEMBER 1980

(£ billion)

Liabilities		Assets	
Notes and deposits		Short-term assets[1,2]	40.0
Sight deposits and notes	27.5	Advances	52.9
Time deposits	57.7	Investment	
Certificates of deposit	5.7	Public sector investments	3.7
Items in suspense and trans-		Other	2.3
mission	3.6	Miscellaneous assets	9.1
Capital and other funds	13.6		
Total liabilities	108.0	Total assets	108.0

Source: Financial Statistics, April 1981, Table 6.5
[1] Notes and coins, balances with the Bank of England, money at call, Treasury and other bills, British Government stocks with up to 1 year to maturity, market loans
[2] Of which, market loans to banks and certificates of deposit, £20.9 billion

reflected the banks' own judgment of their need for short-term or liquid assets. About half of these assets consisted of market loans to banks and certificates of deposit; while these assets satisfy the need for liquidity of the individual bank which holds them, they cannot be regarded as a source of liquidity for the banking system as a whole. When these liabilities of other banks are subtracted, the remaining short-term assets amounted to about 30 per cent of the banks' deposit liabilities to the public.

The banks' principal earning assets are their advances and investments. Advances (£52.9 billion) amounted to about half of total assets. Investments fall into two categories: public sector securities (£3.7 billion, mainly gilt-edged) which form an investment in their own right and also, since they are mostly short-dated, provide supplementary liquidity; and other investments (£2.3 billion), such as investments in subsidiary companies at home or abroad. Miscellaneous assets include 'collections' (payments which have not yet been received from other banks), leased assets, and other assets such as buildings and equipment.

Banks help to transfer funds between surplus and deficit units in the economy – surplus units increase their deposits or repay loans, deficit units run down their deposits or borrow more. The transfer may be between units in the same sector or from one sector to another. No statistics exist to show the extent of transfers within sectors, but figures showing the net amount transferred between sectors are available.

Table 10.2 shows the sector composition of the sterling deposits and lending (including the holding of securities) of the UK banking sector[5] in the period 1976–80. It shows clearly how the banks have extensive dealings with all the major sectors of the economy, and that they have a very important role to play in transferring funds between them. For example, at the end of 1980, the personal sector accounted for 52 per cent of the banks' sterling deposits, but only 22 per cent of the banks' lending was returned to this sector. In contrast, industrial and commercial companies received 40 per cent of the lending but supplied only 20 per cent of the deposits. The other major borrowing sector was the public sector to which 22 per cent of the banks' funds were lent, but which, as noted earlier, holds only a low level of bank deposits. Other financial institutions have a slightly greater weight as depositors than as borrowers. It is noticeable how sterling deposits from overseas have grown in importance in recent years, and by the end of 1980 16 per cent of the banks' deposits were held by overseas residents, whereas only 10 per cent of their lending was channelled to overseas borrowers; much of the latter arises in connection with the finance of UK trade, including medium-term credit for exports.

Table 10.2 also illustrates another aspect of the banks' functions. Because they borrow and lend over the economy as a whole they are able to attract funds from whichever sectors have funds available and lend them to whichever sectors need them in the prevailing economic conditions. Thus, although the personal sector is normally a source of funds for other sectors, in 1977 its borrowing increased by much more than its deposits. And in 1979, when all the domestic sectors were borrowing heavily, and only the personal sector deposits were increasing, the banks were able to provide funds by obtaining more sterling deposits from overseas residents.

It can be seen, therefore, that the banks are the *general* deposit-takers and lenders in the economy; taken as a whole they show no sector preference or specialization. But they are more than this, for they are also the *residual* lenders in the economy. It is to the banks that borrowers turn for funds when they either cannot or do not wish to raise them elsewhere. Thus when times are difficult and companies are short of cash it is typically bank lending that increases,

TABLE 10.2   UK BANKING SECTOR, STERLING DEPOSITS AND LENDING, 1976–80

(£ billion)

End of year	Deposits						Lending					
	Personal sector	Industrial and commercial companies	Other financial institutions	Public sector	Overseas sector	Total	Personal sector	Industrial and commercial companies	Other financial institutions	Public sector	Overseas sector	Total
1976	20.5	8.9	4.2	1.0	4.0	38.5	7.6	18.2	2.6	11.8	3.8	44.0
1977	21.0	10.4	4.9	1.4	5.6	43.4	8.9	20.3	2.8	13.6	4.2	49.8
1978	24.2	11.9	5.8	1.3	5.5	48.6	10.8	22.6	3.4	13.5	5.1	55.3
1979	30.3	11.9	5.5	1.3	8.5	57.5	13.9	26.9	4.5	15.0	5.1	65.3
1980	36.6	14.2	6.8	1.6	11.5	70.6	17.3	32.3	5.3	17.3	7.9	80.1

Source: Financial Statistics, April 1981, Table 6.1

rather than long-term borrowing in the capital market. If the public sector has a deficit which it does not finance through national savings or the long-term capital market, it is the banks which provide the necessary funds. In recent years the public sector has in fact relied relatively little on the banks for money, and the bulk of their lending has been directed towards industrial and commercial companies and persons. But in the past there have been periods when the public sector was the main borrower, when persons actually reduced their borrowing overall, and when the demands of industry were modest.

Banks are the oldest financial institutions and are positioned at the very centre of the financial system. They are involved in all the major functions of the system: providing speedy and cheap payments facilities, mobilizing saving, and transforming the risk and maturity characteristics of assets. How well do banks carry out these functions in the UK?

There is little criticism of the payments facilities provided by the banking system today. The National Giro was set up to provide an inexpensive, convenient and speedy money transmission service, using Post Office facilities. This it does; but a high proportion of transactions are deposits or payments at Post Office counters, as opposed to remittances between giro accounts, and it has not made significant inroads into the clearing banks' business. Nor was it a commercial success – though it may have stimulated improvements in the clearing banks' facilities. However, this is an activity in which the pace of technical change is fast, and further scope for improvement in payments technology clearly exists.

Mobilizing saving entails both collecting saving and channelling it from surplus to deficit units. We have just seen how the banks transfer funds between sectors in a flexible manner. There is also no doubt that they are extremely successful in collecting funds in the wholesale markets and in marshalling very large loans when they are needed. But they have been criticized for their failure to collect a higher proportion of personal deposits. The building societies and, to a lesser extent, the Trustee Savings Banks have tapped markets which the clearing banks had left virtually untouched, and personal deposits with building societies have grown much more rapidly and to a considerably higher level than deposits with banks. How far this reflects a lack of competitiveness on the part of the clearing banks in the past is open to debate – there is no doubt that in some respects, e.g. opening on Saturdays, the building societies satisfy the needs or convenience of their customers better. But the building societies have also benefited from advantages denied to the banks – freedom from monetary controls and privileged tax arrangements – which also help to account for their success. These matters will be discussed further in Chapter 15.

The banks' performance in transforming risk and maturities in the economy has also been the subject of some disagreement. That banks do transform risk is not in question – their loans are risky and their deposits are not, but the issue is whether they do enough in this respect. The techniques which banks (and other financial institutions) employ to control and spread risk were discussed in Chapter 4, one essential element being the containment of the risk on each loan to a low level. The banks' critics allege that in attempting to do this they display excessive caution or impose burdensome requirements on borrowers. Some of these issues have already been aired in Chapter 7, specifically the view that the banks insist on an unduly low level of gearing for companies, that they demand too much security on loans and that the covenants in loan agreements are sometimes undesirably restrictive.

The question of security is fairly straightforward. Banks everywhere take security when they can get it; indeed, in many countries they are legally obliged to take security, though what ranks as security may not in fact be worth very much. Both the form and the amount of the security taken is a matter for negotiation with the borrower. It is difficult to believe that in a banking system characterized by strong competition between banks which are accustomed to the practices in other major countries borrowers would be compelled to concede more security than was reasonable. This must surely be the case in Britain, at least for the large firms with access to the wholesale banks; the situation for small companies may sometimes be more difficult, because the range of choice of lender open to them is much more restricted.

If then security requirements are more stringent in the UK, as is alleged, and since it is certainly true that gearing is lower than in some other major countries, some reason other than excessive caution must be found. A possible explanation lies in the nature of the relationship between bankers and their customers in this country. Before making a loan to a firm a bank has to assess the prospect of repayment and minimize the risk to which it is exposed. One approach is to attempt to judge the quality of a company's management, to examine the strength of its balance sheet, to consider the purpose of the loan, and if on balance the loan seems justified, to take security in case the investment should prove unsuccessful.[6] This approach does not require the company to give detailed, confidential information about its business to the bank, nor does it require the bank to have the expertise needed to assess the technical qualities of the investment proposal or other purpose for which the finance is requested. Some companies in Britain are reputed to be reluctant to take their bankers into their confidence, and so long as they can satisfy their bankers without doing so, they are able to obtain the funds they need and cannot be compelled to alter their behaviour. For their part, the banks are usually ill-equipped to judge for themselves the technical merits of major investment proposals.

The situation is very different in some other countries. In Germany, the banks have a central role, not only in the credit market, but also in the capital market, and it is normal for one or more bankers to sit on the supervisory board of any major company. Thus the bank has full information about the company's strategy and plans, about its current prosperity, and, through its continuing contact with the company's affairs, is able to acquire expertise in the industrial aspects of its activities. In Japan, relations between companies and their bankers are often extremely close, with both banks and companies forming part of larger industrial groups. In France, the banks employ qualified scientists and engineers with the capacity to evaluate both the technical and economic aspects of projects, to assist in assessing lending proposals. Some British banks employ in-house experts to advise on decisions concerning the financing of North Sea oil developments, but as yet the practice has not spread to other areas.

In spite of differences in their practices at home, the foreign banks in Britain do not appear to act in ways which differ from their British counterparts in the UK. This suggests that, if the relationship between bankers and industry is part of the explanation for low gearing in the UK, the attitudes underlying this relationship are to be found at least as much in industry as in the banks.[7]

There are no comprehensive figures of the maturity structure of the banks' sterling assets and liabilities, so it is impossible to measure the extent to which they carry out the function of maturity transformation. But the London clearing banks told the Wilson Committee that in November 1977 50 per cent of their advances, other than to the personal sector, were loans with an initial maturity of more than 2 years. This figure was apparently on a rising trend, and it is almost certain that the proportion of term loans made by the non-clearing banks would be higher. Practically all terms loans in Britain are at variable rates of interest (i.e. the rate of interest charged is linked to a bank's base rate or some market rate) so that the risk of interest rate fluctuations is borne by the borrower.

It is often suggested that banks in Britain should be prepared to lend to industry for longer periods, and it is pointed out that in Germany over half of the bank loans to industry have an initial term of more than 5 years. The clearing banks were rather slow to develop this type of lending; until the 1970s they had little incentive to do so, being sheltered to some extent from competition by a cartel arrangement and discouraged from seeking new business activity by the techniques of monetary control employed at the time. However, with a stable and dependable retail deposit base to work from, there is no doubt that a significant proportion of their advances to industry could reasonably be committed for a longer term. The building societies, which are in many respects in a similar situation, have been happy to provide long-term mortgages for many years. Lending a significant proportion of their funds for longer terms would, however, have implications for the banks' own capital requirements. The risk of loss through a failure to repay the loan increases with its term; the more distant the time at which repayment is expected the greater the uncertainty surrounding the investment it helps to permit. Again, a reluctance to take these risks may be related to the information and expertise which is available to the banks. Moreover, *fixed rate* lending for long periods, which might in some circumstances be attractive to industry, would impose a further heavy commitment on a bank's own capital. For if interest rates rose during the currency of the loan, the bank's refinancing costs could easily exceed the interest earned, creating a running loss which would have to be borne by the bank itself. This is by no means a purely hypothetical problem, as banks in Germany have recently discovered.

SAVINGS BANKS

Savings banks in Britain consist of the National Savings Bank (NSB), which is part of the government's Department of National Savings, and the Trustee Savings Banks (TSB) which are unincorporated societies providing banking services to the personal sector. The savings banks were set up originally to provide savings facilities for the personal sector, and this continues to be the NSBs main function. The TSBs, on the other hand, now provide a full range of banking services for the personal sector, and are currently in a transitional stage towards full banking status.

The NSB operates through the Post Office network in the country. It runs a deposit-taking and withdrawal service through two main facilities: ordinary accounts, from which limited sums can be withdrawn on demand and on which the rate of interest is 5 per cent, and investment accounts on which a higher rate (15 per cent in March 1980) is paid, but for which withdrawals are at 1 month's notice. The ordinary account is attractive to the modest personal saver who is unlikely to accumulate substantial balances, and a standing order service for regular payments is available to depositors. Interest on ordinary account deposits is tax free. The investment account provides savings facilities for people with larger balances, and interest is taxable in the usual way.

Table 10.3 shows that at the end of 1980 ordinary account balances amounted to £1.7 billion, much the same as investment account deposits at that time. But while the ordinary account deposits had grown by only about £50 million per year on average since 1976, the increase in investment account deposits averaged £300 million. Virtually all of the NSBs funds are invested in government securities, including a certain amount of local authority debt. However, unlike competing private sector institutions the govern-

TABLE 10.3   SAVINGS BANKS' ASSETS AND LIABILITIES, DECEMBER 1980

(£ billion)

Liabilities		Assets	
National Savings Bank			
Ordinary account deposits	1.7	Government securities etc.	3.6
Investment account deposits	1.9		
Total deposits	3.6	Total assets	3.6
Trustee Savings Banks			
Sight deposits	2.0	Cash and liquid balances	1.4
Time deposits	3.7	National Debt Office balances	1.1
Other liabilities	0.6	Investments	3.2
		Advances	0.4
		Other	0.2
Total liabilities	6.3	Total assets	6.3

Source: Financial Statistics, April 1981, Tables 3.13, 8.2, 8.3

ment does not have to earn a profit (or contribution to reserves) and is not compelled to limit the interest paid on deposits to the earnings of the account's investment. It is therefore able to manipulate the rate of interest in order to influence the flow of personal savings in this form.

Until the Trustee Savings Bank Act 1976 the TSBs performed very similar functions. There were a large number of comparatively small TSBs, with a few branches each, and they were subject to restrictive statutory limitations on their activities. Since then they have been rationalized through amalgamation, so that there are now sixteen banks working within clearly defined regions and all having assets of more than £50 million. A Central Trustee Savings Bank has been created, and the regional banks hold a substantial part of their liquid balances with this bank.

The TSBs offer four main types of account: savings accounts, on which a modest rate of interest is payable, with withdrawals on demand and a limited range of money transmission services; cheque accounts; investment accounts, in which funds are at 1 month's or 7 days' notice and a higher rate of interest is paid; and term deposits, offering higher rates of interest on fixed term deposits for periods from 6 months to 5 years. Table 10.3 shows that at the end of 1980 sight deposits – savings account and cheque account deposits – amounted to £2.0 billion, while time deposits – those in investment accounts and term deposits – amounted to £3.7 billion. Between the end of 1976 and 1980 deposits increased by an average of about £400 million per year, with time deposits making up well over 80 per cent of the total.

The pattern of the TSBs' assets reflects their history, and over £1 billion of their funds are still held as balances with the National Debt Office; these are being gradually reduced over a period of years by agreement with the government. Like other retail deposit-taking institutions the TSBs hold substantial sums as cash and liquid balances – £1.4 billion at the end of 1980. Their investments, consisting mainly of British Government securities and local authority debt, were £3.2 billion of which £0.8 billion was repayable within 1 year. If these are added to cash and liquid balances the total is nearly 40 per cent of the TSBs' deposits, and over 100 per cent of their sight deposits.

Advances to customers were £0.4 billion. Until the Trustee Savings Bank Act 1976 such private lending was prohibited, and the TSBs have been developing it gradually since their entrance into the more general field of banking.

Most loans are to individuals and small businesses, including a certain amount of mortgage lending for house purchase, and the TSBs are likely to continue to have a special interest in lending to these types of customer. But in early 1980 they took over a major finance company and they have also begun to engage in more general corporate banking. It is therefore possible that with the passage of time their business will come to resemble that of the retail deposit-taking banks more closely.

BUILDING SOCIETIES

Building societies are typical of retail deposit-taking institutions. They collect the bulk of their deposits in retail markets and they also deal mainly in retail markets in investing their funds. There are over 250 building societies in Britain, but most are very small and they are dominated by a comparatively small number of large societies with extensive branch networks. The largest five societies account for over half of the total assets, and less than forty control over 90 per cent. Building societies are mutual organizations, whose reserves have to be built up out of the margin they are able to earn on their business.

Table 10.4 shows building societies' assets and liabilities at the end of 1980. At that time their total liabilities amounted to £53.8

TABLE 10.4   BUILDING SOCIETIES' ASSETS AND LIABILITIES, DECEMBER 1980

(£ billion)

Liabilities		Assets	
Shares and deposits	49.8	Mortgages	42.4
Other	4.0	Short-term assets	3.6
		Investments	6.7
		Other	1.0
Total liabilities	53.8	Total assets	53.8

Source: Financial Statistics, April 1981, Table 8.7

billion, with shares and deposits very nearly £50 billion. Other liabilities include the societies' reserves and certain other items, with the reserves element amounting to about $3\frac{1}{2}$ per cent of total liabilities. About 80 per cent of the societies' assets (£42.4 billion) are held as mortgage loans, practically all to people who own their own homes. The balance is made up of short-term assets (£3.6 billion), and investments (£6.7 billion) including the land, buildings and equipment which they use. The bulk of the investments are highly liquid, and at the end of 1980 nearly 60 per cent consisted of British Government securities with terms to maturity of under 5 years.

The building societies' main function is the provision of finance for home ownership. To this end they collect deposits and lend most of the funds they obtain as mortgage loans, retaining the rest in more liquid forms. Their deposits are not at present guaranteed in any way, but they are generally regarded as safe and trustees are permitted to deposit funds with societies which satisfy certain requirements; these include holding minimum ratios of reserves and of liquid assets to total liabilities.[8] In practice it is inconceivable that any large society would be allowed to fail to the extent that depositors would lose their money, and in recent years on the rare occasions when a small society has failed the other societies have taken over their obligations.

Building societies seek to avoid unnecessary changes in their interest rates. Mortgage loans are at variable rates of interest, but changes cause inconvenience and sometimes hardship to borrowers, and for this reason the level of mortgage interest rates has assumed considerable political importance. Frequent changes also add to the societies' administrative costs. Thus, rather than change interest rates temporarily building societies prefer to balance their assets and liabilities in other ways. Changes in their holdings of liquid assets form one important buffer with liquid assets being run down when there is a shortfall in deposits and increased when deposits flow in more freely, but building societies also frequently control the outflow of funds by rationing the new mortgages they are prepared to provide.

Figure 10.2 illustrates some aspects of the building societies' behaviour. It shows the net inflow into shares and deposits and net outflow for advances during each year from 1970 to 1980, together with the societies' liquidity ratio at the *beginning* of the year. A large gap between the levels of shares and deposits and of advances in any year implies that the societies are acquiring liquid assets, and is

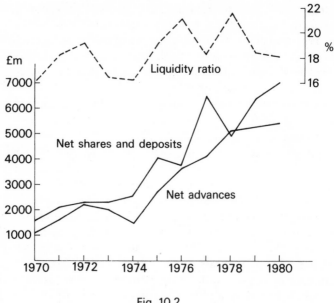

Fig. 10.2

therefore reflected in a rise in the liquidity ratio shown for the beginning of the following year.

When liquidity is high the societies tend to lend freely, and when it is low they restrict their loans. Thus, for example, liquidity was low at the beginning of 1973 and 1974, and lending declined in both years; whereas in 1975, when liquidity had recovered, lending grew more rapidly. Again the more moderate pace of growth in lending in 1979 and 1980 was associated with comparatively low liquidity levels at the beginning of those years. Figure 10.2 also illustrates how the net inflow into shares and deposits is much more volatile than the outflow into lending. The result is that rapid growth of deposits leads to a build-up of liquidity while slower growth is associated with a decline.

Building society interest rates change in response to persistent changes in liquidity, or to the expectation of a sharp increase or reduction in the deposit inflow due to changes in competitive interest rates; in general, deposit and lending rates move closely in line, because the societies' operating costs are relatively insensitive to changes in financial conditions. Table 10.5 illustrates the effects on building societies' net receipts of the competitiveness of their deposit

TABLE 10.5   BUILDING SOCIETIES' NET RECEIPTS, 1973-77

	Receipts less withdrawals (£ million a month)	Indicator of changes in interest rate competitiveness
1973 1st quarter	109	−1.18
1973 2nd quarter	202	+0.19
1973 3rd quarter	109	−2.13
1973 4th quarter	84	−3.48
1974 1st quarter	−7	−4.96
1974 2nd quarter	86	−2.18
1974 3rd quarter	129	−1.59
1974 4th quarter	180	−1.19
1975 1st quarter	248	−0.30
1975 2nd quarter	310	+1.37
1975 3rd quarter	263	+0.48
1975 4th quarter	261	−0.62
1976 1st quarter	348	+1.33
1976 2nd quarter	229	+0.03
1976 3rd quarter	176	−1.46
1976 4th quarter	64	−3.40
1977 1st quarter	164	−0.13

Source: Wilson Committee Evidence, Building Societies' second submission, Table F.

interest rates between the first quarter of 1973 and the first quarter of 1977. In the first quarter of 1974, for instance, when building society interest rates lay well below those available on competitive assets, they suffered a net outflow of deposits; whereas 2 years later when the rates they paid were very competitive they experienced a record inflow. Changes in the rate of interest charged for loans also have an appreciable, though less immediate, effect on the outflow into loans.

Personal sector savers and borrowers make full use of the building societies' facilities. Between 1976 and 1980 over 90 per cent of mortgage loans for house purchase were obtained from building societies; and the lion's share of the personal sector's saving in the form of deposits – over 60 per cent – went to building societies. However, as already noted, the proportion of deposits flowing to building societies varied substantially from year to year, according to the competitiveness of the interest rates they paid.

Building societies have reached their present position after a period of exceptionally rapid growth in the 1960s and 1970s, which reflected both the growth of demand for their facilities and the efficiency with which they gathered funds in response to this demand. A key influence was the attraction of owner-occupied housing as an investment which was likely to maintain or increase its real value in a period of inflation, and the return was enhanced by the tax relief on mortgage interest which was available. As a result, owner-occupied housing was expected to yield a higher rate of return than most alternative assets.

Building societies have also encouraged depositors by extending their branch networks and by remaining open for business at times when the banks are shut (e.g. Saturdays). They have benefited from the arrangements for taxing interest on their deposits; tax has been paid by the societies on behalf of their depositors, who have therefore received the interest free of tax (at the standard rate). Deposit interest paid by most other deposit-taking institutions, such as banks, has been taxable in the hands of the recipient. Since the tax paid by the societies is calculated at the *average* rate applicable to their depositors, which is less than the standard rate of income tax, this enables them to pay higher rates of interest than competitive institutions. Building societies have also received certain tax advantages in respect of their own income.

Some aspects of building societies' growth, particularly the proliferation of branches in the centres of many towns and cities, has been the subject of criticism. Competition on interest rates between building societies has been discouraged by the Building Societies Association's practice of recommending rates of interest to be charged on mortgages and paid on deposits. These rates have been set at levels which leave room for the societies to earn an 'adequate' profit margin – one which provides a profit margin for expansion and which does not put too much pressure on relatively inefficient societies. The method of supervision adopted by the government (discussed in Chapter 14 below) has also militated against fierce interest rate competition between societies. The result is that competition between societies has been directed into other channels, of which branch expansion is the most obvious.

It has been suggested that the abolition (or spontaneous breakdown) of the recommended rate system would be likely to lead to a narrowing of margins, to the benefit of building societies' depositors, who would receive a slightly higher return on their funds, and with the probable effect of improving borrowers' access to mortgage loans in times of shortage – even if possibly at higher interest rates. Inter-mediation costs would be reduced as the more efficient societies expanded at the expense of their less efficient competitors. More-over, fiercer interest rate competition between building societies might well hasten amalgamations amongst large (as well as small) societies, which could lead to a reduction in the number of branches in town centres, possibly matched by an increase in suburbs or outlying areas.

OTHER DEPOSIT-TAKING INSTITUTIONS

Other deposit-taking institutions include the finance houses and other consumer credit grantors and the discount market. Finance houses have traditionally specialized in instalment lending to con-sumers and to industrial and commercial companies, to help to finance the purchase of durable goods. They also make loans for other purposes, and the larger companies engage in leasing, usually through subsidiaries. Their funds are obtained from a variety of sources, mostly from the banks, but a certain proportion (20 per cent at the end of 1976) were obtained by bidding for wholesale deposits from other lenders. Finance house lending is riskier than that of banks, and ratios of capital and reserves to borrowed funds are often about 1:5. The larger finance houses all operate through branch networks and make direct contact with many of their clients, but a substantial proportion of their business emanates from the point of sale, and the seller receives a commission for the business introduced. For example, motor car dealers often arrange credit for their customers, and receive a commission from the finance houses with whom they deal.[9]

The discount market consists of eleven 'discount houses' which play a specialist role in the banking system, money and bill markets. The bulk of their funds are obtained from the banks but a relatively small proportion (6 per cent in December 1980) are obtained from other sources. We shall consider them further in connection with the markets for short-term financial instruments in Chapter 12.

NOTES

1. There is no hard and fast division between these markets in terms of size of loan, and practice varies between banks. However, many banks would be prepared to quote individual terms for deposits of £50 000 upwards.

2. The National Savings Bank is an exception. Since it is part of a government department (see p. 163 below) it does not require capital of its own.

3. The London 'clearing banks' are so called because for many years they operated the clearing system for payments in England and Wales, under which payments on and due to each bank are aggregated and only the net balance is transferred from one bank to another. The National Giro, Cooperative Bank, and Central Trustee Savings Bank now also participate in the clearing system. The Scottish clearing banks perform a similar function in Scotland.

4. The commercial bill is in essence a promise by the company seeking finance to pay the face value of the bill on a stated date in the future. A bank which 'accepts' the bill takes on the liability to make the payment itself if the company should default on its obligation. The guarantee makes the bill a much more attractive financial instrument for potential holders.

5. The statistics for the UK banking sector incorporate deposits with the Banking Department of the Bank of England and with the discount market, and exclude all inter-bank assets and liabilities (which are included in Table 10.1).

6. Companies with good management and sound balance sheets may, of course, decline to give security, and be strong enough to obtain loans without doing so. In other cases, companies may have no assets to pledge as security.

7. Two qualifications are needed. First the US banks pioneered the use of the 'going concern' approach to lending in the UK, though this is now employed widely throughout the banking system. Secondly gearing in other countries with capital markets similar to the UK, e.g. the USA and the Netherlands, does not differ greatly from UK levels.

8. The reserve ratio varies with the size of the building society, being lower for the larger societies.

9. There are no good statistics on finance houses in the UK at present (March 1980). Some finance houses are classified as banks for statistical purposes, and their balance sheets are included indistinguishably with those of other British banks. Others are treated separately.

11 INVESTING INSTITUTIONS

The investing institutions consist of financial intermediaries which specialize in providing funds for long-term investment in the capital market and, to a lesser extent, directly in property. The institutions considered in this chapter all obtain their funds from the general public; *special* credit institutions, i.e. institutions which were originally created to meet needs which appeared not to be satisfied by the financial system, are considered in Chapter 13.

The most important categories of investing institutions are the life assurance companies and the pension funds, with assets of over £50 billion and about £45 billion respectively at the end of 1980. Apart from protecting people (or their dependants) from the vagaries of mortality, these institutions provide facilities for accumulating capital through regular contractual saving or, in the case of pension funds, for enabling people to convert income earned during their working lives into pensions to maintain them in retirement. Next in size are the general insurance funds, amounting to some £12 billion at the end of 1980. These funds are held by insurance companies to enable them to meet claims arising from their general insurance business, e.g. insurance against fires or accidents. Lastly there are the investment trusts and unit trusts, with assets of about £7 billion and £4 billion respectively at the end of 1980, which provide professional investment management services for their clients.

Some of the individual funds, particularly amongst the insurance and pension funds, are very large – in excess of £1 billion – and most large investment and unit trust management groups control several funds. Thus at the end of 1978 there were over forty management groups from the investing institutions controlling funds of £500 million or more, and nearly 150 with funds of over £100 million.

The total assets of the investing institutions are comparable in value to the sterling assets of the deposit-taking institutions (see Tables 2.1 and 2.3). But it is not only the assets that are important. The flow of saving through the investing institutions in the UK amounted to about £11 billion in 1980, or 5 per cent of GDP. This is unusually high by international standards, and is one of the note-worthy features of the UK capital market.

The fundamental principle governing the operation of the investing institutions is that of matching – the nature of the assets they hold reflects the characteristics of their liabilities. Thus the bulk of the liabilities of the life assurance and pension funds do not fall due for many years, so these institutions have a strong preference for long-term assets corresponding to the term of their liabilities. The claims on general insurance funds are liable to arise much sooner, so general funds have a greater need for liquid assets in their portfolios, although they too invest a considerable part in long-term assets. Investors in investment trust shares or in unit trusts expect their funds to be held largely in ordinary shares,[2] so the funds controlled by these institutions are employed mainly in the equity market.

The institutions make the great majority of their investments by purchasing securities in the financial markets at home and abroad. By careful selection of their portfolios, they aim to maximize the income of the fund, and by holding a diversified portfolio they virtually eliminate the specific risk attached to the shares of individual companies. Fund management involves selling as well as buying securities, and the funds continuously monitor the performance of the companies whose securities they hold, in order to form their own opinion of the value of each security. If a company's shares seem to them to be worth more than the market price they may attempt to add to their holding, whereas in the reverse situation they might reduce their holding or sell it altogether. They are always on the look-out for companies in whose shares they might hope to invest profitably, and they are subjected to a continuous flood of recommendations from stockbrokers or other investment advisers.

Most of the larger funds have several hundred distinct security holdings, whose values range from, say, a hundred thousand to several million pounds. They limit the maximum size of any normal holding by reference to the scale of their own portfolio – say 3 per cent – and the value of the company's share capital available in the market – say 2 per cent. Any larger holdings are treated as exceptional, requiring special justification. The larger the holding, both in absolute terms and as a proportion of the ordinary shares outstanding, the more difficult it becomes to dispose of it, should the institution wish to do so; the institutions set considerable store by the marketability of their assets. At the other end of the scale, few of the larger institutions would normally seek to buy or sell securities in lots of less than, say, £200 000, because deciding on acquisitions and sales, and monitoring the performance of companies whose shares are held, are time-consuming and costly activities.

The institutions do not have any preference for new issues (or rights issues) of securities over purchases of existing securities in the market, though a rights issue frequently presents them with a good opportunity to obtain a significant holding in a company or to acquire a large block of shares at one time. Otherwise the minimum size of holding which is of interest to the institution may be difficult to acquire, unless some other large institutions are willing sellers.

In normal circumstances the institutions do not seek to influence the policy or management of the companies whose shares they hold. However, when an institution takes an abnormally large, or strategic, stake in a company it will try to maintain close contact with the company's management. In some of these cases the investing institution will have representation on the company's board. Strategic investments of this kind in small- or medium-sized companies are becoming more common.

The scope and scale of the institutions' holdings of assets have implications for the capital market, which we shall return to at the end of this chapter and in Chapter 12. The possibility of moving further in the direction of strategic investments will be considered in the final chapter of the book.

LIFE ASSURANCE AND PENSION FUNDS

Life assurance business can be divided into three broad categories: term assurance, whole of life and endowment assurance, and annuities. Under a term policy the insurance company pays benefits (a capital sum or an annuity) if death occurs within the specified period. No benefit is paid if the person insured survives beyond the end of the term. Since most people do survive to the end of the term, the annual premiums are low relative to the sums assured. With policies of this type the insurance company builds up a small fund during the early years when the probability of death is low, but runs it down later when, as the person insured gets older, the probability of death is higher.

With a whole-of-life policy the insurance company pays a capital sum on the death of the person assured, and with an endowment policy the sum is paid out at some prescribed date when the policy matures, or earlier if the assured dies previously. The premiums are much higher than for term insurance because the company is committed to paying out the sum assured eventually, either at death or on maturity. It follows that the life assurance company has to accumulate a substantial fund, out of which the payments are made when they fall due. Whole-of-life and endowment policies may be 'without profits', in which case the money value of the benefit is fixed in advance, or 'with profits', which means that the agreed sum may be augmented by bonuses declared by the company. These bonuses reflect the return earned by the life company on its funds and its expenses during the currency of the policy.

Annuities provide the policy-holder with a regular income for some defined period, usually the annuitant's life, but often with a guarantee that a minimum number of payments will be made even if the annuitant dies earlier. Annuities may be purchased either by the payment of premiums for a period of years or by means of a single premium before the annuity starts. In any event the life assurance company accumulates and holds a capital fund, which is gradually run down through annuity payments.

Life assurance company liabilities specify guaranteed minimum money values,[3] but the sums paid out on with-profits policies are expected to be higher. This means that to enable it to meet its legal commitments a life assurance company has a preference for assets whose money values at maturity are guaranteed, and which have a fixed rate of interest. But at the same time life companies wish to earn as high a yield as possible on their funds, since this benefits their with-profits policy holders. Life companies, therefore, normally choose to hold a mixture of fixed-interest and equity investments (including property), the latter in the hope that the return will exceed what is earned on fixed-interest securities. Competition between life companies is often focused on the level of bonuses they have been able to pay in the past, so a company's investment performance is crucial to its competitive position. Since the bulk of life assurance funds in the UK reflect whole of life, endowment or annuity business, the liabilities are mainly of a long-term nature, thus justifying the preference, by companies, for long-term assets.

The considerations governing investment by pension funds are in most respects similar to those affecting life companies' annuity business. Pension funds are created from the pension contributions made by individuals and their employers during the employees' working lives. These contributions are invested and, with the earnings on the investments, accumulated until the employees retire. At retirement the employee frequently receives a capital sum, and for the rest of his life he receives a regular pension.[4] In principle the pension, like an annuity, is paid out of the capital fund and the income derived from it. In practice, however, pension schemes normally contain both contributing and retired members, so that the pensions can be paid partly or wholly out of current contributions. The contributions and benefits of pension schemes are treated as a whole, and there is no link between an individual's pension and the size of his own contributions.[5] The most common practice is to calculate a person's pension by reference to his final wage or salary, or to his earnings in some period shortly before retirement, while contributions are fixed as a percentage of the wage or salary earned. In some pension schemes the money value of pensions is increased after retirement to compensate partly or fully for inflation.

The cost of a pension scheme depends on the return which is earned on the fund's investment[6] – the higher the return on investment, the lower the level of contributions required to finance the benefits of the scheme. Pension funds therefore aim to earn as high a yield as possible (consistent with prudence) on their funds. Since the bulk of their funds relate to pension commitments to people who are still in employment, they are concerned with the return in the long run, and can afford to make long-term investments and take a long view. Moreover, since their pension liabilities are linked to wages and salaries, at least up to the time of retirement, it is the *real* value of their assets which is of most concern to them. Pension funds therefore have a preference for those assets – equities and property – whose real values are least vulnerable to inflation in the long run.

The composition of the assets held by life assurance and pension funds at the end of 1979 is shown in Table 11.1. Neither category has much need for liquidity, and for both the proportion of short-term assets in the portfolio was less than 5 per cent. The holdings of fixed-interest securities for the funds are shown in the next three items in the table – government securities, mortgages and loans, and fixed interest company securities, for life assurance they amounted to about 40 per cent of the total, compared with only about 25 per cent for pension funds. The difference reflects the much greater importance of liabilities with a fixed money value for life assurance companies.[7] So far as these institutions are concerned there is little to choose between the different types of fixed-interest security, provided that the interest received on mortgages and loans and on fixed-interest company securities allows an adequate margin over gilt-edged securities to compensate for their poorer marketability and greater default risk.

TABLE 11.1   LIFE ASSURANCE AND PENSION FUNDS:
COMPOSITION OF ASSET PORTFOLIOS, END 1979

	Life assurance (%)	Pension funds (%)
Short-term assets	4.3	4.8
Government securities	27.6	22.3
Mortgages and loans	7.3	2.2
UK Company securities		
Fixed interest	4.4	1.8
Ordinary shares	25.0	42.3
Unit trust units	2.6	0.6
Overseas securities	2.9	5.5
Property	24.2	19.4
Other	1.7	1.1
Total assets	100.0	100.0

Source: Financial Statistics, April 1981, Table 8.13, 8.14

Ordinary shares in UK companies and unit trust units (often held in connection with 'unit-linked' life business) together with overseas securities are the main equity assets. For life assurance funds they amounted to 30 per cent of the portfolio, whereas for pension funds the total was nearly 50 per cent, the relatively high proportion of equity assets held by the latter being the counterpart of their lower holdings of fixed-interest securities. The proportions held in overseas securities have been artificially depressed. Until 1979 investment in overseas securities was impeded by exchange control, with new investment having to be financed by foreign currency borrowing if tax and other disadvantages were to be avoided. Since exchange controls were abolished in 1979 both categories of fund have taken the opportunity of increasing their overseas holdings.

The last major type of asset is direct investment in property, amounting to nearly 25 per cent and 20 per cent of total assets for life and pension funds respectively. The higher ratio for the former reflects the size of the life companies' portfolios and the fact that they have a longer history of this form of investment. The expertise required for direct investment in property differs from that which is needed for managing a security portfolio, and only large institutions find it worthwhile to employ the necessary teams.

The distribution of the asset portfolio at the end of 1979 results from the combined effects of past purchases of securities and property and of changes in the capital values of these assets. Since equity assets and property are more likely than fixed-interest securities to show capital gains consistently, the proportionate distribution of new investment is rather different. This is illustrated in Table 11.2 which shows the distribution of the net purchases by life assurance and pension funds of assets of different kinds from 1976 to 1980.

TABLE 11.2   LIFE ASSURANCE AND PENSION FUNDS:
INVESTMENT, 1976–80

	Life assurance (%)	Pension funds (%)
Short-term assets	2.9	2.5
Government securities	59.3	36.2
Mortgages and loans	3.1	0.6
Company and overseas securities		
Fixed interest	−1.4	−0.2
Ordinary shares	19.0	41.9
Unit trust units	2.1	0.4
Property	14.3	16.5
Other	0.6	2.2
Total	100.0	100.0

Source: Financial Statistics, Table 8.13, 8.14.

On average in this period only a small proportion of the money available was devoted to increasing short-term asset holdings, though this proportion can fluctuate considerably from year to year. Over 60 per cent of the life assurance and over 35 per cent of the pension funds' new money was used to purchase fixed-interest securities, with government securities accounting for virtually the entire amount. This was a consequence of the high level of public sector borrowing, together with firms' unwillingness to issue new long-term fixed-interest securities at the prevailing level of interest rates, so that there were significant net repayments of long-term debt by companies. Purchases of ordinary shares (of UK and overseas companies) and of unit trust units absorbed just over 20 per cent of life assurance and 40 per cent of pension fund money; while purchases of property amounted to around 15 per cent in both cases. The proportions of new money devoted to both shares and property are of course less than the balance-sheet ratios, reflecting the accrued capital gains included in the latter.

ROLE IN THE SAVING/INVESTMENT PROCESS

We have already noted in Chapter 6 that the volume of personal saving through life assurance and pension funds has risen in the last 20 years. This is demonstrated in Table 11.3, which shows that from 1958 to 1962 saving through life assurance and pension funds averaged just over 3 per cent of GDP, but that saving in these forms had risen to nearly 5 per cent of GDP by 1980. During the 1960s and 1970s there was quite a rapid extension of the coverage of pension schemes to include a broader cross-section of the population, and this was coupled with improvements in the benefits provided. Contributions have increased correspondingly. Inflation has also played a part, by raising the nominal yield on the funds' holdings of fixed-interest securities and short-term assets, and so augmenting the funds' income.

While saving through life assurance and pension funds has grown relative to GDP, it has in fact fallen from about 50 per cent to 40 per

TABLE 11.3   SAVING THROUGH LIFE ASSURANCE AND PENSION FUNDS, 1958–80

Saving through life assurance and pension funds	1958–62	1963–67	1968–72	1973–77	1978	1979	1980
Per cent of GDP	3.1	3.3	3.6	4.3	4.5	4.9	4.8
Per cent of financial saving by the personal sector[1]	50	52	48	41	43	38	39

Sources: Wilson Committee Report, Table 10.3; *Financial Statistics*, April 1981, Table 1.10
   [1] Liquid assets, public sector long-term debt, company and overseas securities, life assurance and pension funds

cent of the personal sector's total financial saving, as Table 11.3 shows, largely because inflation has had a much more pronounced effect on saving in the form of liquid assets. Nevertheless, the growth of saving through long-term institutions is probably more important: even if inflation fell, a high level of saving through life assurance and pension funds would be likely to persist; and whereas savings held as liquid assets cannot readily be made available for investment in risky assets, the funds channelled through the investing institutions are available for long-term borrowers and for risky ventures.

We drew attention in Chapter 6 to some of the structural, legislative and market factors which influence saving through life assurance and pension funds. Structural factors include a desire for security, and to obtain security by combining contractual saving with life-assurance protection through an endowment or whole-of-life policy makes good sense. So does the purchase of an annuity to provide a regular, continuing income in old age. But the most important structural factors have to do with the social arrangements employed to support the retired population.

The present system of pension provision in Britain is firmly embedded in our social and economic structure. It consists of a basic state scheme, including an element which is graduated with income, supplemented by occupational pension schemes which often replace the graduated element in the state pension. The relationship between the state Retirement Pension scheme and the occupational schemes is determined by legislation, and it is the significant role accorded to occupational schemes which generates the flow of saving in this form.

The use of life assurance and pension funds for saving in the UK is also supported by important tax concessions. Through the tax system most life assurance premiums receive a subsidy of 15 per cent (in 1981) from the government, contributions to pension funds are fully deductible from income before tax, and the revenue earned by pension fund investments is free of UK income and capital gains tax. These tax concessions are not available to people who choose to save in other ways, and there is no doubt that they have a considerable effect in channelling saving through life assurance and pension funds.

It would, however, be a mistake to assume that these structural and legislative factors are the whole story; market factors are also important. The life assurance companies are in keen competition with other institutions for the management of savings, some of which also receive favourable tax treatment, and the choice between direct investment in, say, owner-occupied housing and accumulating capital through a life-assurance policy is also available to most savers. Competition amongst life-assurance companies focuses on their costs, which are reflected in their premium rates for both with profits and without profits policies – and on their investment performance over a long period of years, which is reflected in the bonuses paid on with profits policies. For example, comparisons are often made of the sums which a policy-holder would have received on maturity if he had taken out policies with different companies at various times in the past.

The life assurance companies and pension funds are the central institutions concerned with mobilizing long-term saving in the economy. They gather together the savings of millions of individuals, and make them available in large sums in the long-term capital markets. The size of some of the individual institutions, and the total volume of funds available, ensure that very large sums of money can be provided to borrowers when required.

While the nature of their liabilities does lead the institutions to prefer assets with similar characteristics, they are prepared to alter the sector composition of their assets readily in response to changes in the pattern of demand. Thus, if industrial and commercial companies wish to issue long-term fixed-interest securities, the life-insurance companies will purchase them in preference to gilt-edged securities at a yield margin which compensates them for the differences in quality. Moreover, in recent years, when the state of the economy and the size of the public sector borrowing requirement led to a concentration of demand in this area, they have invested extremely heavily in gilt-edged securities even though, at least for pension funds, these are not particularly suitable assets. Thus the institutions are prepared to depart from the asset portfolio structure which minimizes risk in relation to their liabilities; but to persuade them to do so it is necessary to offer compensation for additional risk in the form of a higher prospective yield.

These institutions also play an important part in asset transformation in the economy, although it is the transformation of risk rather than of liquidity which is their concern. Life assurance and pension funds have no need to convert short-term liabilities into long-term assets, because their liabilities are by and large already long-term. As we have seen, they hold only a small proportion of their assets in a liquid form. But risk transformation is an important function. Although the money value of the institutions' liabilities may not be fixed, people expect, quite reasonably, that their savings through life assurance policies and their future pension rights will be safe. As already noted, diversification within categories of assets eliminates much of the risk, and a further reduction is achieved by spreading portfolios amongst different categories of asset, e.g. fixed-interest securities, UK equity shares, property, and overseas securities.

PENSION PROVISION

At one time most people in Britain depended on their families for support in old age. Some, including businessmen and members of the professions, aimed to save enough from their incomes to provide a capital sum sufficient to keep them in retirement, but they were very much in the minority. Others, who did not have families or former employers willing to support them, relied on the communities in which they lived. But nowadays the system is quite different. Practically everyone is covered to some degree by the state retirement pension scheme; about half the working population are also included in occupational pension schemes which will provide additional pensions when they retire; and many people build up some savings of their own to provide themselves with a measure of extra security. Since about 60 per cent of the current annual saving through life assurance and pension funds results from pension schemes (many of which are operated through insurance companies), the importance of occupational pension schemes for saving in the UK is clear.

Most state pension schemes run on a pay-as-you-go basis, in which current pensions are financed from current contributions, and state retirement pensions in Britain are no exception. With this kind of scheme the notion that people are saving up during their working lives to build up a capital sum from which their pensions will be paid in due course is abandoned. Instead, the scheme depends on an implicit social contract between generations: the working population of today pay the pensions of their predecessors, in the hope that the next generation will do the same for them. Rather than relying on the ownership of property (an accumulated fund) for their pension, people rely on the political process to ensure they get a fair deal. Each individual's contributions depend on his income, and his pension entitlement may also depend on the size of contributions (relative to the average level at the time) and the period for which he has contributed, but the scheme as a whole works on the principle that total contributions and total benefits in any period will balance.

Pay-as-you-go schemes are popular for a number of reasons. In particular, they have the great advantage that they are not undermined by wage inflation: wage and salary inflation is reflected automatically in higher contributions, which provide the revenue needed to allow pensions to keep pace with changes in wage levels. Schemes of this kind also appear to be relatively cheap for the working generation, when the pensions which society pays to the present retired generation are less than those which the working generation expects to receive itself. (This is in fact a feature of the British scheme at present.) But there are also difficulties. Pay-as-you-go schemes may prove burdensome if there is a decline in the size of the working population or if, due to great longevity or other demographic reasons, the retired population increases. Then the resources given up by the working population to pay for current pensions may seem excessive. Moreover, pay-as-you-go schemes are not really desirable on an enterprise basis, because the continuity of an enterprise cannot be guaranteed and the pension entitlement of the scheme's members is therefore insecure. In practice, in countries such as France where pay-as-you-go pension schemes are the general rule, they are operated on a very wide basis – so wide that they can effectively rely on the state for support.

The alternative is to have *funded* pension schemes, operated on principles which we have already described briefly. The contributions of working members are paid into a fund, which is invested to yield an income in the future. Current pensions are a charge on the fund, and may be financed from current contributions, the income of the fund, or by selling some of its assets. Contributions are normally related to income, and pensions benefits are usually calculated by reference to the individual's final salary. Within a funded scheme there is no identification of individual contributions or of assets purchased from them, but the general level of contributions reflects the typical career patterns and expected mortality experience of the scheme's members, and the funds are valued actuarially at regular intervals to test whether sufficient funds exist to cover the liabilities. Thus any improvement in benefits for the working members of the scheme has to be paid for immediately in the form of higher contributions.

If wage and salary levels were constant, the relative sizes of the working and retired members in the scheme did not change, and entitlement to benefits was the same between generations, a scheme would be 'mature', and while a substantial fund of assets would be held there would be neither saving no dis-saving. The contributions from working members to the fund, plus the income earned on its assets, would be just enough to pay the pensions of the retired members. But these conditions are not likely to be satisfied in Britain in the foreseeable future, and there are several reasons why the volume of saving through funded pension schemes is likely to continue to be large.

First, pension payments normally depend upon the number of years during which a member has paid contributions. With the increase in the coverage of schemes in recent years existing pensioners have many fewer years of relevant service than current contributors expect to have when they retire; the pensions currently paid are therefore relatively low. Secondly, while under most schemes pensions are related to the members' final salaries, only a minority of pension schemes take account fully of changes in wage and salary levels after the individual's retirement. Schemes in Britain seldom adjust pensions in line with any growth of real incomes in the economy, and it is only in the public sector that pensions have generally been fully up-rated for inflation. Failure to raise pensions in line with higher contributions also boosts saving. Thirdly, high nominal interest rates have raised the incomes of pension funds, and apparently contributed to saving, although in reality part of the interest payment is required to maintain the real value of the fund's assets. Finally, the real rate of return earned by many funds in recent years has fallen short of what had been expected. As a result deficiencies have emerged in many funds, and companies have found it necessary to make additional contributions to the funds over a period of years in order to make these deficiencies good.

The contribution which funded occupational pension schemes in Britain make to saving is, of course, one of their chief attractions. But they also have the merit of allowing diversity in pension arrangements – pension provision differs between firms and occupations. Provided that the funding principle is adhered to, differences in promised benefits are reflected in costs now, not deferred into the indefinite future. Thus employers who wish to offer superior benefits, or workers who wish to receive them, can do so – but only if they are prepared to accept the implications for their costs, or their net wages respectively.

Funded schemes do, however, have two serious disadvantages. The first is connected with the failure of most schemes to index pensions for inflation, with the result that some existing pensioners have found the real value of their pensions seriously eroded by inflation. In the absence of suitable securities it is difficult for private pension schemes to guarantee the real value of pensions, though the introduction of index-linked gilt-edged securities may help in this respect. The second problem concerns the cost of funded schemes. The funding principle presupposes that an adequate real rate of return will be earned on the funds' assets, and if the real return proved to be very low the level of contributions would have to be much higher than it is today, placing unbearable burdens on industry and commerce. In that event, firms would choose to abandon occupational pension schemes and their workers would rely upon the state scheme. It is conceivable that while investment may continue to yield a positive real return to the economy as a whole, that return may be reflected in higher wages and salaries rather than in profits on the capital invested, so that the return received by savers would be very low.

We shall return to the subject of index-linking in Chapter 16, and the questions of the real rate of return on investment, and to whom it accrues – whether labour or capital – raise more fundamental issues concerning the working of the economy, which cannot be pursued here. Nevertheless, provided that we do not suffer from high inflation for a protracted period, and in the absence of radical changes in the ownership of and return to capital, the present system of pension provision is likely to survive and to continue to sustain a high level of long-term personal saving in the economy.

GENERAL INSURANCE

The assets of the general insurance funds amounted to some £12 billion at the end of 1980. There were some 400 general insurance funds in the UK, of which the twenty largest held over 70 per cent of the total assets.[8] The funds (or *reserves*) of general insurance companies are held to enable them to meet claims on the policies they have issued. Since most policies run for a year and most claims are made very soon after the event giving rise to the claim occurs, the liabilities are mostly short term. But in some instances claims may be delayed or a settlement may not be reached until several years after the event, during which time a reserve has to be retained to cover possible payments. In addition to the specific (technical) reserves which an insurance company maintains to meet the claims it expects, companies also hold general reserves in case their loss experience is worse than they have anticipated.

General insurance companies hold a significant proportion of their assets in a liquid form, because claims are expected to arise in the near future and underwriting experience is liable to deteriorate quite quickly, e.g. the costs of repairing damage may rise faster than

had been expected, so that claims turn out to cost more than anticipated at the time that premiums were set. Most of their longer-term
assets are also readily marketable. But liquidity is not the sole consideration: they also seek to protect the real value of their reserves
from the effects of inflation, and therefore invest part of their assets
in ordinary shares and property; and they are naturally concerned
with the yield they earn on their funds – competitive conditions may
compel them sometimes to accept an underwriting loss, to be
recovered out of earnings on investments. Thus a balance between
liquidity, real value certainty, and return has to be struck.

The composition of general insurance funds at the end of 1979 is
shown in the first column of Table 11.4. At that time short-term
assets amounted to just under 14 per cent of the total, but these
could easily be supplemented from the government security holdings
(nearly 25 per cent of assets), of which over 40 per cent were short-
dated, and nearly 30 per cent medium-dated, gilt-edged securities.
Ordinary shares of UK and overseas companies made up less than
25 per cent of the total portfolio, and other fixed-interest securities
amounted to under 10 per cent. Since many of the insurance offices

TABLE 11.4   GENERAL INSURANCE FUNDS:
ASSETS, END 1979, AND INVESTMENT, 1976–80

	Assets end-1979 (%)	Investment 1976–80 (%)
Short-term assets	13.8	12.1
Government securities	24.5	37.1
Mortgages and loans	3.0	1.6
Company securities		
UK ordinary shares[1]	19.0 ⎫	
Overseas ordinary shares	3.4 ⎭	5.0
UK fixed-interest	4.2 ⎫	
Overseas fixed-interest	1.6 ⎭	10.5
Overseas government securities	2.9	5.6
Property	10.1	6.7
Other	17.5	21.4
Total assets	100.0	100.0

Source: Financial Statistics, Table 8.13
[1] Including unit trust units

undertake business in other countries, certain overseas government securities also appear in their portfolios. Property comprises 10 per cent, and other investments – mainly premiums collected by agents but not yet handed over to the insurance companies – for nearly 20 per cent.

General insurance companies increased their asset holdings by about £1 billion per year in the period 1976–80. This very large net flow of funds onto the capital market is mainly a consequence of inflation – as the general price level rises so does the level of insurance cover required in the economy, and the insurance companies' reserves have to rise *pari passu*. Most of the additional funds are generated directly by higher premium income and from the insurance companies' own retained profits, but in a number of instances companies have raised additional equity capital in the stock market to support the higher value of their business.

The second column in Table 11.4 shows the distribution of general insurance funds' net purchases of assets from 1976–80. In this sector too, government securities absorbed an above average proportion (37 per cent) of the funds available. There was very little investment in ordinary shares, but fixed interest investment in company and overseas securities took over 10 per cent of the funds available. Property investment (7 per cent) was comparatively low, but agents' balances (21 per cent) rose very sharply in this period.[9]

General insurance funds should not be expected to make an important contribution to the supply of funds in the capital market in the longer run. Though their asset portfolio has always been substantial, and in managing that portfolio they account for a significant proportion of trading on the stock market, the net inflow of funds was comparatively small when the price level was reasonably stable. Some growth of funds can, of course, be expected from retentions and as a result of any increase in the real volume of insurance business. But the holding of investments is, as it were, a by-product of general insurance, whereas for life assurance and pension business it is central to their main activity.

INVESTMENT AND UNIT TRUST

Investment and unit trusts are the other important groups of investing institutions. The value of their funds at the end of 1980 amounted to £11 billion. The principal services offered to clients are portfolio diversification to spread risk, and professional management of funds.

Investment trusts are companies set up for the purpose of collective investment in shares and other securities. The members of the Association of Investment Trust companies managed about 200 trusts at the end of 1978, with many management groups controlling several trusts. At that time the nine largest groups, each of which had over £200 million under management, accounted for over a third of the total funds, which by the end of 1980 amounted to £7.2 billion.

Shares in investment trusts can be bought or sold in the same way as any other shares, at whatever price prevails in the market. The share price is influenced by the value of the trust's assets and by the past success of its management, but it will not generally be the same as the value of the underlying assets. In recent years investment trust shares have stood at a discount on the value of the underlying assets.[10]

An investment trust shareholder obtains, in effect, a proportion of a diversified asset portfolio. He is protected from the extremes of risk associated with holding shares in only a small number of companies, and he benefits from the relatively low transactions costs which apply to purchases or sales of large blocks of shares. He hopes that the trust's management will be expert, and successful in earning an above-average return on assets. Investment trusts also have the advantage that they can borrow to augment their asset portfolio if they wish (which might be more difficult or expensive for the individual shareholder); and many trusts have a long tradition of investing a significant proportion of their assets overseas, thus giving their shareholders the benefit of international diversification, or indeed the opportunity of holding overseas assets with much less trouble than would be the case if they were held directly. For these benefits the shareholder has to incur the cost of remunerating the trust's management.

Since the abolition of exchange control in 1979 investment trusts have taken steps to increase the proportion of overseas assets in their portfolios. Some trusts show a considerable degree of regional specialization and others have a sector specialization, though the majority are general trusts. In recent years a number of trusts have increased the scale of their direct investment in the shares of unlisted companies, and one major group now makes a practice of taking substantial strategic stakes in companies whose shares it holds, forgoing the benefits of marketability for the closer involvement which a strategic stake allows. In spite of these trends there is still an overwhelming emphasis on the traditional skills of portfolio management.

With their shares standing at a discount on the underlying assets it has not been practicable for investment trusts to raise new equity capital in recent years, and thanks to the high level of interest rates there has been little borrowing in sterling either. The investment trusts have not therefore been a significant source of saving to the UK capital market; indeed, there has been a net shift of resources from UK into overseas securities in the last 5 years. Nevertheless, in the secondary market they are an important group of holders who wish to buy or sell shares in substantial packets, and in the primary market, with the large sums at their disposal, they are in a position to subscribe to new issues by selling other assets, or to underwrite new issues even if they do not wish to subscribe themselves, thereby assisting in the process of raising new capital by industry.

Unit trusts fulfil similar functions. Their liabilities, unit trust units, are sold by the trust's managers to the public. The value of each unit is calculated regularly, frequent daily, as a fraction of the value of the fund's assets. The managers undertake to buy or sell units on request, at prices which lie within a prescribed margin of the unit's value. Since regular valuations are required, unit trusts are not permitted to invest any substantial proportion of their funds in unlisted securities, whose true value may not be easy to establish.

At the end of 1980 there were 475 authorized unit trusts in the UK managing a total of about £4.1 billion. There are about ninety management groups in the Unit Trust Association, but at the end of 1978 the largest seventeen groups, all with funds under management of over £100 million, accounted for over 80 per cent of the total assets. Unit trust units are frequently held by individuals with comparatively small sums to invest – there are nearly two million separate holdings, though many individuals have holdings in more than one trust. In comparison with direct investment in company securities the transactions costs for such individuals are low. The trusts have a wide range of objectives, including investment in the UK market as a whole, sector and regional specialization. Unit trusts have traditionally placed less emphasis on overseas investment than the investment trusts, but since the abolition of exchange control such investment has increased. Tax changes in 1980 also make it practicable to create unit trusts specializing in investment in fixed-interest securities, though it is too early to tell whether this will develop on a large scale.

Unlike investment trusts in recent years, unit trusts play a continuing, though comparatively minor, part in the process of mobilizing saving. The annual inflow into new investment in the last 5 years has averaged about £100 million. But their participation in the secondary market is probably of greater significance. Since their liabilities can be bought or sold effectively on demand, unit trust management groups are under continual pressure to maintain their investment performance at all times; comparisons of their perform- ance over short and long periods are readily available. Funds are therefore managed very actively, and the rate of turnover of unit trusts' assets is considerably higher than for other major institutional investors (see Chapter 12). On average, however, this has not led to superior investment performance – the return on unit trust units seems to be broadly comparable with that in the market as a whole. The principal benefits obtained by their unit-holders are therefore diversification at comparatively low cost, and, with the wide range of specialist trusts at their disposal, an opportunity to obtain this diversi- fication within any particular sector or geographical region of their own choice.

INVESTING INSTITUTIONS AND THE CAPITAL MARKET

We are now in a position to consider some of the implications of the investing institutions' behaviour for the capital market. On the investment side of their activities these institutions have very similar objectives, and seek to obtain their objectives by very similar means. Thus they all attempt to maximize the return on their portfolios, subject to certain constraints determined by the nature of their liabilities, which influence the optimum (risk-minimizing) structure of each institution's portfolio. Departures from the optimum, which expose the institution to extra risk, have to be justified by the prospect of additional return.

The institutions all hold portfolios of financial assets, and some- times also property, and buy or sell at the margin when they believe that conditions are favourable. The portfolio managers are bound to act prudently: they are under fiduciary obligations to their liability- holders, and cannot take unreasonable risks with their clients' money. Prudence demand that they hold a diversified portfolio, and that they have regard to the nature of their own liabilities, but subject to these considerations they are free to vary the proportions of the various categories of financial instruments – e.g. equity or debt – in their portfolios in favour of those on which they expect the return to be relatively high. Within each category they select stocks on which they hope the return will be above average. Since investment overseas may offer the prospect of a higher return than investment in UK securities, and since international diversification adds to the stability of a portfolio, life assurance and pension funds, whose liabilities are entirely in sterling, are entitled to invest some of their funds abroad. How much of its portfolio would be regarded as reasonable for any single institution to invest abroad can only be judged by reference to the practices of other, similar institutions.

All the investing institutions place considerable weight on the marketability of their assets. They put a premium on being able to dispose of at least part of holdings which they regard as over-priced, and on being able to buy new holdings or add to holdings which seem under-priced. Poor marketability has to be justified by a higher expected yield. They are not unwilling to take risks – risk-taking is inherent in investment – but they are unwilling to take *unnecessary* risks or to purchase a risky asset if their expectation of the rate of return falls short of what is available on other investments. High risk in itself does not rule out an investment if the expected return is adequate – as investment in North Sea oil and certain other activities has demonstrated. Nevertheless, since investment managers must be able to show that they are behaving in a responsible fashion, the proportion of their assets devoted to abnormally risky investment is seldom high.

The effects of the institutions on the securities market will be considered in more detail in the next chapter. At this stage it is only necessary to point to some of the effects of the very large size of their holdings of securities, both in aggregate and in terms of individual stocks, and of the annual flow of saving which passes through their hands. First, when one of the larger institutions wishes to deal, substantial volumes of stock and large sums of money are involved; the market organization and arrangements for dealing have to be able to cope with these requirements. Secondly, the flow of saving through the institutions makes it comparatively easy for public sector bodies or large companies to raise the capital funds they require, provided they can satisfy the risk criteria applied by the institutions. Finally, while most of the institutions are too large to wish to hold shares in many smaller or unlisted companies, this does not necessarily imply that finance for these companies will not be available. Funds may be provided through specialized companies, some of which have been created by institutional investors for this purpose, rather than by the larger institutions investing directly themselves.

NOTES

1. I.e. mainly the personal sector (including employers' contributions to pension schemes).

2. Some unit trusts specializing in investment in fixed-interest securities have been launched recently (1981).
3. Life assurance companies also issue some 'unit-linked' life policies, in which the value of the policy is linked to the value of particular investments.
4. Pension provision for widows is also common.
5. Though pensions do depend on the number of years for which contributions have been made.
6. Strictly, it is the *real* return, or the return relative to the increase in wage and salary costs, which matters.
7. Since life companies carry out a considerable volume of pension business the proportion of the ordinary life and annuity portfolio held in fixed-interest securities will have been even higher.
8. Figures refer to the end of 1978.
9. The relatively low level of equity investment – ordinary shares and property – in this period was a consequence of some companies' experience in 1974, when the collapse of share and property prices seriously eroded their general reserves. This has led most companies to follow more cautious investment policies.
10. I.e. the share price has been less than the value of the trust's assets (less liabilities) divided by the number of shares.

12 FINANCIAL MARKETS

In this chapter we shall consider the contribution made by the major financial markets to the working of the financial system. These markets can be divided into the *securities* markets, which exist to allow trading of stocks and shares and to enable new issues of these financial instruments to be made, and the *money* markets, where highly liquid financial instruments are traded. They are *organized* markets, in the sense that they have a defined membership and that market practices are regulated, with the object of ensuring that users of the market are provided with the facilities they need, for example, access to the information required to reach well-informed decisions and the ability to deal speedily and cheaply at prices which reflect overall supply and demand in the market.

The security markets can be divided in turn into the *primary* or new issue market, which is concerned with the raising of new capital, and the *secondary* market, which covers trading in existing securities. Our main concern will be with the mostly highly developed securities markets – the markets for *quoted* securities, i.e. those which have a regular quotation on the Stock Exchange – but we shall also consider the market for unlisted securities briefly.

We have already seen in Chapter 10 how the banks and some other deposit-taking institutions hold a considerable proportion of their funds as market loans and other short-term assets. These are normally obtained through the money markets, which consequently make an important contribution to the liquidity of the financial system, whilst at the same time enabling some of its ultimate users, such as local authorities, to raise considerable amounts of short-term finance. The money markets are often divided into the *discount* market, in which the discount houses deal as principals, and the *parallel* markets, which are organized mainly by brokers.

The *foreign exchange* market will not be discussed in detail. Individuals or companies who wish to buy or sell foreign exchange normally do so through their banks, which in turn buy or sell foreign currency in the foreign exchange market. This is a telephone and telex market, in which most deals are arranged through foreign exchange brokers, and dealing takes place between banks in London and with bankers in other financial centres. The market is generally active, and the rate of exchange for any currency responds quickly to changes in the balance between supply and demand. Deals are carried out for 'spot' delivery (i.e. for delivery 2 business days later) or for other terms. As noted in Chapter 9, the prices prevailing in the spot and forward currency markets have a bearing on the flow of international funds into or out of the UK. Government policy towards the exchange rate is often implemented through official transactions in the foreign exchange market; the Bank of England buys or sells foreign exchange against sterling in the markets, thus altering the supply/demand balance, and hence the equilibrium price.

THE SECURITIES MARKETS

The Stock Exchange is the principal trading market in securities in the UK. It provides facilities for trading in 'listed' securities, i.e. securities for which prices are quoted regularly. The Stock Exchange Council prescribes rules which must be observed by the members of the Stock Exchange, who are responsible for all trading, and by the issuers of the securities listed.

The types of security listed, their number and market value at the end of December 1980 are shown in Table 12.1. Much the most important categories of domestic securities are ordinary shares, with the shares of over 2600 companies listed, and British Government stocks. Companies whose shares are listed are known as 'quoted companies'. There are also very large numbers of company loan stocks and preference shares listed, though the average value of each issue is small, and many local authority and public boards also have quoted stocks. Although the securities of overseas companies represent over half the total market value of all listed securities, this exaggerates their importance because they are usually listed – and the bulk of the dealing takes place – elsewhere. The Stock Exchange also lists a substantial number of stocks issued by overseas public authorities, as well as Eurobonds (foreign-currency bonds) issued by UK and other borrowers.

TABLE 12.1   SECURITIES LISTED ON THE STOCK EXCHANGE
AT 31 DECEMBER 1980

	Number of securities	Market value (£ billion)
Public sector and foreign stocks		
British Government and Government guaranteed	110	70.7
UK local authorities and public boards	592	2.6
Overseas public authorities	253	3.3
Company securities		
UK companies		
Loan capital	1799	3.8
Preference shares	1256	0.8
Ordinary shares	2205	85.9
Overseas companies	621	185.5
Eurobonds		
UK companies	85	1.5
Overseas companies	432	6.7
Total	7353	360.7

Source: The Stock Exchange Fact Book

THE SECONDARY MARKET

The members of the Stock Exchange in Britain are divided into two categories, 'stockbrokers' and 'jobbers'. Holders of securities listed on the Stock Exchange do not deal directly with each other, but instead instruct a stockbroker to buy or sell securities on their behalf. The stockbroker does not buy or sell on his own account, but goes to the jobber who acts as a principal in the market, buying or selling shares. The jobber's obligation is to quote two prices – a buying price and a selling price – at which he is prepared to deal up to some maximum number of shares. His function is that of a market-maker – by being prepared to trade at all times he ensures that buyers and sellers are able to deal – and he alters the price he quotes in an effort to maintain balance between supply and demand. As a trader, the jobber makes his profit from the difference between the price at which he buys securities and the price at which he is able to sell them. To carry out his market-making function the jobber has to be prepared to hold a stock of securities in his own portfolio. Moreover, in order to satisfy the demands of buyers, he may sometimes find himself committed to sell more of a security than he possesses, and has to fall back on arrangements to borrow the security temporarily from other holders, until an opportunity arises to purchase the security himself.

The stockbroker is the agent of his client. It is his duty to obtain prices from all the jobbers trading in the security and to deal with the jobber who quotes the most favourable price. He is also responsible for all the paperwork involved in transferring the ownership of securities. For these services he receives a commission, calculated on a tapering scale by reference to the nature of the security and value of the transaction. For example, the minimum commission on long-dated gilt-edged securities ranges from 0.625 per cent on sums up to £2000 to 0.03 per cent on the excess of deals over £10 million; on ordinary shares the commission is 1.5 per cent up to £7000, 0.5 per cent on the next £93 000, and then falls by stages to 0.125 per cent on the excess over £1.75 million.[1] As well as carrying out their clients' dealing instructions, stockbrokers usually also provide their customers with other services, including investment advice, portfolio valuation, and tax matters. There is normally no separate charge for these services, and brokers receive their remuneration in the form of commission on transactions in securities carried out for the client.

The level of Stock Exchange turnover[2] in the most important types of security in the three years, 1978–80, is shown in Table 12.2. Turnover in British Government securities accounted for over 80 per cent of the total, amounting to well over twice the market value of

TABLE 12.2   STOCK EXCHANGE TURNOVER, 1978–80

			(£ billion)
	1978	1979	1980
British Government securities	103.7	129.0	151.7
Local authority securities	4.2	4.4	3.8
Loan capital and preference shares	1.7	1.8	1.8
Ordinary shares	19.2	24.1	30.8

Source: Financial Statistics, April 1981, Table 12.2

the stock outstanding each year. But the average value of deals is high, and the percentage rate of commission correspondingly low. Ordinary share turnover (which includes turnover in the shares of overseas companies listed on the exchange) averaged just over 15 per cent of the total, representing about a third of the market value of UK ordinary shares annually.[3] Since purchases and sales are counted separately, this implies that on average about one-sixth of UK ordinary shares change hands in a year. Local authority securities make up only a small proportion of the total, but are traded actively (turnover per year exceeds the market value of the securities); whereas turnover in loan capital and preference shares is even less, and under 30 per cent of the value of the securities each year. Tax considerations help to explain the comparatively high level of turnover in fixed interest securities – the capital gain on stocks due to accrued interest is worth more to many taxpayers than the interest itself, which creates opportunities for profitable trading between taxable and tax-free funds.

The system of trading in the UK Stock Exchange has a number of desirable features. First of all it ensures that all buying and selling interest in shares is reflected in the market, and because the brokers take their business to a small number of jobbers, there is no danger of the market becoming fragmented with trading in different parts taking place at different prices. Secondly, where several jobbers deal in the same stock, competition between the jobbers should ensure that buyers and sellers of shares deal at fair prices. Thirdly, during Stock Exchange opening hours there is continuous dealing, and a security holder can be sure of being able to buy or sell shares (in limited amounts) without delay. Finally, the separation of the market participants into brokers and jobbers, each with distinct functions (each operates in a 'single capacity') is an important feature of the UK stock market, which makes it comparatively easy to prevent certain malpractices which can arise from potential conflicts of interest.[4] In most other countries stockbrokers also act as dealers, sometimes carrying out the market-making function by holding securities themselves – a situation which makes close regulation necessary if abuses are to be avoided.

The jobbing system of market-making requires the jobbers to be prepared to take substantial positions in the securities in which they trade, i.e. if sellers prevail temporarily, they must be prepared to build up their own holding of shares in a company, whereas if buyers are preponderant, they must be willing to run their own holding down or even take an open position, in which they are committed to sell stock they do not hold. In either event, if they misjudge the temporary nature of the buying or selling pressure, they are vulnerable to changes in price and may find that they have to sell at a loss shares which they have purchased, or buy in shares at a price which is higher than that at which they are committed to sell. The system works most satisfactorily when the majority of buyers or sellers are dealing in fairly small lots, so that the capital requirement for the jobbers is not excessive. However, the growth of institutional shareholdings has imposed considerable strains on the system, because jobbers do not have the capital to quote prices for the large quantities of shares which many institutions often require. As a result, if an institution wishes to buy or sell a significant shareholding in a company, the broker instructed to carry out the order frequently has to attempt to find counterparts from amongst his own clients, thereby discharging the market-making function himself. When this happens the deal is known as a 'put-through', because the order is put through the market, that is it is offered to the jobber, who certifies that the price is fair and may take or supply some of the shares himself. But the bulk of the transaction goes through without the jobber's involvement in his trading capacity.

Although the number of members of the Stock Exchange has fallen back only slightly from a peak reached in 1974 and now seems reasonably stable, the numbers of both jobbing and broking firms had fallen, to twenty[5] and 245 respectively at the end of 1979. The decline in the number of jobbers has been particularly marked, from 117 firms in London alone in 1957.

The Stock Exchange accounts for practically all of the trading in UK listed securities. However, since 1974, some financial institutions have made use of an alternative system for trading in company securities – Automated Real-Time Investments Exchange Limited (ARIEL) – which is computer-based and bypasses the Stock Exchange. The subscribers to this system deal directly and anonymously with one another using computer terminals, but turnover has been less than a half per cent of turnover on the Stock Exchange in the relevant classes of security, even though the costs of dealing are significantly less than the commission payable to brokers. A major difficulty with computer-based systems such as ARIEL is that there is no provision for the function of market-maker, and institutions which wish to buy or sell find difficulty in making contact with counterpart traders. This is the function carried out by the broker in a put-through, who by telephoning clients individually actively seeks out counterparts for buying or selling orders. Moreover, institutions which are acting on investment advice supplied by brokers, or receive other services from them, are under some obligation to place business with them.

THE PRIMARY MARKET

The Stock Exchange also supplies the primary market to which borrowers turn for capital. When a company wishes to raise new share or loan capital it normally approaches an issuing house (usually a merchant bank) for advice and assistance, and a sponsoring broker. The former advises on the terms on which the company should seek to raise capital and on the mechanics of the issue, while the latter is responsible for seeing that the necessary documentation is provided for the Stock Exchange. The sponsoring broker also sometimes doubles as issuing house.

The timing of issues for £3 million or more is controlled by the Bank of England, which tries to ensure that large issues do not coincide, that the total number of new issues open in the market at one time is not excessive, and that cash demands are spread out in a reasonable fashion. The result is sometimes a queue of prospective borrowers. But the Bank does not attempt to influence the nature of the borrowers or the amounts of capital they raise; the object is purely to avoid congestion in the market which could lead to unnecessary temporary price movements.

New issues of shares to the public entail the preparation and publication of a prospectus, setting out in considerable detail information about the company and its affairs to satisfy both legal requirements and the requirements of the Stock Exchange. With a public issue of shares in a company which does not already have a Stock Exchange quotation, the public are invited to subscribe, usually at a fixed price; alternatively, a minimum price may be specified and tenders at that or higher prices are invited. In some instances the issuing house buys the new shares outright from the company concerned, and itself offers them for sale to the public subsequently. When public interest in the shares is likely to be limited the issuing house may instead place the bulk of the shares at a negotiated price with a group of institutions or other large investors, selected by the issuing house and sponsoring broker on the client's behalf. Although it is cheaper than a public issue or offer of sale, this method is used only infrequently for issues of shares, because there is a danger that the interests of the existing shareholders may not be fully protected – a small group of new share-holders might be allocated shares on unduly favourable terms. Under Stock Exchange regulations, placings of shares in excess of £$1\frac{1}{2}$ million are not permitted, other than in exceptional circumstances.[6] In their evidence to the Wilson Committee the Stock Exchange estimated that the costs of a public issue or offer for sale raising £2 million would be of the order of $8\frac{1}{2}$ per cent of the proceeds (including 1 per cent for capital duty and nearly as much for VAT).

The normal method by which a company already listed on the Stock Exchange obtains new equity capital is the 'rights' issue. The company gives its existing shareholders the right to subscribe for new shares, allocated *pro rata* to their existing shareholdings. The price asked for the new shares is usually set at a discount of some 15–20 per cent below the share price at the time of the announcement. Shareholders who do not wish to take up their allocation of new shares can sell their rights in the market, and so avoid any financial loss which might otherwise result from setting the rights issue price below the prevailing market price. The cost of a rights issue of £2 million was estimated as $4\frac{1}{2}$ per cent of the proceeds (including $1\frac{1}{2}$ per cent for capital duty and VAT). Placings represent a cheaper alternative (under 3 per cent), and can be made at a much smaller discount below the market price, but as with other new issues the the Stock Exchange normally limit placings to a maximum of £$1\frac{1}{2}$ million.

Companies frequently issue shares as 'vendor consideration' in connection with takeovers, when the shareholders of the company being taken over receive shares in the other company in exchange for their own shares. Very often there is an element of cash consideration (which may be optional) and the company may arrange for shares equivalent to the cash consideration to be placed with institutional investors. The £$1\frac{1}{2}$ million limit does not apply in this case.

Placings are the most common method employed for issuing loan capital, though an offer for sale or rights issue is sometimes used, particularly for convertible debentures where there is an equity element. The cost of a placing was estimated as under 3 per cent, compared with about 6 per cent for an offer for sale.

New issues and rights issues are usually underwritten; that is arrangements are made to ensure that any shares for which there are no other subscribers are purchased. In the case of a rights issue this will occur only if the price of the existing shares falls below the rights issue price. A period of at least 3 weeks elapses between the announcement of the rights issue and the date on which subscriptions are due, and since there is always the risk that the share price will fall during this period there is a genuine risk that in the absence of underwriting the company might fail to obtain its money – though the risk diminishes with the size of the discount at which the new shares are offered. Normally the issuing house acts itself as the principal underwriter, but arranges sub-underwriting from a number of institutions, who receive a fee for their services. This is generally $1\frac{1}{4}$ per cent of their commitment, and represents a significant element in the cost of raising new capital. Underwriting is, of course, unnecessary for placings.

Gross capital issues on the UK market, which raised new capital for UK companies, from 1975 to 1979 are shown in Table 12.3.[7] Capital issues averaged over £1.2 billion per year in this period, with rights issues accounting for nearly 80 per cent of the total. Placings contributed 10 per cent, with only about 7 per cent raised through public issues and offers for sale, whether at a fixed price or by tender. Thanks to the high nominal interest rates prevailing, rights issues of preference and loan capital were very low.[8]

TABLE 12:3   CAPITAL ISSUES ON UK MARKET BY UK LISTED
COMPANIES, 1975–79

					(£ million)
	1975	1976	1977	1978	1979
Public issues and offers for sale	103	103	61	18	22
Tenders	36	31	28	14	22
Placings	71	101	275	106	81
Rights issues					
Ordinary shares	1226	1025	812	920	946
Preference and loan capital	104	32	7	9	33
Total	1539	1291	1183	1067	1103

Source: Wilson Committee Report, Table 3.63

THE GILT-EDGED MARKET

The gilt-edged market comprises British Government and government guaranteed stocks, and stocks issued by local authorities and some other public bodies. Though the gilt-edged market is part of the primary market, the techniques for issuing new government securities differ from those in the company securities market. The Bank of England does not employ an issuing house to act on its behalf, though the government broker does act as sponsoring broker for it, and issues are not underwritten. In practice, however, the bulk of a new issue is often taken up by official bodies, for sale subsequently in the secondary market.[9] In effect, recently issued stocks, known as 'tap' stocks, are continuously on offer to the market, instead of the market having to provide the entire sum on the day of issue. In recent years the government has issued some stocks which were payable in instalments, thereby also spreading the period over which payment was received.

The government has been the dominant borrower in the capital market in recent years. As Table 12.4 shows the average level of gross capital issues from 1976 to 1980 was almost £11½ billion – nearly ten times as much as was raised by companies in this period. Net issues to non-official holders averaged £7½ billion. In addition to government securities there have been significant issues of negotiable bonds (bonds with a maturity of 1–5 years) by local authorities. About £750 million of these bonds were issued in 1980, although this was only about £50 million more than the maturities of that year.

TABLE 12.4   ISSUES OF BRITISH GOVERNMENT SECURITIES, 1976–80

(£ billion)

	Total cash issues	Total cash redemption etc.	Net issues	Net purchases by non-official holders
1976	8.3	2.4	5.9	5.4
1977	12.6	2.6	10.0	7.3
1978	7.3	2:4	4.9	5.1
1979	14.1	3.6	10.5	10.1
1980	14.9	3.6	11.2	10.7

Source: Financial Statistics, April 1981, Table 3.9

New issues of government securities have a very wide range of maturities, ranging in 1980 from about 3 to nearly 30 years. Practically all gilt-edged securities have fixed rates of interest (there are a few variable-rate issues outstanding) but an important innovation in 1981 was the issue of index-linked stocks, in which the rate of interest (or coupon) was fixed, but the monetary value on which interest payments and the capital sum to be repaid at maturity is calculated is revalued regularly to take account of inflation.

INFLUENCE OF THE SECONDARY ON THE PRIMARY MARKET

While the functions of the primary and secondary markets differ it is no accident that the institutions participating in them are often the same, because an efficient secondary market, in which existing securities can be bought or sold easily, contributes in several important ways to the strength of the primary market. First and foremost it is the secondary market which provides the liquidity, the ability to turn securities into cash if desired, which makes it reasonable for many savers to hold long-term assets. This is undoubtedly the case for most individual savers, who may wish to realize part or all of their assets without being involved in costly and extended negotiations.

A second way in which the primary market depends upon the secondary market is in the pricing of new securities. The price which new shares issued by a company will fetch depends upon the prices of similar securities at the time the issue is made – the company's own securities in the case of a rights issue. In principle, an active secondary market, in which holders of shares who have access to information about the company are able to deal freely, will lead to share prices accurately reflecting informed views about a company's prospects. This in turn should lead to accurate pricing of new issues.

Thirdly, the secondary market contributes to the operation of the primary market by enabling a wider range of institutions to participate in underwriting new issues. The underwriter has to be sure that he will be able to take up shares if called upon to do so, and for this he has to be able to obtain the necessary cash. While most institutions can rely on borrowing for short periods, the risks associated with underwriting would be greatly increased if institutions were unable to dispose of some of their existing assets quickly to provide cash (or repay short-term borrowing) should it prove necessary.

Finally, most of the institutions involved in the primary market, whether as providers of funds or as arrangers of new issues, are also heavily involved in secondary market activities. They are engaged continuously in seeking out information about companies, and in analysing and monitoring their performance. This continuous appraisal helps to determine the prices at which securities are traded and makes it much easier for the institutional investors to reach a swift decision when they are invited to subscribe to or underwrite a new issue; in the absence of the secondary market the time required to raise new capital would be prolonged and the costs involved increased.

Questions have been raised, however, concerning the necessity of active secondary market trading for the working of the primary market. It has been suggested that Britain suffers from over-active trading in the secondary market for company securities, combined with a comparatively low level of issues in the primary market.

While secondary market trading undoubtedly enhances liquidity it is not obvious that some of the major institutional investors have the same need for liquidity in their portfolios as private individuals. Liquidity clearly is important for general insurance funds, where the ability to realize funds in order to meet claims quickly is essential, and for unit trusts, which are bound to encash units on demand. But, it matters less for the other long-term institutions – the life assurance companies, pension funds and investment trusts – who do not expect to have to find large sums of cash at short notice, and can plan their realizations of assets accordingly. These institutions are prepared to invest part of their assets in relatively illiquid property, and the equivalent institutions in some other countries seem to be able to operate successfully with a higher proportion of their portfolios invested in relatively illiquid assets. However, rightly or wrongly, the institutions do place considerable weight on the marketability of their assets even though they sometimes find difficulty in disposing of a large holding of shares in a company without having to accept a substantial reduction in the price, and so long as they can deal at the margin of their holdings they are able to adjust the balance of their portfolios and find funds to take advantage of any particularly attractive investment opportunities which arise. In the absence of the liquidity provided by the secondary market these institutions – particularly those without a substantial inflow of accruing funds – would have much less flexibility in the management of their assets.

Criticism of the secondary market usually rests on the belief that there is excessive speculative activity which distorts market prices and casts doubt on the extent to which share prices actually reflect informed views of companies' prospects. Some speculative activity, in the sense of purchases or sales of shares by people who think that the current share price is either too low or too high, but who are not necessarily permanent holders, is virtually essential to the smooth functioning of the market, since it is traders of this kind who even out temporary imbalances between supply and demand for a company's shares. This, indeed, is one of the jobbers' functions. However, speculative activity may go much farther, and lead to the purchase of shares, not because the share price is deemed too low in relation to the company's prospects, but because purchasers think that prices will continue to rise and that they will then be able to sell out at a profit. Speculation in this case depends more on a short-term view of market prospects than on a careful analysis of the fundamental considerations affecting the company's future and hence the value of its shares.

It is difficult to argue against the proposition that fundamental considerations will dominate in the end – the shares of companies which prove to be very profitable rise in price, and the shares of companies that fail fall. But many people are not convinced that some of the more violent fluctuations in share prices are caused entirely by new information about companies becoming available or by a careful reassessment of existing knowledge. On the contrary, they seem sometimes to be affected by moods of exaggerated optimism or pessimism, or by fashion which leads comparatively uninformed investors to make speculative purchases or sales in the hope of making a quick profit.

In spite of these qualifications it is undeniable that the primary and secondary markets *together* make an important contribution to the functioning of any financial system. Together with the financial institutions which use their facilities the markets are a powerful force for mobilizing saving in the UK, even though in recent years a very high proportion of the savings mobilized have been directed towards the government rather than to the private sector. Without the securities markets it would be much more difficult and costly for asset-holders to diversify their portfolios and so reduce the risks to which they are exposed. And it is the securities markets which make it easy for the saver to realize long-term assets, and so have the advantage of liquidity. Finally, the effect of organized markets on transactions costs should not be overlooked. The purchase or sale of securities in a small company, whose shares are not traded on an organized market, frequently involves employing members of the accountancy and legal professions, at costs which may be considerable in relation to the sums involved. Costs of this kind can be avoided entirely when dealing takes place in the organized markets.

UNLISTED SECURITIES

Until recently the Stock Exchange set out to cater for the needs of the 2600 or so listed companies. But listing was not open to all companies, nor was it always wanted. Before a company can be granted a Stock Exchange listing, or quotation, it is obliged to satisfy certain conditions. It must for example be of a minimum size, have traded for at least 5 years, have sufficient of its securities available in the market to allow an acceptable degree of marketability, and sign a listing agreement with the Stock Exchange governing the way in which it will conduct its affairs and the information about its business which it will make available in future. These conditions are intended to ensure that listed companies conform with high standards of behaviour, that the market has sufficient information for dealing to be fair, and that prices are not affected unduly by narrow markets with little trading. Indeed, the jobbing system in the UK stock market presupposes that there will be a reasonable degree of trading activity, and is not really suitable when trading in a company's shares is only sporadic.

No similar organized market existed for trading in unlisted securities. Stockbrokers were able to arrange occasional deals in shares of unlisted companies; but for many years this was not actively encouraged by the Stock Exchange. Outside the Stock Exchange dealers helped to find buyers for shares in unlisted companies, and one firm attempted to fill the role of market-maker for the shares in a limited number of companies. But generally, if a company wanted to raise new capital or if existing shareholders wished to dispose of their shares, they had to approach a merchant bank, stockbroker or other dealer, who would attempt to place the shares for them through their own contacts. The market was extremely fragmented, and the terms on which new capital could be raised reflected the illiquidity of unlisted shares.

During 1980 the Stock Exchange (after much prompting) took steps to develop a market in unlisted securities on a more formal basis, and such a market now exists under their aegis. The conditions for access to the Unlisted Securities Market are less rigorous than those for a Stock Exchange listing, and the obligations placed on companies are also less onerous.[10] Stockbrokers acting for clients who wish to buy or sell unlisted securities are still bound by the rules of the Stock Exchange.

The procedures employed in the Unlisted Securities Market differ in some important respects from those for listed securities. In particular, jobbers are not necessarily involved at all, and a broker may organize trading in a company's shares. Moreover, there is more scope for the use of placings in new issues, and a higher degree of direct involvement between companies and institutional investors is practicable.

Since the Unlisted Securities Market was created there has been a steady flow of companies arranging to have their shares traded on it. Companies which continue to grow are likely in due course to find the status and liquidity offered by a full listing advantageous, but they are under no pressure to apply for a listing if they do not want to and may continue to have their shares traded as unlisted securities indefinitely.

THE INSTITUTIONS AND THE SECURITIES MARKETS

The last 25 years has seen a gradual but persistent change in the character of the securities markets in the UK, brought about by a change in the pattern of ownership. Table 12.5 shows how institutional ownership of UK securities has grown steadily, and this has been accompanied by a corresponding decline in the direct ownership of securities by the personal sector. Thus in 1957 the investing institutions held only 17 per cent of the total stock of British government securities outstanding, whereas by 1978 this had risen to 46 per cent. For *long-dated* securities the percentage of ownership must have been considerably higher. Even more important, the institutional ownership of ordinary shares had risen from 19 per cent in 1957 to 47 per cent at the end of 1978, a figure which by the end of 1980 will have exceeded 50 per cent. Thus, whereas in the 1960s the ownership of UK equity shares was dominated by private individuals and trusts, by 1980 there is no question but that the institutions were the dominant force. Changes in the ownership of company loan capital and preference shares have also been substantial, but have had less to do with the growth of the institutions; changes in the tax system resulted in preference shares becoming concentrated in the hands of certain institutional investors, while

TABLE 12.5   OWNERSHIP OF LISTED UK SECURITIES BY
INVESTING INSTITUTIONS,[1] 1957-78

	At end year; per cent of total market value in issue					
	1957	1962	1967	1972	1977	1978
British Government securities	17	24	27	34	41	46
UK local authority securities	23	26	21	10	16	20
UK company securities						
Loan capital	75	79	77	51	45	42
Preference shares	36	37	59	52	69	72
Ordinary shares	19	24	31	35	44	47

Source: Wilson Committee Report, Table 3.68
    Insurance companies, pension funds, investment trust companies and unit trusts

company loan capital was for a time regarded by private trusts as an attractive alternative to gilt-edged securities.

The influence of the institutions in the secondary market has been enhanced by a change in their investment behaviour during this period. Table 12.6 shows the sales activity in ordinary shares of the investing institutions for 1963 to 1977. In this case sales activity (rather than the purchases plus sales recorded in Table 12.2) is an appropriate measure of turnover because most of the funds were expanding (or at least not contracting); by concentrating on sales from their portfolios the effects of investing new money on turnover are excluded. There was a marked increase in the sales rates of all the major groups, with a trebling overall, and a quite remarkable increase by the unit trusts (whose investment performance in the short-run receives the greatest publicity). In relation to their assets the turnover of the institutions is now clearly greater than for the market as a whole, with the result that they now account for the lion's share of turnover in the equity market.

These changes have implications for the system of market-making in the UK. We have observed already that the jobber in a share is obliged to quote a price for dealing – a slightly higher price for a sale than for a purchase – and that since his own capital is limited he will quote a firm price for only a limited number of shares. To earn his profit he relies on temporary imbalances between supply and demand in the market, so that he can buy shares more cheaply

TABLE 12.6   SALES ACTIVITY IN ORDINARY SHARES BY
INVESTING INSTITUTIONS, 1963–77

	Sales during year as per cent of market value of holdings[1]		
	1963–77 average	1968–72 average	1973–77 average
Insurance companies	4.2	6.7	12.6
Pension funds	4.3	10.2	16.3
Investment trust companies	10.4	14.5	21.7
Unit trusts	10.2	30.7	45.6
All investing institutions	6.5	11.7	19.3

Source: Wilson Committee Report, Table 7.2
 [1] Average of beginning and end-year holdings

than he sells. The larger institutions, however, control funds which dwarf the capital available to the jobbers, and their shareholdings in the individual companies are often very large in relation to the amount a jobber could reasonably take on to his own book or supply from it. Thus the size of lot in which the institutions wish to deal is often greater than the jobbing system can cope with, leading to the emergence of the put-through as a common means of arranging the purchase or sale of large lots. This aspect of the brokers' services is extremely important to the large institutional investor, and it seems possible that an ever-increasing proportion of institutional trading will be handled by the brokers in this way. In addition, the jobber relies on trading taking place for a variety of reasons, and not merely a belief that shares are under or over-priced. But when institutions dominate the market there is a fair chance that they will react in a similar way to new information, so that one-way dealing, in which there is a preponderance of buyers or sellers but little interest on the opposite side of the market, will develop. This leaves the jobber in a very vulnerable position, because prices are likely to move quite sharply before he is able to correct any imbalance in his own portfolio.

One consequence has been the decline in the number of jobbing firms which we have already mentioned. The remaining firms have, of course, a much stronger capital base, but there is no doubt that the decline in the number of jobbers has led to a reduction in competition; agreements exist on the minimum spread between buying and selling prices that jobbers will quote, and on some occasions competing jobbers operate a joint book. Thus the competition, on which the system relies in order to ensure that the cost to the users of the Stock Exchange is kept as low as possible, has been sharply diminished.

Conditions are different in the gilt-edged market because the government broker, acting for the Bank of England, is often prepared to respond to bids for stock from the market, supplying the necessary stock from official holdings. This reduces the strain on the jobbers' capital resources. Nevertheless, occasions do occur when the scale of market dealings appears to be greater than the jobbers can easily handle.

The jobbing system is enshrined in the Stock Exchange regulations, which compel brokers to offer all their business to the jobbers in the first instance, and prevent the jobbers from dealing directly with clients on their own account. These, and all the other regulations of the Stock Exchange, are to be tested in the Restrictive Trade Practices Court, and if it is found that they are not in the public interest the regulations will need to be abandoned. In that event the jobbing system is unlikely to survive.

The growth of the institutions may also have important implications for the organization and practices in the primary market. In spite of the changed situation as regards the ownership of shares and the dominant position of the institutions in bringing new saving to the market, the techniques for raising new capital do not appear to have altered significantly. In the gilt-edged market, for the most part, the government still employ the tap method of issuing stock, though occasionally they have resorted to a tender method. Selling stock by the tap method, and varying the price to encourage sales, may eventually succeed in raising the desired volume of finance, but the timing of sales has sometimes caused difficulties for the government – with periods when sales were low interspersed with sudden surges. A tender system, probably with some underwriting by the institutions, might well be preferable and more in tune with the fact that a high proportion of the stock is likely to find its way into institutional portfolios.[11]

In the equity market too the fact that the bulk of the funds subscribed for rights issues are likely to emanate from the institutions, many of whom will already be substantial shareholders in the company, might well be recognized. The time when companies had to rely on being able to gather funds together from a very large number of small shareholders is past. The institutions with substantial shareholdings in a company sometimes commit themselves in advance to take up their share of a rights issue, and this part of the issue does not need to be underwritten. It might well be appropriate to extend this practice to a wider range of institutions, so that only that part of the issue allocated to non-institutional or smaller shareholders would need to be underwritten. Indeed, if shareholders as a body agreed to give up their pre-emptive rights to new shares, a placing rather than a rights issue might be more convenient and less costly for the company.

Any changes of this kind could come about only if the contacts between companies and the institutions which held their shares were close, so that institutional shareholders could be called upon to provide additional capital when it was needed. The issue of the relationship between companies and institutional investors is important; we shall return to it in the final chapter.

THE STERLING MONEY MARKETS

In contrast with the securities markets, which are of direct relevance to many of the ultimate users of the financial system, the sterling money markets are much more the concern of certain specialized users. Nevertheless, they are of considerable importance for the financial system. They help to create the liquidity on which the banking system depends; they act as the channel through which the Bank of England influences financial conditions generally; and they provide a very significant source of relatively short-term finance for some important categories of borrower.

The money markets comprise three broad categories of financial instrument: secured loans, bills and unsecured loans. Secured loans and bills are the province mainly of the discount market, whose members act as principals, while transactions in unsecured loans are usually carried out by money brokers who do not take a position themselves but simply bring lenders and borrowers together. Table 12.7 contains estimates of the size of the various components of the London sterling money markets at the end of 1979, the total identified amounting to almost £45 billion. Over half of this represents business between financial institutions rather than lending to ultimate borrowers; inter-bank deposits, deposits with finance houses, most of money at call and a considerable proportion of sterling certificates of deposit all come in this category.

TABLE 12.7   THE LONDON STERLING MONEY MARKETS, 1979

	(£ billion)
Money at call with discount market	4.4
Treasury bills	2.5
Commercial bills	5.6
Local authority bills	0.6
Sterling certificates of deposit	3.7
Other local authority temporary debt	5.1
Deposits with finance houses	1.1
Inter-bank deposits	16.4
Other market loans by the banking sector	5.3
Total identified	44.8

Source: Wilson Committee Report, Table 3.70

The discount market consists of the Discount Houses, which are members of the London Discount Market Association, and certain other institutions. They borrow sterling, either overnight or at call for a fixed period, mainly from the banks, though a small proportion of their funds is obtained from other lenders Money at call with the discount market has traditionally been regarded as the most liquid and safe part (after cash) of the banks' assets. The default risk is negligible because money at call is secured on the Discount Houses' assets. Instead of holding non-interest-bearing cash banks with surplus funds lent them to the discount market, whilst those with a deficiency withdrew call loans, thus minimizing the cash balances the banks had to hold. This is a function which the discount market continues to perform, though the amount of call money – £4.4 billion at the end of 1979 – is also influenced by the market's need for funds to carry out its other functions effectively.[12]

The Discount Houses' funds are invested in a variety of financial instruments including treasury bills, commercial and local authority bills, certificates of deposit, local authority bonds and short-dated gilt-edged securities. The Discount Houses act as market-makers in the bill and certificate of deposit markets, by standing ready to buy or sell these instruments at quoted prices. At the end of 1979 Treasury, commercial and local authority bills outstanding amounted to £2.5 billion, £5.6 billion, and £0.6 billion respectively, with sterling certificates of deposit of £3.7 billion. As noted in Chapter

10, all these instruments form part of the banks' liquid assets, and the fact that the discount market stands ready to buy them adds considerably to their liquidity. As can be seen from the figures – nearly £9 billion altogether – the bill markets are also an important source of finance to ultimate borrowers.[13]

The remaining items in Table 12.7, which amounted in total to over £25 billion, are traded in what is known as the 'parallel' market, as are sterling certificates of deposit. The suppliers of funds in this market are the banks and the discount market, together with the local authorities, building societies and other financial institutions, and many industrial and commercial companies. The takers of funds cover a similar range. Funds are generally placed through brokers, and while rates of interest differ between the various categories of borrower (according to perceived difference in risk and other factors, including transactions costs) the market is essentially a unitary market, with rates of interest moving very closely together. These instruments too account for a high proportion of the banking system's liquid assets, but in contrast with money at call with the discount market, inter-bank deposits are unsecured. Most money-market instruments have maturities ranging from overnight to 1 year, but sterling certificates of deposit may be issued for periods of from 3 months to 3 years.

The ultimate liquidity of the system rests with the Bank of England, which can supply cash either by purchasing bills (usually from the discount market) or by advancing funds to the Discount Houses. The latter used to be the more common procedure, but since the end of 1980 purchases of commercial bills have become the preferred method.[14] The Bank of England does not intervene directly in the parallel money markets, which rely for their liquidity on the ability of some participants to withdraw funds from the discount market (which in turn relies on the Bank of England).

The sterling money markets therefore have a key role in the financial system, for it is through them that the Bank of England influences financial conditions generally. The terms on which the Bank supplies cash have a pervasive influence on interest rates throughout the money markets as a whole, and spread out from there to the rest of the financial system.

NOTES

1. For small deals brokers also charge a minimum commission, which varies from one broker to another, of say, £10.

2. Calculated as purchases plus sales.
3. Transactions in overseas securities are not distinguished separately, but UK turnover undoubtedly accounts for most of the business.
4. E.g. a security dealer might be tempted to advise a client to buy securities of which he wished to dispose.
5. Of which fourteen were in London.
6. Companies may also be introduced to the Stock Exchange without any new capital being raised. The purpose of a Stock Exchange introduction is to improve the marketability of the company's shares, which may be helpful to existing shareholders and gives the company access to improved capital-raising facilities in the future. Other new issues may also be a means of enabling existing shareholders to dispose of some of their shares, rather than a source of new capital to the company.
7. The figures for rights issues of ordinary shares in 1978 and 1979 include nearly £450 million and £150 million respectively for issues by British Leyland, 99 per cent of which were taken up by the National Enterprise Board.
8. Placings of loan stocks were, of course, affected by similar considerations.
9. The government broker responds to bids for stock from the market, and usually makes known a price at which he is prepared to sell.
10. The less rigorous requirements are reflected in the fact that unlisted securities do not have 'trustee status', i.e. the trustees are not automatically permitted to invest in securities of this kind without the specific authority of those setting up the trust.
11. For further discussion see Wilson Committee *Report*, pp. 181–83.
12. The Bank of England has requested banks whose acceptances are eligible for rediscount at the Bank to hold money at call with the discount market in order to enable the discount houses to continue to hold substantial bill portfolios.
13. Some of the commercial bills are in fact issued by non-bank financial institutions, such as finance houses.
14. Hence the Bank of England's efforts to ensure that the discount market is not short of funds to finance a substantial bill portfolio.

13 SPECIAL CREDIT INSTITUTIONS

Most financial institutions in the UK economy evolved spontaneously as a result of initiatives taken by individuals or groups in the private sector. Usually they saw an opportunity for commercial gain and set up a business to take advantage of it, but philanthropic motives have also been important, as for example in the creation of the Trustee Savings Banks and building societies.

The origins of the Special Credit Institutions (SCI) differ from those of the rest of the financial system, because these institutions were created in an effort to satisfy needs for which the existing financial system did not appear to cater adequately. The predecessor of the National Savings Bank, the Post Office Savings Bank, was set up with the social function of providing facilities for saving in small amounts by ordinary people, but nowadays SCI in Britain operate on the investing rather than the saving side of the financial system, with a view to influencing the availability and terms on which borrowers are able to obtain funds.

There are two main reasons for creating SCI. First, gaps or weaknesses in the provision of facilities by the private sector may be detected. One possible response is to create a new institution to fill the gap or strengthen the system. Secondly, for reasons of public policy, the government may wish to promote or assist certain activities. An institution with the power to take initiatives (or respond to initiatives taken elsewhere) by providing finance on favourable terms may help the government to achieve its aims. Instead of using SCI for this purpose the government can, of course, adopt other courses of action, such as making grants or subsidies available to favoured categories of borrower. But an institution, whose decisions are not subject to everyday parliamentary scrutiny, is probably more able than a government department to offer support selectively and take initiatives itself.

In some countries SCI occupy a central position in the financial system. France is one example, in which a high proportion of capital funds are channelled through the Caisse des Dépôts et Consignations, mainly into investment by local government authorities and into housing. Another institution, the Crédit National, helps to increase the supply of long-term loan finance to industry in France, and was used by the government to channel funds in accordance with the priorities of the French National Plan. SCI of this type often stem from weaknesses in the supply of long-term capital, which have threatened to hold back capital investment in the economy.

Thanks to the long-standing strength of the capital market in Britain the need for SCI has been much less keenly felt. The supply of general-purpose loan finance has usually been covered adequately by the banks, and long-term loan capital has been available (at a price) through the securities markets. Equity finance for listed companies has also been readily available, provided that the company's record of profitability seemed to warrant entrusting additional capital to it. Public sector bodies have had no difficulty in raising loan finance (provided they were prepared to pay the interest-rate demanded in the market) and, although sometimes rationed, long-term mortgage finance for housing has been available from building societies and other lenders. SCI in Britain have therefore tended to operate on the fringes of the financial system, to help to satisfy specialized needs for finance and to promote certain activities.

One area of difficulty, to which we have already referred in Chapter 7, is the provision of long-term equity and loan capital to small firms (the Macmillan gap). In an effort to fill this gap the Industrial and Commercial Finance Corporation (ICFC) – now the main operating division of Finance for Industry (FFI) – was created in 1946. An experimental loan guarantee scheme, started in June 1981, is a further attempt to deal with this problem. Possible problems in the availability of long-term capital to medium-sized or larger companies are recognized by the existence of the Finance Corporation for Industry (FCI), which is now also part of FFI, and by Equity Capital for Industry (ECI).

Difficulties experienced in the funding of innovations led to the National Research Development Corporation (NRDC) which finances development expenditure and initial commercial production of relatively small-scale innovations. On a larger scale the National Enterprise Board (NEB) can assist with the funding of high-risk investments, particularly where new technology is involved, and indeed has been able itself to take the initiative in promoting such enterprises. The NEB, together with the Scottish and Welsh Development Agencies (SDA and WDA respectively) also have the function of helping firms which operate in the assisted areas of England and in Scotland and Wales.

Finance may also be provided directly by government departments. Under the Industry Act 1972 the Department of Industry provides grants and subsidies in the form of regional development grants, selective financial assistance, and grants for certain categories of investment. The Export Credits Guarantee Department (ECGD) also acts as a medium for subsidizing export credit, although its main function is to act as an insurance organization providing insurance cover for export business. Although not strictly SCI these departmental sources of finance and assistance for industry will be discussed at the end of the chapter.

FINANCE FOR INDUSTRY

FFI was formed in 1973 as a holding company for ICFC, FCI, and several other specialized subsidiaries including Finance for Shipping (FFS) and Technical Development Capital (TDC).

ICFC was set up in 1945, at the request of the government, in an effort to fill the Macmillan gap. Its shareholders were the Bank of England, London and Scottish clearing banks, and it has always operated as a commercial enterprise which has sought to earn a (modest) profit on its capital. It provides finance in sums from £5 thousand to £2 million, by means of loan and equity capital, and leasing facilities are also available through another of FFI's subsidiaries. New investments in the year to March 1980 amounted to £105 million, divided between 900 customers. ICFC frequently provides additional finance for existing clients; about a third of its customers in 1979/80 came in this category. The bulk of ICFC's finance for small firms consists of medium and long-term loan capital, but equity is also available, and ICFC may insist on taking some equity capital in addition to making loans if the risk is high, so that some prospect of an additional return is required to justify the provision of loan finance. Equity capital is also provided when other lenders insist on the equity base of a firm being strengthened before making loans themselves. ICFC finance for small firms is often part of a package, involving co-operation between ICFC and the clearing banks, with the Department of Industry participating when government grants or loans are involved.

ICFC do not seek control of the companies to which they provide equity capital, and they view themselves as long-term holders of capital; they do not disinvest or dispose of shareholdings unless this is in the interests of the company concerned. There is keen competition between ICFC and development capital companies,[1] particularly in the provision of equity capital to companies which stand a good chance of experiencing rapid growth. But development capital companies typically have a greater need for income in the short-term than does ICFC, and since they rely on turning over their funds many do not regard themselves as permanent holders of equity in individual companies and invest in the hope that they will be able to dispose of their equity shareholding at a capital gain within a short period of years. ICFC rarely invests in totally new enterprises, but its subsidiary, TDC, provides finance for the initial stages of worthwhile technological innovations.

FCI was formed by the same group of shareholders in 1945, to provide longer-term finance for larger companies. Its facilities have not been heavily used in recent years, mainly as a result of the high prevailing level of interest-rates but also because other sources of finance, e.g. medium-term bank loans, have been available. FCI is also in a position to provide limited amounts of equity finance, and there are signs that this side of its activities may grow and that it may become more involved in the provision of a combination of equity and loan finance to companies which have been experiencing difficulties. FFS provides finance for the construction of shipping and for chartering activities. At the end of 1979 FFI had total assets of over £850 million. Apart from its share capital and reserves it obtains its funds by borrowing short-term deposits in the money markets and by issuing its own loan stocks. Deposits at the end of March 1980 amounted to over £370 million of which £300 million had maturities of less than 1 year, and as much as £200 million were repayable within 1 month. FFI's risk investments are financed from its own equity capital, and very substantial standby credits from its shareholding banks protect it from any shortage of finance for loans.

EQUITY CAPITAL FOR INDUSTRY (ECI)

ECI was set up in 1976, at the instigation of the Bank of England, by a consortium of financial institutions. Its initial share capital was £41 million, subscribed by 365 institutions in all. It aims to provide equity capital for industrial companies which warrant support but which cannot readily raise new equity through the normal channels, and is usually prepared to invest in the range £250 thousand to

£2 million, with an absolute upper limit of £4 million – 10 per cent of its present funds. ECI expects to have a continuing involvement with the companies in which it invests, and usually appoints a non-executive director to the Board. Considerable controversy regarding the need for ECI preceded its creation, and the demand for its facilities has not yet been very great. Its investments have inevitably been in high-risk situations – where the risk is low companies seldom have difficulty in obtaining funds from other sources – and some have proved unsuccessful. There seems, however, to be scope for ECI to play a significant part in injecting new equity capital into companies which are in trouble, but have a reasonable prospect of survival, and it is possible that, since ECI is itself under the control of institutional shareholders, it may come to play a catalytic role in obtaining equity funds directly from the more important institutional shareholders of the companies in which it takes a stake.[2]

NATIONAL RESEARCH DEVELOPMENT CORPORATION
(NRDC)

NRDC was established by the government in 1948 with the function of securing the development or exploitation of inventions, where adequate finance was not available from other sources. It is enjoined, taking one year with another, to earn sufficient revenue to meet its outgoings. Initially NRDC was financed by Department of Industry loans, but these have now been repaid and finance is provided out of NRDC's own accumulated surplus and reserves.

In practice NRDC provides help to private individuals or small companies. Usually it operates on a joint venture basis, putting up part of the finance required and hoping to recover its money (and help to pay for losses elsewhere) through a levy on sales. This method is particularly appropriate when an investor can find an existing company which is prepared to help to exploit his ideas, with the aid of some outside support. However, NRDC can also provide equity and loan finance for companies directly. At the end of March 1980 NRDC had spent or committed £62 million in respect of 608 development projects in existence.

NATIONAL ENTERPRISE BOARD AND THE
REGIONAL DEVELOPMENT AGENCIES

The NEB is a public corporation, set up under the Industry Act 1975. Its statutory purposes are to develop or assist the economy of

the UK; to promote industrial efficiency and international competitiveness; and to provide, maintain or safeguard productive employment. It draws its funds partly from the National Loans Fund but
mainly as public dividend capital, which is analogous to share capital
for private companies.

The main function of the NEB is to provide finance for industrial
investment, particularly the expansion and modernization of productive facilities in manufacturing industries. But at the outset the
NEB was also given the function of acting as a holding company for
shareholdings in industrial companies which were already owned by
the government, e.g. shares in British Leyland Limited and, at that
time, Rolls-Royce Limited. The needs of these companies have
absorbed the lion's share of the NEB's investment.

The NEB is able to provide equity, and sometimes also loan,
finance for industry more generally. The conditions under which
NEB finance would be appropriate are not unlike those which concern ECI – companies may have difficulty in generating sufficient
internal cash for their investment, they may have no spare equity
on which they could base further borrowing, and their performance
might throw doubt upon the success of a conventional rights issue.
When the NEB provides loan finance it does so on terms which are
no more favourable than could be obtained by a company of high
quality borrowing in the capital market, and the intention is that
it should look for a commercial return on its investments, with the
qualification that it may be prepared to wait longer for income to
be generated from projects it supports than would be the case with
most private organizations.

The guidelines laying down the Board's remit have been a matter
of some political contention. At the end of 1980 the Board's remit
fell under four main headings:

the Board shall pursue a catalytic investment role especially in
connection with:

i   companies in which they already have an interest when this
    direction takes effect;
ii companies engaged in the development or exploitation of
    advanced technology;
iii companies carrying on (or intending to carry on) an industrial
    undertaking which is (or will be) wholly or mainly in the assisted
    areas in England;
iv loans of up to £50 thousand to small firms.

The NEB's role in developing and exploiting advanced technology may prove to be of considerable importance. Such investments frequently involve the commitment of considerable resources, and unless an existing UK company already had interests in the technology and a desire to extend farther in that direction, particular branches of industry might not be adequately represented in the UK. There are cases where the minimum economic scale is high and the risks are large, circumstances which, when they occur together, may represent a barrier to private financing. The NEB has in fact taken significant initiatives in the development of microchip projects, and other examples include investment in biotechnology and the development of specialized metals for use in aero-engines. The regional functions of the NEB have their counterparts in the responsibilities of the Scottish and Welsh Development Agencies. Their concern is mainly with medium-sized firms with a strong regional base, though on occasions they do also participate in providing equity finance to large enterprises. Both the regional development agencies have divisions specializing in finance for small firms. They too are expected to earn a commercial rate of return on their assets, and, like the NEB, obtain their funds from the government.

The extent to which the NEB and regional development agencies should be encouraged or permitted to depart from private sector criteria in assessing the case for supporting investment proposals has been the subject of considerable debate. If finance is provided on deliberately concessional terms this may have implications for other enterprises, which are in competition with those in receipt of support but do not enjoy cheap finance. On the other hand, since one of the objectives of an organization like the NEB is to provide selective support in order to strengthen firms which are thought likely to be of long-run importance to the economy, some discrimination of this kind may be unavoidable.

GOVERNMENT FINANCIAL ASSISTANCE

The central government also exerts a direct influence on investment through a number of channels. The first and most important is the tax system, through the use of accelerated depreciation allowances. Instead of writing off assets at a rate which reflects their useful lives, when calculating their taxable profits firms are allowed to write off 100 per cent of expenditure on plant and equipment and 50 per cent of industrial building in the first year. For firms with sufficient profits this means that a tax saving in the first year amounting to about half of the cost of plant and machinery and a quarter of the cost of building is made.[3] Stock relief has a similar effect in helping to finance the additional stock required for new projects.

Tax allowances act as an across-the-board incentive to investment by industry. Other aspects of central government financial support come under the Industry Act 1972 and are more selective. The first category is regional aid (Section 7 of the Act) – Regional Development Grants are available in assisted areas to meet part of the costs of providing buildings, plant and machinery. All qualifying expenditure in the assisted areas is eligible for grants. In addition, selective financial assistance, usually in the form of an interest relief grant which reduces the interest-cost borne by the borrower, is also provided for projects that create or safeguard employment.

The second category (Section 8 aid) is aid granted under schemes set up for specific purposes. Examples are the Accelerated Projects Scheme, designed to bring forward investment projects in the period April 1975–July 1976 which would otherwise have been deferred (aid was normally in the form of interest-relief grants) and a number of sectoral schemes to promote investment in particular branches of industry, such as the Ferrous Foundry Industry Scheme and the Instrumentation and Automation Industry Scheme.

The final category (also Section 8 of the Act) is aid to individual firms – rescue cases, of which British Leyland is the most notable example. About half of the aid granted under Section 8 falls in this category.

Local authorities also have powers to assist industry in their areas, usually by way of advance factory construction and by provision of loans or grants.

EXPORTS CREDITS GUARANTEE DEPARTMENT (ECGD)

ECGD was set up as long ago as 1919, and is a separate government department. Its main function is to encourage exports by providing export credit insurance to UK exporters, but in addition it provides some insurance against loss on overseas investments. ECGD's aim is to operate its insurance business at no cost to the government, and the premiums charged are expected to be sufficient to meet the cost of claims. The proportion of British exports insured by ECGD had risen to as much as 33 per cent in 1978/79.

ECGD is also a medium for providing subsidized finance for medium-term credit. The government agrees a fixed rate of interest at which the banks will provide the necessary finance – a rate which is intended to be in accordance with international agreements – and ECGD reimburses the banks for the difference between this fixed rate and an agreed commercial rate of return. The terms offered by different suppliers are a major consideration in the award of export contracts, and the government has taken the view that subsidies to exports are justifiable in the light of the competition faced. Export credit insurance is often required by firms, both to limit their own exposure to loss and because the banks which advance the necessary finance require insurance as part of the security for their loans.

In attempting to cover its costs ECGD behaves in a similar fashion to other insurance organizations. It insists on a spread of business – it does not permit a company to insure only its more dubious risks – and it operates limits on the total credit granted to particular countries to avoid undue exposure to political risks. Insurance against the straightforward commercial risks could in principle be provided by the private insurance market, and the ordinary techniques of risk assessment apply to such risks, but political risks are generally too concentrated and unpredictable for private insurance. In fact, in 1980 ECGD suffered quite heavy losses due to payments embargoes and disturbed political conditions in some countries.

NOTES

1. See Chapter 7.
2. The scheme to provide new equity capital for Stone-Platt Industries in March 1980 is an example of what may occur more frequently in future.
3. The tax saving in the first year can be converted into an implicit reduction in the cost of capital. Since allowances are used up in the first year the tax bill is in principle higher later, but firms with a continuing investment programme can defer tax indefinitely. Many firms, however, do not have sufficient profits to make full use of their potential tax allowances – though by leasing rather than purchasing assets they are able to obtain the benefit of the allowances indirectly.

14 REGULATION AND CONTROL

Some of the reasons why governments control the activities of financial institutions and regulate the securities markets have already been indicated in Chapter 1, notably the prevention of failure by institutions and of fraudulent dealing in markets. Governments try to ensure that financial institutions are able to honour their commitments, that savers have access to the information they need to form a proper judgment about the prospects and risks attached to the securities they buy, and that dealing in financial markets is fair. Controls imposed for these purposes are described as *prudential* controls.

Governments also control the financial system as part of their financial and economic policies. We saw in Chapter 5 how the rate of growth of money affects rates of interest in the economy: through this and other channels monetary policy influences economic activity and prices. The methods which governments employ to conduct their monetary policies frequently involve restricting the activities of financial institutions, notably banks. Governments also often attempt to influence the allocation of resources in the economy, sometimes through taxes or subsidies, sometimes by requesting or obliging financial institutions to provide finance for certain categories of borrower on favourable terms, and sometimes through their policies with regard to competition, restrictive practices and mergers, which impinge on the financial institutions. Regulations and controls applied for these reasons come under the general heading of *economic* controls.

In this chapter we shall deal first with the need for prudential controls and regulations, and with their function in the UK, after which we shall consider economic controls and their influence on the financial system briefly. No attempt is made to give a detailed description or critique of the current system of monetary and other controls in the UK.

THE NEED FOR PRUDENTIAL CONTROLS

Before considering the forms taken by prudential controls and regulations in the financial system it is worthwhile pausing to consider why prudential controls are required at all. Why can institutions not be permitted a free rein within a market system, with the users making their own assessments of the quality of the liabilities issued by the different institutions? Presumably then the institutions which built up a good reputation over a long period would be in a strong competitive position to attract business, while savers would turn away from shakier enterprises. As with many other things which are bought and sold, the obligation to satisfy himself on the quality of the product he was buying would lie with the user.

There are several reasons why 'leaving it all to the market' may not be desirable. It is not easy for the customers themselves to evaluate with any confidence the quality of the services they are buying. Services are sold by description, the commitments entered into may be for long periods, the services are frequently not consumed at the time that payment is made and a high reputation gained through sound business practices in the past may no longer be fully justified. It may be very difficult for the private individual to obtain access to the information he would require in order to form a judgment about the strength of a financial institution, and even if the information was available the great majority of people lack the expertise to appraise it properly; the process of evaluating the soundness of financial institutions is highly technical. In any case, for each individual to have to carry out such an appraisal himself would be time-consuming and inefficient, and it is something which can be avoided by a degree of standardization in the financial instruments offered. If, for example, bank deposits are known to be safe then consumers do not have to spend the time and trouble in making enquiries about the bank with which they deposit their funds. So long as the constraints placed upon banks to ensure that their deposits really are safe do not seriously impede the activities of sound institutions, there would be a substantial net cost saving to society from standardization.

Prudential controls on financial institutions which ensure that consumers obtain the services they think they are purchasing must also be seen in the context of consumer protection. In the UK the doctrine that the buyer should beware does not generally apply, and producers are under an obligation to supply products which perform the functions claimed for them. Prudential controls on financial institutions attempt to ensure that the same conditions apply within the financial sector. There is also the practical consideration that when, in the last decade, financial institutions have failed their liability holders have in general been protected. During the secondary banking crisis of 1973–75 depositors with banks that failed eventually got their money back; and the same has been true of building society failures. Policyholders with failed insurance companies have not invariably been so fortunate, though they too have received some of the benefits they expected. By and large the consensus of opinion amongst the sound institutions has been that the reputation of the industry as a whole would suffer if savers or policyholders lost their funds through failures, and they have seen it as in their own long-run interest to take over the obligations of failed institutions. Where society as a whole is biased towards protecting the consumer, and where the institutions themselves see it as in their own interest to offer protection retrospectively, there is clearly a strong case for attempting to avoid failures.

It would, however, be a mistake to suppose that all the arguments are in favour of protecting the customer, at the expense of inhibiting the freedom of action of financial institutions and other participants in financial markets. A balance has to be found between opposing interests. Controls and regulations on institutions and markets are by no means costless: they inevitably impede competition, which is the main spur to efficiency and innovation in the economy. Rigid controls are all too liable to lead to inefficiency and to stifle new developments. Moreover, while controls may make financial institutions' liabilities more attractive in some respects, they may simultaneously reduce their attractions in other ways – for example by reducing the rate of return on funds or raising the cost of insurance. Regulations designed to improve the efficiency of markets may also have damaging side-effects, and the costs of enforcing control must not be overlooked. How far society goes in controlling institutions and markets must depend then on the priority given to promoting efficiency and innovation – a priority which is best pursued by allowing the institutions freedom of action – as against protecting their customers, including the ignorant or foolish, from loss.

INFORMATION AND BARGAINING POWER

Any proper evaluation of the financial strength of institutions or of the value of securities depends on access to information. Everybody accepts that there should be an obligation on the issuers of securities to provide some information: the debate concerns the kinds of information which should be supplied, and the quantity and frequency of information which is needed. The main area of concern in the UK relates to securities.

The companies acts specify *minimum* information requirements which companies must make available for inspection through their annual accounts and through prospectuses prepared in connection with new issues of securities to the public. But the requirements for *listed* companies go much farther, because the Stock Exchange regulations for these companies require them to publish their accounts in greater detail and at more frequent intervals and to make public announcements of any material changes in their business. The press plays a very important part in ensuring that this information is disseminated widely.

Fair dealing involves more than the mere *provision* of information, and that there is an equality of bargaining power between lenders and borrowers. Unequal access to information is reflected in the problem of 'insider' trading, now banned under the Companies Act 1980, where one of the parties involved in a security transaction has access to information which is not generally available. The avoidance of conflicts of interest, which often arise when one party has information not available to the other, is one of the objects of the regulations which the Stock Exchange imposes on its members, and provides some justification for the jobbing system; since the jobber does not know whether he will be required to buy or sell shares at the price he quoted, he is not a position to make use of any inside information.

Equality of bargaining power is difficult to ensure, because it depends largely on the range of choice open to both borrowers and lenders, and on independent decision-taking amongst them about the terms to be offered. For example, a small company seeking a loan may be at something of a disadvantage in negotiation with his banker, whereas the large company with access to facilities from a wide range of banks can rely on competition between them to ensure that he obtains a fair deal. The existence of agreements amongst institutions, such as the recommended rate agreement amongst building societies, also puts borrowers at a disadvantage, because even by shopping around they are unlikely to improve upon the recommended rate.

REGULATION OF INSTITUTIONS

The regulations governing financial institutions in Britain derive from a number of Acts of Parliament including the Banking Act 1979, the Insurance Companies Act 1974, the Policyholders Protection Act 1975, the Trustee Savings Bank Act 1976 and the Building Societies Act 1962. Responsibility for enforcing the regulations and supervising the institutions rests with a variety of bodies: the Bank of England (banks and some aspects of Trustee Savings Banks), Department of Trade (insurance companies) and Registrar of Friendly Societies (building societies and some aspects of Trustee Savings Banks). The approaches to regulation differ from one category of financial institution to another, but they generally include some or all of the following elements; powers of authorization, controls on balance sheets, restrictions on persons who may carry on business, insurance against loss for customers.

In all cases the institutions may not engage in business unless they have received prior authorization from the relevant body, to obtain which they must satisfy certain specified criteria. One criterion is the nature of the business carried out by the institution. For example, in order to trade as a bank an institution must either provide a highly specialized banking service or a wide range of banking services including; current and deposit account facilities or accepting of deposits in wholesale money markets, overdraft or loan facilities or placing of funds in wholesale money markets, foreign exchange services, bill finance, financial advisory or investment management services. Financial institutions which carry out some, but not all, of these functions may not describe themselves as banks but may be authorized to act as 'licensed deposit-taking institutions'.

Secondly, regulations may confine authorization to financial institutions which are of some minimum size and whose balance sheets satisfy criteria designed to ensure that they can honour their liabilities. For example, insurance companies are subject to *solvency requirements*, relating the value of their assets to their outstanding liabilities; and (wide-ranging) banks must have minimum net assets of £5 million, maintain capital which the Bank of England deems adequate to the business in which the banks engage, and satisfy other prudential liquidity requirements.

Thirdly, before authorization is given the authorizing body must be satisfied that institutions have a 'high reputation' (banks) or be run by 'fit and proper persons' (insurance companies). The criteria for deciding which persons are 'fit and proper' are not stated, but some categories, e.g. persons with previous convictions for fraud, to take an extreme example, would clearly be ruled out.

Finally, in case the regulations to avert the failure of institutions should themselves prove inadequate customers may be further protected by insurance arrangements. If a bank should fail these arrangements guarantee that depositors will receive at least 75 per cent of the first £10 000 of their deposits with any institution; for insurance policyholders there are similar guarantees in respect of 90 per cent of the cover provided. There is no official scheme at present (1981) for building society deposits, though, as already mentioned, on the few occasions that building societies have failed in recent years other societies have taken over their obligations and the depositors have been paid in full.

REGULATION OF SECURITIES MARKETS

The basis of regulation in the securities markets is somewhat different. It is a combination of statutory regulation, through Acts of Parliament like the Companies Acts 1967 and 1980 and the Prevention of Fraud Act 1958, and non-statutory regulation through bodies such as the Stock Exchange, Takeover Panel and Council for the Securities Industry (CSI). The regulations embodied in statute law apply to all who buy or sell securities, and represent standards of conduct which society regards as the minimum acceptable practice. The ambit of non-statutory regulations is confined to participants in the organized financial markets, but are intended to ensure that higher standards prevail – good, rather than merely acceptable, practice.

Under the Companies Acts companies are obliged to provide accounting and other information, without which it would be impossible for their liability-holders to reach an informed view of the risks they ran. Additional information requirements apply when a company is seeking to raise new capital from the public. The Companies Acts also prescribe standards of conduct for directors and employees of companies, particularly in regard to the use which may be made of confidential or unpublished information to which they have access. As noted above, under the Companies Act 1980 'insider' dealing is prohibited, i.e. persons in possession of price-sensitive unpublished information are not permitted to deal in the company's securities.

The Prevention of Fraud Act 1958 sets out the conditions under which persons may engage in business as dealers in securities. Dealers either need a license from the Department of Trade, in which case they are subject to 'licensed dealers' rules', or they must be granted exemption (e.g. most banks), or they must be members of recognized bodies, of which the Stock Exchange is the most important. Exempt dealers are expected to conform to practices which are consistent with the licensed dealers' rules, and the recognized bodies have their own rules, binding on their members and imposing obligations at least as stringent as the licensed dealers' rules. The object of the rules is to prevent unfair dealing practices, such as might arise if a dealer had a conflict of interest, e.g. selling shares from his own portfolio when ostensibly acting for a third party.

While statutory regulations provide a back-up for non-statutory bodies, it is in fact the latter which have the main influence on practice in the organized financial markets. Stock Exchange regulations are binding on their own members and thus determine the terms on which users of the market can trade in securities and the mechanisms employed. The Stock Exchange listing requirements for securities also have a pervasive influence on the information which is available in the market, since companies and other borrowers must abide by the Stock Exchange rules if they wish their securities to be traded through Stock Exchange facilities.

The dangers of distorted information and unfair dealing are particularly acute when a takeover bid is made. The Takeover Panel has, therefore, published rules to be observed by contestants. The Panel is drawn from City institutions and has no legal backing, but its sanctions on offenders include public criticism and exclusion from the securities markets – sanctions which are sufficiently serious for those with a public position or who earn their livelihood in the financial system to ensure compliance. The Takeover Code contains a number of general principles to which those involved in takeover bids should adhere, together with more specific rules designed to ensure that the information provided by contestants is fair and that all shareholders are given the same opportunities to sell their shares to takeover bidders.

The Takeover Panel is one arm of the CSI, which consists mainly of representatives of the financial institutions, with a Chairman and Deputy Chairman appointed by the Governor of the Bank of England and a small number of lay members. Its objectives include keeping a watch on the ethical standards of the securities industries, reviewing codes of conduct, and considering new developments including proposals for legislation.

The role of non-statutory regulation and the balance between it and statutory regulation have been the subject of some debate. There is a danger that non-statutory regulation may come to reflect the interests of the regulators, rather than those of the users of the market. Though this is not necessarily the case, the suspicion that it might be arises particularly where the regulators are elected by those to whom their regulations apply. For example the Council of the Stock Exchange is elected wholly from its own members. There have been suggestions that some of the Stock Exchange regulations, for example those concerning minimum commissions, may not be in the interest of the public, and that the obligations placed upon companies whose securities are listed by the Stock Exchange may be unduly onerous.

In comparison with statutory regulation, non-statutory rules have several advantages. First, non-statutory regulation is flexible. It can be changed quickly in the light of changing circumstances, whereas statute law involves new or amending Acts of Parliament, and even rules such as the licensed dealers' rules promulgated under statutes are changed only infrequently. Secondly, non-statutory regulation is generally carried out by people who are knowledgeable about the markets, and are usually actively engaged in the markets themselves. Thirdly, since it is based on the consent of those who are regulated, rather than on law, it can place more weight on the spirit rather than the letter of the rules. Fourthly, and this applies particularly to take-overs, decisions on whether something is permissible can be obtained very quickly. Finally, non-statutory regulation is cheap; it does not involve an army of lawyers or expensive legal battles.

Non-statutory regulation, however, does also have weaknesses and dangers. First, it is not comprehensive in its coverage, and however pervasive its influence over the organized securities markets, it leaves a considerable area untouched. Secondly, it cannot operate effectively where the consent of market participants is lacking, and compliance is not always easy to secure. Thirdly, as noted above, there is a risk that non-statutory regulations may give too much weight to the interests of the regulators, and too little to those of the regulated. There is a danger that the public interest may be overlooked.

The regulation of the securities markets inevitably involves a combination of both statutory and non-statutory rules, and the optimum point of balance is subject to continual change. There is consequently a need for statute law to be brought up-to-date periodically, in order to ensure that the practices observed throughout the financial system are in accordance with what society generally regards as acceptable, and to fill any loop-holes which non-statutory regulations are unable to deal with.

ECONOMIC CONTROLS

Governments also impose controls on the financial institutions for reasons of general financial and economic policy. These include policies to maintain overall macroeconomic balance in the economy, to influence the allocation of resources between activities or sectors, and to sustain effective competition. Regulations for these purposes may affect the size and composition of balance sheets, involve controls on particular types of deposit-taking and lending, or prohibit restrictive agreements or mergers between institutions.

Banks everywhere are subject to regulation in the context of monetary control. The regulations may involve lending or deposit ceilings, ceilings on the rates of interest paid to depositors or charged to borrowers, and compulsory holdings of specified categories of assets. Banks in the UK have been no exception. They were subject to ceilings on their private lending for much of the 1960s, restrictions on their ability to compete for sterling deposits for most of the 1970s, occasional controls on interest rates, and they had an obligation to conform to minimum balance-sheet ratios throughout. They have also at times been subject to guidance on the scale of lending for particular purposes, with high priority being given to manufacturing industry and exports, and correspondingly low priority to lending to persons and for property development. Consumer instalment lending has been affected directly by regulations governing minimum down-payments and maximum repayments periods.

The government has also attempted to influence the scale and terms of building society lending. The overall level of lending is discussed in a Joint Consultative Committee, in which the government indicates the level of mortgage lending which it believes to be compatible with its economic objectives. The larger building societies are, in effect, asked to ensure that their lending does not exceed the indicated level. In efforts to prevent mortgage interest rates from rising, building societies have also been the recipients of government loans, subsidies, and tax relief. Only the insurance and pension funds have been free of significant interference, for economic reasons, with their freedom to select their own assets.

Economic controls on institutions weaken competition amongst them and, except when subsidies are paid, place controlled institutions at a disadvantage relative to others which escape the net. Ceilings on deposit-taking or lending weaken competition within the categories of institution subject to control, and stifle initiatives for new developments. The change in the monetary control system, known as Competition and Credit Control, introduced in Britain in 1971, undoubtedly led to improved efficiency and innovation by the major banks. Interest-rate controls make it harder for institutions to attract funds they need, and balance-sheet controls affect the earning capacity of the controlled institutions, making them less able to compete for funds with those outside. For example, the banks' compulsory holdings of reserves, which have in practice yielded only a relatively low rate of return, have made it easier for other institutions to bid funds away from them.

Economic controls which affect the competitive strength of the regulated institutions are of only temporary value to the authorities. The financial system adapts in ways which circumvent the controls. Controls on some institutions lead to induced growth by others, not subject to the controls, and of types of contract which avoid regulations. Examples abound from many countries. In the UK the use of commercial bills and inter-company loans has increased substantially, in place of bank advances backed by deposits which were subject to control; in the consumer field, television rental grew rapidly at the expense of hire purchase, when only the latter was subject to control; and growth of the non-clearing banks in the 1960s was due, in part, to the fact that the clearing banks were subject to limits on their lending. There is therefore a strong case for devising schemes of monetary control which interfere as little as possible with competitive conditions in the financial system.

The government's concern with competition in the financial system has a positive side too. It has an interest in ensuring that competition is maintained, that the users of the system have an adequate range to choose from, and that economic power does not become unduly concentrated. Competition within the financial system is the principal means of ensuring that its users are well served.

In part this is a question of preventing mergers of institutions to the point where choice, and competition, is unduly restricted. There are sound economic reasons why the number of clearing banks should be small – clearing bank economics dictates the need for a large branch network, and in many localities there is imply not room for many competing banks. Nevertheless, the government refused to permit a merger between Lloyds Bank and Barclays Bank, which would have reduced the number of large clearing banks from four to three. Questions of monopoly, or undue concentration of economic power, would also arise if banks sought to enter activities such as insurance or stockbroking, and unless compelling cost advantages from an extension of their activities into these aspects of finance could be demonstrated, it is unlikely that the government would allow it to occur.

Restrictive agreements also interfere with competition. We have already commented in Chapter 10 on the distorting influence of the Building Societies Association's recommended rate system, and on the stultifying effects of the clearing banks' cartel before the 1970s. Tariff agreements (now abandoned) in insurance had similar results. Some agreements of this kind fall foul of the Restrictive Trade Practices Act – though the building societies are exempt from its provisions.

In many branches of the economy there is an intrinsic tension between the benefits which arise from competition, in the form of choice, quality and service, and the cost and risk-reducing advantages of size. This tension is particularly acute in the financial system, because competition between financial institutions adds to the risk of failure, and so runs counter to prudential considerations; and attempts to avoid risk of failure through prudential controls often blunt the edge of competition. The Registrar of Friendly Societies, for example, has sought at times to discourage individual building societies from paying high interest rates, lest their margins should be too narrow or they should be encouraged to take too much risk in their lending. While this protects depositors from risk, it could also make it more difficult for efficient societies to expand at the expense of their competitors. Another example is the solvency requirements for insurance companies, which make it difficult for new enterprises to enter the insurance industry. Thus in forming its policy the government has inevitably to adopt a compromise position, trading some of the benefits of competition for the greater security which regulation offers.

PART V ISSUES

Now that the components of the financial system have been considered individually we are in a position to consider some issues pertaining to the system as a whole. Chapter 15 looks at the *efficiency* of the system, when judged by reference to criteria derived from the tasks imposed upon it. While the UK financial system scores highly on some of the criteria, for example its ability to mobilize saving and channel funds to major borrowers, in terms of others, such as stability, the verdict is less favourable.

Chapter 16 draws together some of the effects of *inflation* on the financial system and examines the implications for the quality of the facilities provided to savers and investors. Possible means of easing the problems created by inflation for the system's users are discussed, including index-linking of long-term securities.

The final chapter takes up the issue of whether, and if so how, the financial system can help to *promote industrial investment*.

15 THE EFFICIENCY OF THE FINANCIAL SYSTEM

Before beginning an examination of the efficiency of the financial system it may be helpful to review its objectives briefly. The most basic function of any financial system, which we have virtually taken as read throughout this book, is the provision of payments facilities. The responsibility for this function lies with the monetary system, the note-issuing authority and the banks, and is the concern therefore of only one part of the system. The broader objective of the system as a whole is to meet the needs of society with regard to saving and investment. The financial system must provide savers and investors with financial instruments which have characteristics suited to their diverse needs. It must ensure that the terms available to individual savers are 'fair', in the sense that no group should be exploited or denied favourable opportunities which are open to others. The resources made available for investment should be allocated to those projects where they are likely to be most productive, i.e. where the return to society is highest. Finally, it is a function of the financial system to maintain the balance between total saving and investment, and it is important that this balance should be achieved at a high level of economic activity.

We can classify these objectives into two categories. First, there are objectives concerned with microeconomic efficiency. Questions of *microeconomic efficiency* include the range of financial instruments available, the choices open to savers and investors, the ability of the system to cater for their needs regardless of who they are and of the sums involved, the effects of risk on the volume of saving and the supply of funds to investors, the prices which prevail in the financial system, intermediation costs and the capacity of the system to innovate and adapt to changing needs. The pricing of funds is a crucial element which involves not only the efficiency with which pricing takes place in the organized markets, but also the effects of market structure, regulations, taxes and subsidies on the cost of funds, and the question of divergences between social and private returns. The second category, *macroeconomic efficiency*, is concerned with aggregate saving and investment. Questions here concern the extent to which the financial system helps to meet society's objectives regarding the levels of saving and investment in the economy, which may be influenced by general social considerations as well as private preferences; the stability of both the volumes of saving and investment and the rates of interest which prevail; and how far the financial system can be relied upon to balance saving and investment at a high level of economic activity.

RANGE OF FINANCIAL INSTRUMENTS

Our first criterion for judging the microeconomic efficiency of the financial system relates to the range of financial instruments which are available to savers and investors. Does the range of instruments available meet the needs of the ultimate users of the system?

With one important exception the British financial system performs well when judged by this criterion. Savers have a wide range of assets to choose from, ranging from deposits which are completely safe and highly liquid to ordinary shares which allow those who seek a higher return at the cost of greater exposure to risk to achieve their aims. The quality of the organized securities market and the activities of specialized institutions ensure that savers who wish to avoid undue risk through diversification are able to do so. Borrowers too have access to a very wide range of financial instruments, including ordinary shares, long- or short-term loans, hire purchase facilities, and the ability to lease assets or rent property.

The only major weakness is the lack of widely-available financial instruments which provide real value certainty. Some do exist, for example index-linked savings certificates for older people, and save-as-you-earn national savings contracts which anybody can enter into. In addition, pension funds (and insurance companies in respect of pension business) are now able to hold index-linked gilt-edged stock, though only a limited amount has been issued. The monetary value of these forms of saving increases with the general price level. However, the real return on index-linked savings certificates and save-as-you-earn contracts is close to zero, and the restrictions applied to saving in these forms render them unsuitable for many savers. Index-linked private securities are not available, and the high level of nominal interest rates on ordinary debt instruments has created considerable problems for many borrowers. This is a subject to which we shall return in the next chapter.

ELASTICITY AND CHOICE

Next we consider a set of criteria, all of which have to do with the *allocative efficiency* of the financial system, that is the extent to which its functioning will lead to resources for investment being applied where their return to society is likely to be highest. A market economy relies heavily on competition to bring this about: for any given degree of risk savers will place their funds with those who offer the highest price for them, and those potential borrowers with the highest yielding investments in prospect will bid the highest prices. There may be difficulties in evaluating returns and assessing risks, particularly for much of the investment in infrastructure carried out by the government, and in some cases the return to the investor may differ from that to society. Clearly there must be some mechanism for ensuring that socially desirable investment is properly assessed and that the appropriate amount of funds is made available, matters which cannot be left entirely to a market system. But throughout the private sector it is generally left to the price system (often operating through financial intermediaries) to determine the allocation of funds, and the efficiency of this system depends on competition.

An adequate degree of competition within the financial system implies that the range of choice amongst similar financial instruments open to savers and borrowers must be satisfactory. Savers in Britain can make use of a variety of outlets for their saving – banks, building societies, Trustee Savings Banks, insurance companies, and the stock market to name only some of those available. In some instances competition may be moderated by agreements, as with building societies, or because the number of competitors is small, as with the retail deposit-taking activities of the clearing banks. But even if this limits the range of choice within any category the saver still has the option of placing his savings with a competing type of institution, and competition between the categories of financial institution is unrestricted. Savers with large amounts of funds at their disposal can, of course, place them in highly competitive markets.

Borrowers seeking large amounts of funds are also well placed, because they too have access to the securities markets, and have a large number of banks competing for their business. They can be fairly sure of obtaining funds at the going rate of interest, taking account of the risk characteristics of the financial instruments they wish to issue. In the new issue market competition by issuing houses for their business is also keen. The breadth of choice available to small companies is much more limited, and occasionally they may have little option but to turn to the bank with which they customarily deal. But most small companies could obtain finance from competitor banks if they wished to do so, and they also have access to financing in other forms, such as hire purchase or leasing. The position of the consumer is similar in many respects to that of the small firm; provided his credit is good he should have no difficulty in obtaining a consumer instalment loan from a number of competing banks or finance houses. Opportunities for mortgage finance were, until recently, more restricted, due to the dominant position held by the building societies and the recommended rate system, though the recent entry of the banks into this area of financing represents a material improvement into the range of choice open to house purchasers.

Choice is one aspect of elasticity in the financial system. In an elastic system, if funds are more readily available from one source than from another borrowers can readily switch their business. For savers, elasticity implies that, if one group of borrowers is seeking funds more actively than another, they can easily direct their savings to those who wish to take them without the inconvenience of accepting an unsuitable financial instrument. An elastic financial system has the ability to direct funds from wherever financial surpluses arise to those economic agents with financial deficits, regardless of the sectors in which the deficit units are found.

The UK financial system is extremely elastic in this respect, due partly to the absence of any strong sector preferences on the part of the banks, partly to the willingness of the life assurance and pension funds to alter the *sector* composition of their asset portfolios, and partly to the existence of the sterling money markets (see Chapters 10–12). In bank or institutional portfolios, and in the money markets, a small change in relative interest rates is sufficient to cause a substantial redirection in the flow of funds. For example, insurance companies are just as happy to hold company loan stocks as gilt-edged securities provided that the yield margin compensates them for the additional risk and inferior marketability, so that an increase in the demand by companies needs only to raise this yield-margin slightly in order to attract funds. Similarly, in the sterling money markets, if local authorities are short of finance at a time when, for example, company borrowing is slack, they have only to bid up rates slightly to obtain the money they need.

There is one respect in which the UK financial system may not in fact be very elastic – that of the maturity preferences of the different financial institutions. Banks have traditionally preferred to make short- or medium-term loans at variable rates of interest, whereas the institutional investors wish to hold long-term fixed-rate loans or equity assets. This does not cause problems so long as the preferences of borrowers broadly coincide with the relative availability of funds from the different categories of institution. But if borrowers' preferences change it may not be easy to shift savings flowing through one category of institution (e.g. the investing institutions) into the financial instruments normally provided by the other (e.g. the banks). Inflation has in fact altered the maturity preferences of company borrowers, and we shall return to this question in the next chapter.

SCALE AND RISK

Resources will be allocated where their prospective return is highest only if finance is available irrespective of the scale of the investment and with due account being taken of the risk that investments will prove unsuccessful. One aspect of the efficiency of a financial system is therefore its ability to mobilize saving for large-scale investments. In this respect the UK financial system appears to be very satisfactory, so long as the risks entailed fall within the usual range. The high volume of funds available for long-term investment in the capital market makes it possible to raise very large sums in the securities markets. Rights issues and other sales of ordinary shares running into hundreds of millions of pounds are not unknown, and long-term debt issues of a similar order of magnitude are possible. Indeed, though the British Government typically employs the tap method of selling stock, issues of £1 billion can be sold by tender if desired. The banking system too is capable of providing extremely large loans when required, as financing of North Sea oil development showed.[1] For example, a syndicated loan amounting to US$468 million plus £180 million – the currency combination reflecting the expected distribution of costs – was provided by sixty-six banks in 1972 to finance the development of the Forties Field.

If scale causes problems in the UK financial system it is at the other end of the range. Provided that banks are satisfied about the risks involved there is no problem for borrowers in obtaining small amounts of loan finance; the problem lies in obtaining equity finance for small companies, even when the risks involved are no more than average. This is a topic which we have already discussed in Chapter 7, and we should note that the specialist institutions and other measures considered there go some way to overcoming the difficulties which small firms encounter.

From society's point of view it is generally the expected return from an investment which matters, rather than the risk attached to it. An efficient financial system would therefore be characterized by the absence of any bias against risky investment projects. The only exceptions are *very* large projects, so large that the future welfare of the country as a whole is affected by the outcome of the project. Examples are the Channel Tunnel and the Nuclear Power programme. For other projects, including projects which are very large by the standards of the firms which carry them out, diversification across the economy as a whole virtually eliminates all the specific risks. Thus while it is desirable for the financial system to impart a bias against risky projects which are likely to yield only a low rate of return, there should be no bias against risk *per se*.

The risk to which an investor is exposed depends both on the project itself and on who is carrying it out. A large project need not be unduly risky if it is carried out by a large enterprise, which has sufficient management and financial resources to see it through even if unexpected problems arise. Similar unexpected problems might be well beyond the capacity of a small firm to deal with. Most investment projects are in fact carried out by existing firms, using finance which is not specifically tied to the project in question. For the lender or equity shareholder it is the profitability of the firm overall, including the new risky project, that counts. It is only when the success of a particular project is likely to affect the viability of the enterprise as a whole that the financial investor is concerned with the specific risks.

Where individual projects, or individual high-risk firms, are concerned, there is evidence that equity finance can be obtained in the UK capital market, so long as the risks can be assessed reasonably objectively and the prospective returns are thought to be adequate. In the equity market as a whole there is no evidence that high specific risks (as opposed to a strong correlation with market-risk) lead to investors demanding a higher rate of return. Difficulties do, however, sometimes arise when a combination of high risk and large scale occur together. The project may be too large, or the return too conjectural, for existing firms to embark on, and a brand new company set up for the purpose would face enhanced risks of failure. In these conditions most countries find it necessary to give some government assistance, possibly in the form of research and development contracts, by guaranteeing loans, or creating new enterprises under the aegis of a state agency such as the NEB.

In the absence of special credit institutions it seems likely that some bias against high risk investment would exist. But this is the principal function of the NRDC and ICFC's subsidiary TDC (see Chapter 13), and is included in the areas of activity of the NEB. These institutions must have gone some way to reducing any bias against risky investment, particularly when it is concerned with new technology.

However, an absence of bias against risk in the financial system depends on the ability of people concerned to make a proper appraisal of the risks involved. Any tendency on the part of financiers to exaggerate the risk of failure, would lead to an under-estimation of the expected returns from risky projects, the degree of under-estimation increasing with the risk, and this would reduce the number of projects carried out. Businessmen frequently allege that there is a bias of this kind and that bankers and other financiers are unduly cautious; they reply that businessmen are frequently over-optimistic when it is other people's money which is at stake. Both points of view may well have some validity.

The financier's caution and scepticism is a necessary safeguard against the businessman's optimism and enthusiasm. But it may easily go too far, because few financiers have the expertise to judge risks accurately. The people proposing the investment project generally are, and certainly ought to be, more expert – more able to judge the prospective return and risks – than the financiers to whom they turn for funds. Moreover it is they, rather than the financiers, who will be in control, who will have the opportunity to put things right if difficulties arise. Thus, with the information, expertise and control at their disposal, the risk must necessarily be greater in the eyes of the financier than of the project's proposers.

For the lender, as opposed to the equity shareholder, it is the risk of loss rather than the possibility of unexpected gain, which matters, because it is he who is liable to suffer the loss and someone else who receives the gain. Thus a bias against lending for risky (or difficult to assess) projects is natural. Indeed, the difficulty of assessing projects, and of exerting control, is one important reason why the banker puts as much weight on his judgment of the company or person seeking funds as on the precise purpose for which the funds are required.

For companies with access to new equity capital, a bias against risky investment on the part of bankers need not restrict their investment activity. (It is perhaps worth recalling that sound banks need to keep default risk to a very low level.) Any similar bias amongst equity investors would be more damaging, and may well exist. Dispersed share ownership ensures that no single investor can exert much control, detailed (and often complicated) information cannot be made available to the shareholder, and few shareholders claim expertise in the activities of the companies seeking funds. Moreover, the distance between shareholders and company managements may create problems for the latter if things go wrong, and they too may choose to avoid the more risky possibilities.

We shall return to the relationship between investors and company managements in the final chapter. In the meantime it is sufficient to note that there is some reason to suppose that companies seeking funds for specific risky projects in the market[2] may encounter some bias against risk, a bias that reflects the difficulty of appraising risks properly and the separation of fund-provision from control.

SECURITY PRICES AND RATES OF INTEREST

The next condition which the financial system must satisfy in order to allocate funds efficiently is that the prices, or rates of interest, on financial instruments must be equal after allowing for differences in risk and transactions costs. Notice that by and large the financial system sets a price for funds, rather than allocating funds directly to selected users. Anybody can approach a bank for a loan and, provided they satisfy the bank's criteria regarding capacity to repay, are eligible for a loan at the going rate of interest. In the securities market, prospective borrowers or issuers of equity can come to the market and raise funds at the going price. The question for efficiency is whether there are any systematic biases in pricing, which lead to some borrowers obtaining funds too cheaply and others having to pay too much.

The first part of the system in which biases of this kind might conceivably exist is the stock market. Certain categories of share might be underpriced in relation to others; or new information might not be fully reflected in stock market prices. If information is reflected fully in prices, so that (after allowing for risk) the expected rate of return on the shares of different companies is the same, the market is said to be *technically efficient*.

Prima facie the British stock market, with substantial numbers of professional investors continually scrutinizing share prices and assessing the effects of new information on the value of shares, might be expected to be technically efficient, since otherwise investors would be able to detect opportunities for buying underpriced shares and selling them subsequently, and their activities would quickly eliminate under or overpricing in the system. In fact, studies which have been carried out suggest that new information is rapidly absorbed into share prices, and without any bias. This does not mean that the response is necessarily accurate initially; it implies only that when new information is received the response of share prices is as likely to be too little as too much; the behaviour of a share price in future cannot be deduced from its recent history.[3]

One would, however, hope for more than this from a stock market that purported to allocate funds efficiently. If the expected total return from shareholdings in different companies was the same (after allowing for market risk) shares with a low dividend yield could be expected to have greater future earnings growth, and consequently higher future dividends, than shares with a high dividend yield. In fact neither dividend yields, nor price/earnings ratios, have proved to be good predictors of future earnings growth. But that does not necessarily condemn the pricing process as technically inefficient, because a company's future earnings are inherently uncertain and a very wide margin for error around the best estimate may be unavoidable. What matters for fair pricing of funds is that the average earnings growth of companies with high price/earning ratios should be above those with low price/earnings ratios, and by an appropriate amount.

Most of industry's new equity capital does not in fact pass through the capital market at all, since it is accumulated out of each firm's own retained profits. We saw in Chapter 7 that recently about 75 per cent of the increase in firms' equity has been obtained in this way. In principle, if firms judged investment proposals by reference to an external cost of capital, the fact that part or all was financed from retained profits would have no influence on the allocation of resources. But in practice, most firms will demand higher prospective returns from investment which has to be financed by raising external equity capital, so the fact that so much of new equity does not pass through the market may have a distorting effect on resource allocation.[4]

The rules governing public sector investment may also introduce distortions. Social capital can seldom be appraised in these terms, and investment by public corporations is subject to different rules. In particular, the external financing limits applied to public corporation at present (May 1981) may easily prevent these enterprises from carrying out investments whose prospective return is higher than that of marginal projects in the private sector.

MARKET STRUCTURE, TAXES AND SUBSIDIES

The prices which prevail in the security markets are seldom subject to distortions as a result of restrictive practices, and are comparatively little affected by regulations, taxes or subsidies. Security holders are concerned with the after-tax return on their funds, and since many of the major institutions pay neither income nor capital gains tax the gross and net returns for them are the same.[5] By contrast, the terms on which financial institutions do business are sometimes significantly affected by these considerations.

In the first place rates of interest may be affected by market structure. The small number of clearing banks may result in them paying less for retail deposits and charging more for retail loans than would be expected in a more competitive situation. The recommended rate system for building societies is likely to have a similar effect. Building societies generally charge more for large than for small mortgages, though the transactions costs are proportionately lower in the former and the risks of loss are no greater; but it reflects what the market will bear, and the lack of competition. However, it is easy to exaggerate the importance of these distortions, which probably have only minor effects on resource allocation.

Secondly, government regulations, taxes or subsidies may have significant effects on resource allocation. Prudential regulations often increase the costs or reduce the earnings of the regulated institutions, to the detriment[6] of those who use their services. If the effect is substantial the regulated institutions are likely to find their role in the financial system reduced, as credit flows pass through unregulated channels. Economic controls may have similar effects. Distortions of this kind interfere with 'competitive neutrality' – a condition in which the actions of the state do not affect the relative prices prevailing in the market. The UK financial system is comparatively free of such distortions at present, though in the past controls on the banks have had a considerable effect on credit flows, which by-passed the controlled banks – though the effect on rates of interest was probably rather small.

The effects of taxes and subsidies are much more substantial. Sometimes the government deliberately sets out to create 'privileged circuits', to alter the prices prevailing in the market in order to favour certain categories of borrower, the most notable in the UK being house purchasers. This is a particular example of a more general case. Circumstances may arise in which the benefit to society from allocating resources in a particular way differs from the benefit received by the private economic agent – investment which creates jobs in an area of high unemployment is an example. Or, social preferences may differ from the preferences of private individuals – for example, the government may decide that it is desirable to raise the level of saving and investment in the economy, for the benefit of future generations, even if left to their own devices the present generation would prefer to have a higher level of consumption now. By giving relief from taxes or making grants the government alters the cost to borrowers, so that the outcome of individual decisions accords more closely with what the government sees as social needs. Departures from neutrality for reasons of this kind add to the efficiency of the financial system if they lead to an outcome which accords with social objectives. But many of the effects of taxes are less easy to justify, being the unintended side-effects of policies pursued for quite different reasons or the result of measures which, while justified in the past, have outlived their usefulness. When this occurs the distortions in the financial system which result can only detract from its efficiency.

Tax reliefs (and other grants) are employed fairly widely in the UK as a means of influencing investment. Accelerated depreciation allowances and other grants provided by the government are the most important measures for firms; these have already been discussed in Chapter 13. Private individuals are encouraged to invest in owner-occupied housing through mortgage interest relief, which permits them to set off mortgage interest (within limits) against their income for tax purposes, or through equivalent grants. These measures bias investment in favour of the specified purposes relative to other kinds of investment which are not treated similarly, for example the purchase of consumer durable goods by private individuals or the construction of office blocks.

As already noted in Chapter 6 tax reliefs and other arrangements have a considerable effect on the pattern of personal saving in Britain. Contributions to pension funds are free of tax, as is the income on their assets, and this undoubtedly encourages saving for retirement through occupational pension schemes. The tax treatment can be justified as a form of income spreading – tax is not charged on contributions at the time they are earned, but the pension which is received subsequently is taxable. Nevertheless, this form of tax treatment is not open to people who choose to provide for their own retirement in other ways; and there is a clear anomaly in the fact that lump sum payments are often made to employees at the time they retire, and these payments escape tax altogether.

Most of life assurance premiums are eligible for tax relief, amounting at present to 15 per cent of the premium payments. The original purpose of this concession was to encourage people to take out life assurance and so to provide for their dependants, but the main effect nowadays is to encourage saving in this form. The existence of this relief has led to the attachment of life cover to other forms of saving so that they too qualify.

The tax treatment of interest on deposits depends on the institution with which the deposit is held. Building society deposit interest is free of tax (at the standard rate) in the hands of depositors, though the building societies themselves pay over tax at the average rate of their depositors to the government. Tax on bank deposit interest[7] is, however, collected from taxpayers individually. There is no doubt that the building societies' arrangement gives them a marketing advantage, though it can be defended in terms of administrative convenience.

The government grants a variety of tax privileges to its own securities. Gains on gilt-edged securities are free of capital gains tax if the securities are held for more than a year, and the interest on national savings certificates is free of all taxes – to name only two concessions. These privileges allow the government to borrow more cheaply than would otherwise be the case, and while this probably does not affect the total sum raised by the government in the financial markets it does conceal the true cost of government borrowing.

It seems unlikely that all these tax reliefs accord with current social or economic needs. The size of some is much greater than was originally intended. For example the rise in nominal rates of interest has greatly increased the value or mortgage interest relief. Assuming a standard rate of income tax of 30 per cent, relief when the rate of interest is 5 per cent is equivalent to a subsidy of 1.5 per cent, but this rises to 4.5 per cent with a mortgage rate at 15 per cent. Equally, it seems likely that the life assurance relief applies to much more saving than was originally envisaged.

There is no doubt that the existing patterns of saving and investment are materially affected by tax provisions. While proposals to remove or reduce reliefs invariably arouse strong political resistance, these political costs must be weighed against the damage to the system in the longer-run from allowing distortions to continue unchecked. A thorough review of the tax treatment of saving and investment is overdue.

OPERATIONAL EFFICIENCY

The next aspect of microeconomic efficiency in the financial system is the question of its operational efficiency, the intermediation costs which have to be borne by the system's users. Competition is the chief weapon for cutting intermediation costs, since the more efficient institutions will be able to undercut their less efficient rivals and so attract business from them. It is difficult to devise objective standards by which to measure the efficiency of institutions within the system, but there is no evidence that intermediation costs in the UK are generally excessive by international standards.

Nevertheless, in those parts of the financial system where competition is restricted, there is a prima facie case for supposing that intermediation costs may be unnecessarily high. The cases of the building societies and the clearing banks have already been mentioned. The minimum commissions stipulated in the stock market are another example of the same kind, and one effect of the introduction of ARIEL as a competitor for the Stock Exchange was a substantial reduction in the commissions charged by the Stock Exchange on large deals.

Intermediation costs in the securities markets are also affected by taxes. Stamp duty at the rate of 2 per cent is payable on the purchase of ordinary shares, and is therefore a very significant element in the total cost of buying and selling shares. Companies which issue new shares have to pay a capital duty of 1 per cent, again a significant element in the transactions cost.[8] Most of the other intermediation costs also bear Value Added Tax (VAT) at the normal rate. The VAT merely puts capital market transactions on all fours with other aspects of economic activity, but the capital and stamp duties are imposts which discriminate against activities in the financial markets.

DYNAMIC EFFICIENCY

The final aspect of microeconomic efficiency to consider is the dynamic efficiency of the financial system – its ability to innovate and adapt to changing needs. There are many examples of innovating behaviour affecting the banking system – the development of the parallel markets, the introduction of medium-term project loans (led by the US banks in London), and the facilities provided for North Sea oil development, are examples. Commercial bills, while being a financial instrument of very long standing, have seen a resurgence of use. Leasing has grown, and been extended to cover a much wider range of plant and equipment, in response to companies' changing tax situation.

The investing institutions have also shown great adaptability in their competition for savings; unit-linked life assurance and custom-designed pension arrangements are two examples. Whether they have been so adaptable on the investment side of their activities is more questionable. Initiatives have been taken by some institutions to improve the supply of funds to small firms. But there has often seemed to be a reluctance to depart from well-tried practices, and considerable dispute as to whether the situation demands any change. The response to the proposals for the creation of ECI was one of reluctant acceptance, rather than warm enthusiasm – though it has to be said that ECI has not yet demonstrated that it has an important continuing function in the system. The Stock Exchange as an institution has given the impression that it preferred the status quo, and has reacted to outside pressure – as for example in the development of the Unlisted Securities Market – rather than set out to adapt its practices to the changing environment. This institutional response from the Stock Exchange stands in sharp contrast to the imagination and innovation shown by many of its members in pro-viding for the needs of their corporate and institutional clients.

MACROECONOMIC EFFICIENCY

The financial system should make an important contribution to the macroeconomic efficiency of the economy. One aspect is the *levels of saving and investment* which prevail. It is often argued that saving and investment in the UK are too low, certainly when judged by the standards of many other advanced industrial countries.

Whether this is the fault of the financial system is open to ques-tion. The financial institutions have been a powerful force for encouraging and mobilizing personal saving in the economy. Notable examples are the marketing efforts made by insurance companies and pension brokers in promoting saving through life assurance and

encouraging the spread of occupational pension schemes. The building societies have also been outstandingly successful in attracting
deposits throughout the country. Moreover, the process of encouraging saving has been greatly assisted by the tax incentives to which we
have referred. If there is a problem of insufficient saving it seems to
lie in the low level of industrial profitability and retentions, which
has reduced saving by the company sector, and by the small contribution to saving made by the government itself. One component of
saving in which the UK lags behind other countries is saving by the
public sector, and if public sector saving could be restored to the
level of the 1960s total saving in the UK would rise to much the
same level as our international competitors.

On the investment side the financial system has a permissive rather
than a promotional role. Funds are made available to those who seek
them, on terms which reflect prevailing market conditions, and many
of the financial institutions respond to the demands made on them
rather than actively encouraging their clients to spend more. This is
true of most of the investing institutions and of some of the deposit-
taking institutions. However, the banks, which do generally go out of
their way to promote the lending side of their business, are an important exception. The somewhat muted promotional role does not have
any damaging effects so far as investment by the personal sector or
government is concerned, but there is the possibility that, quite apart
from the price, the other terms attached to the supply of funds may
deter some potential industrial borrowers. Whether the financial
system could do more to promote industrial investment is considered
in the final chapter.

The second criterion for judging the macroeconomic efficiency of
the financial system is *market stability*. In terms of the volume of
long-term funds passing through the financial system the UK performs well. There is a large and steady flow of funds available
through the contractual saving institutions, which is available for
investment in the capital market. Unlike some other countries, such
as Germany, the bond market is not dominated by banks which are
liable to withdraw or even to attempt to sell their holdings if their
liquidity comes under pressure. While the supply of long-term
mortgage finance for house purchasers is more variable, reflecting
variability in the deposit inflow to building societies, the flow of
mortgage lending is protected from these fluctuations to a considerable degree through variations in building society liquidity, as noted
in Chapter 10.

When it comes to stability in the price of funds the performance
of the UK financial system has been much less satisfactory. The

ordinary share index rose to a peak in August 1972, before falling by 70 per cent by the end of 1974; debenture yields rose from an average of under 10 per cent in 1972 to nearly $16\frac{1}{2}$ per cent in 1974 (about 19 per cent at the peak), fell to under 13 per cent in 1978 and were back at nearly 15 per cent at the end of 1980. The Bank of England's minimum lending rate has oscillated violently. From under 10 per cent in the spring of 1975 it rose to 12 per cent by October; it fell to 9 per cent in March 1976 and was back at 15 per cent by October that year; then down to 5 per cent by October 1977 and back up to 14 per cent by February 1979; it fell to 12 per cent in April but jumped to 17 per cent by the following November.

When interest rates behave like a yoyo it is difficult for savers or investors to know where they stand, and the amplitude of these fluctuations suggests that the financial system has not been working well. But it does not follow that the cause lies in any inherent weaknesses in the structure of the financial system; on the contrary, it may reflect instability in the economic environment. Changing expectations of inflation, changes in exchange rate policy, and the actual conduct of monetary policy have all contributed to interest-rate instability. But market reactions to changes in the environment may also have played a part. While the boom and subsequent slump in share prices from 1972 to 1974 was partly a result of monetary policy it is difficult to believe that it did not also reflect exaggerated optimism followed by exaggerated gloom, in relation to any changes in objective economic conditions.

There is another aspect of stability in the financial system which is important – its structural stability. Financial institutions, particularly the banking system, are so central to the functioning of the economy, that failures can have significant adverse macroeconomic effects. In the financial crisis of 1974 the Bank of England had to arrange, and to some extent itself provide, support for a considerable number of institutions. The regulatory structure at the time was clearly defective to have allowed failure on such a scale to arise. But prudential controls have now been improved and the risk of structural instability has been greatly reduced.

The final criterion for judging the efficiency of the financial system is its contribution to *macroeconomic stability*, or the maintenance of a high level of economic activity. Just as changes in price play an important part in balancing supply and demand in many goods markets, so the rates of interest which prevail in financial markets have the function of balancing saving and investment in the economy. If rates of interest fail to adjust to maintain balance between saving and investment this has implications for economic activity. A rate of interest which is too high will cause aggregate demand to be depressed and economic activity to contract; too low a rate of interest helps to generate a boom and inflation. To avoid these damaging consequences governments frequently take action to alter the fiscal balance with a view to managing the level of aggregate demand.

Short-term rates of interest are under the control of the authorities (provided that the exchange rate is allowed to float) and are governed by monetary policy considerations. An excess of investment demand over saving will be reflected in accelerating monetary growth, and may cause the authorities to respond by raising interest rates. Long-term rates of interest are less subject to direct control by the authorities, and are governed more closely by the balance between demand and supply in the securities markets. But demand and supply reflect not only current saving and investment flows, but also monetary conditions and expectations of future security prices, which may cause both savers and investors to alter the timing of their transactions.

Keynesian economists have argued that savers' behaviour is likely to delay or prevent a downward adjustment in interest rates which is required to maintain the level of activity during a recession. If they do not expect recessionary conditions to last savers (and investing institutions) would view such a downward adjustment as short-term, and rather than purchase securities at temporarily high prices will prefer to build up liquidity. Unless the authorities permit a corresponding expansion in the liquidity of the economy, and borrowers too are prepared to borrow in short- rather than long-term markets, this will have a depressing effect.

These arguments have generally been applied to the 1930s when interest rates were already at very low levels. It is possible, however, that inflationary expectations may have a similar result in the early 1980s, if uncertainty concerning the future rate of inflation makes institutional investors reluctant to purchase fixed-interest securities at lower nominal rates of interest. If this were to occur real rates of interest on long-term debt instruments could remain at levels which were higher than warranted by the state of the economy. This possibility will be discussed further in the next chapter.

The sensitivity of the general level of market yields (as opposed to relative yields) to the overall supply of saving and demand for investment is in doubt. The adjustment to changes in the underlying balance may sometimes be delayed, with consequences for the economy at large. In a sense this is the reverse of the problem of instability in market yields to which we have referred above. However, both under- and over-adjustment give rise to problems in the economy, and may call for an appropriate response from the government, either by helping the market to bring about the necessary change in yields or by compensating through fiscal policy[9] for the failure of interest rates to adjust.

CONCLUSION

The UK financial system scores well when judged by most of the microeconomic criteria we considered. The only significant deficiency amongst financial instruments is the restricted provision of real-value certainty. Savers and borrowers usually have plenty of choice, and for the most part there is sufficient elasticity in the system for funds to flow easily from savers to borrowers. Large-scale funding seldom presents problems, but there is a question-mark over the provision of finance for risky projects which cannot readily be carried out by companies as part of their usual activities. Pricing is generally fair, though the predictive ability of the stock market is not particularly good. It does not follow, however, that any feasible alternative could do better. Regulations, taxes and subsidies do distort prices, and while some of the effects are certainly intended and easy to defend, others are less justifiable. Operational efficiency seems to be satisfactory on the whole, and dynamic efficiency is good in the banking sector and related activities, but more debatable amongst the capital market institutions.

   In terms of macroeconomic efficiency the performance of the system is more questionable. There are doubts about its performance in promoting investment, in terms of price stability its performance is undeniably poor (though the fault may lie largely with the environment and the actions of the regulators rather than with the other participants in the system), and the fact that changes in rates of interest have not been sufficient to prevent booms and slumps in the economy is also plain. However, the financial system had to operate in an extremely difficult environment in the 1970s, and could hardly have been expected by itself to compensate for the other disturbances which affected the economy.

NOTES

1. See 'The Financing of North Sea Oil', *Committee to Review the Functioning of Financial Institutions*, Research Report No. 2.

2. As opposed to projects carried out with internal finance or with funds raised on the strength of their balance sheets as a whole.

3. A systematic tendency to underestimate the final effect of new information would mean that investors could expect shares which fell after some news to fall further subsequently, and those that rose to rise further subsequently; this does not in fact occur.

4. Against this, it can be argued that firms may be more willing to undertake *risky* investment projects with retained funds, whose use they do not have to justify publicly, than with external finance, and this may help to counter a bias against risk-taking in the system.

5. Taxes do affect yields if the market is segmented, so that securities of a particular kind are held by groups with one tax status, while other securities are held by groups with a different tax status. The most important instances are preference shares, which are typically held by taxable funds, and low-coupon gilt-edged stocks, which are also attractive to tax-paying private investors.

6. Of course, prudential regulations are intended to provide other benefits to users to set against these costs.

7. Trustee Savings Banks are now in the same position as the clearing banks.

8. Though comparatively unimportant for the 'cost of capital' – it would raise the cost from, say, 10 per cent to 10.1 per cent.

9. Changes in the fiscal balance which compensate for excessive or deficient aggregate demand in the private sector remove the underlying imbalance between saving and investment, and so negate any tendency for interest rates to adjust (albeit slowly) to the appropriate level.

16 INFLATION AND THE FINANCIAL SYSTEM

Inflation has had a profound influence on the UK financial system. In earlier chapters we have shown how inflation affects the level of nominal interest rates, alters the level and composition of personal saving, and discourages long-term borrowers, and we have noted the consequences for the behaviour of the financial institutions. Our object now is to draw these effects together and carry the analysis a stage further, before discussing some of the ways in which the system might adapt to ameliorate the more damaging effects of inflation.

INFLATION AND SAVING

Inflation has affected the *level* of saving by persons, firms and the government. We saw in Chapter 6 how personal saving has risen from under 10 per cent of personal disposable income in 1970 to over 15 per cent in 1980; both liquid assets and contractual saving have risen, the former by more than the latter. One important reason for the increase in liquid saving is the erosion of the real value of liquid assets caused by inflation. High nominal rates due to inflation have also boosted the incomes of life assurance and pension funds and so contributed to contractual saving. In addition companies have been required to top up their pension funds because – in spite of the high interest rates – the value of the assets has failed to keep pace with inflation-induced increases in the liabilities. The composition of personal saving has also been influenced by inflation, with a trend towards investment in bricks and mortar.

At the same time as personal saving has increased, saving by industrial and commercial companies has fallen. Company profits have failed to keep pace with inflation – costs have risen faster than prices – but the reduction in saving by industrial companies has been much less than the increase in personal saving, and saving by financial companies has also risen so that private saving as a whole has increased.

One of the most striking features of the 1970s has been the reduction in public sector saving (see Table 8.5). Amongst the important causes were the government's deliberate attempt to stimulate the economy in 1972 and 1973 by raising expenditure and cutting taxes, further measures of the same kind in an effort to offset the deflationary effects of the OPEC price rise at the end of 1973, and a tendency for inflationary pressures on wage costs to cause government expenditure to rise faster than tax revenue. The reduction in public sector saving has more or less matched the rise in private saving, so that there has been no clear trend overall.

INFLATION AND BORROWING

Inflation affects the demand for funds for investment in a variety of ways. First, it increases the uncertainty surrounding estimates of the profits which an investment project is likely to yield in future, and probably reduces them. Inflation distorts the economic environment, and that in itself heightens uncertainty. In their efforts to control inflation governments are liable to interfere with the pricing policies of firms; or they may curb demand by raising taxes, including taxes on companies; or they may use monetary policy, thus raising interest costs as well as cutting demand. If any of these occurs company profitability will be reduced.

Lower profits also affect firms' ability to invest. Their retentions are lower, so they have less scope for investment out of internally generated funds. Possibly more important, their willingness to seek external funds is adversely affected. Today's investment will often not contribute to a firm's cash flow for some time; meanwhile external funds have to be serviced. It is uncommitted profits on existing activities which provide the finance for this purpose, and when profitability is low there is less available. Again, a firm's ability to borrow depends upon the strength of its balance sheet, which is enhanced by retentions. Without the additional equity to provide security, financial institutions may be reluctant to increase their lending; so caution prevails and investment is curtailed.

Inflation also gives rise to the so-called 'front-loading' problem for borrowers, which is illustrated in Table 16.1. Suppose that a firm borrows £100 000, repayable over 20 years by equal annual instalments, and suppose further that it could borrow at 5 per cent in a

TABLE 16.1   FRONT-LOADING DUE TO INFLATION
(£100 000 loan repayable over 20 years by equal annual instalments)

(£ thousand)

	Year							
	1	2	3	4	5	10	15	20
A *No inflation*								
1. Interest (5%)	5.00	4.75	4.50	4.25	4.00	2.75	1.50	0.25
2. Capital (5%)	5.00	5.00	5.00	5.00	5.00	5.00	5.00	5.00
3. Total	10.00	9.75	9.50	9.25	9.00	7.75	6.50	5.25
B *10% inflation*								
4. Interest (15%)	15.00	14.25	13.50	12.75	12.00	8.25	4.50	0.75
5. Capital (5%)	5.00	5.00	5.00	5.00	5.00	5.00	5.00	5.00
6. Total (£ current)	20.00	19.25	18.50	17.75	17.00	13.25	9.50	5.75
7. (£ real)	18.18	15.91	13.90	12.12	10.56	5.12	2.27	0.86

non-inflationary situation. The cash cost to the firm – the burden on its cash flow – consists of interest (line 1) and capital repayment (line 2), with the total shown on line 3. In the first year the firm pays £10 000, falling to £9500 in the second year and so on down to £9000 after 5 years, and then gradually diminishing to £5250 in the last year. Now consider what happens if inflation runs at an annual rate of 10 per cent and if the nominal interest rate rises to 15 per cent to compensate the lender for the loss of capital value. Interest in this case is shown in line 4, and the capital repayment (line 5) remains at 5 per cent per year. In the first year the firm has to find £20 000 falling to £17 000 after 5 years, and reducing to £5750 in the last year. In money terms all the figures are considerably higher in the second case, but the comparison is hardly fair because the value of money is declining by 10 per cent a year throughout the 20-year period. The last line of Table 16.1 expresses the payments in real terms (i.e. in terms of purchasing power when the loan is made) and shows that in the first year the payments still amount to over £18 000 falling to about £10 000 after 5 years, and to practically nothing at the end of the period.

The result is clear: inflation raises the real cash flow cost of borrowing in the early years of a loan, even though the real cost becomes substantially less later. This is what is meant by front-loading – over the life of the loan the firm pays out no more in real terms but repayments have to be made much sooner. For an investment project to be viable, either it must begin to produce cash very early in its life, or alternatively the investor must have sufficient spare income from his other activities to service debt until the project matures. Front-loading is therefore a deterrent to long-term investment in projects which yield a relatively low return sustained for many years, or for which the period until the project matures is lengthy.

It is not only industrial investment that suffers; in the housing market too the cash flow cost of borrowing restricts the amount that people are able to borrow. Lenders generally limit what they will permit a household to borrow to the amount they think the household can afford to service. If interest rates rise the capital sum corresponding to this limit falls.[1] Since building societies compete in the deposit market for their funds, and the rates of interest on mortgages are variable, moving broadly in line with deposit rates, changes in short-term interest rates can have substantial effects on the demand for housing. For example, the 15 per cent mortgage interest rate which prevailed through most of 1980 in Britain was associated with very weak demand in the housing market and a low level of house-building for the private sector.

The effects of inflation on borrowing have not been confined to the private sector. The fall in public sector saving has had repercussions on the government's own funding needs, and in an effort to cut its borrowing requirement the government has placed stringent curbs on the investment programme of the public sector. In some instances these curbs may have been justified by a low expected return, or social priority, for the investment, but in others they reflected nothing more than the political costs attached to reducing government current expenditure or raising taxation.

Inflation affects the form as well as the level of financing. In Chapter 7 we noted that companies were unwilling to issue long-term fixed interest stocks at high rates of interest because, while their best guess might be that inflation would continue apace, if in the event inflation fell to a low level the real cost of servicing debt would rise sharply. They chose instead to borrow from the banks for short or medium terms at variable rates of interest. On the other side of the market lenders are unwilling to lend at low nominal rates of interest in a period of inflation, even if their best guess is that inflation will fall appreciably, because if they are wrong the real rate of return will prove unacceptably low. This asymmetry regarding risk, with potential borrowers fearing the consequences of over-estimating and potential lenders of underestimating inflation, has meant that practically no issues of long-term debt by companies have taken place. Only the government has issued long-term fixed interest debt – in very large quantities – apparently unconcerned by the effect that a substantial fall in inflation would have on its real debt servicing costs.

FINANCIAL INTERMEDIATION

These effects of inflation on saving and borrowing have had impor-tant consequences for the activities of the financial intermediaries. They have had much more work to do, as Table 16.2 illustrates. This shows how the financial surplus of the personal sector has risen since the end of the 1950s, implying that a much larger volume of funds had to be channelled to other sectors. The company sector (including financial institutions) has swung from a small surplus to a small deficit, and the public sector, after moving almost into

TABLE 16.2   FINANCIAL SURPLUSES AND DEFICITS OF
UK DOMESTIC SECTORS, 1958-80

	Personal sector	Company sector	Public sector
	(Per cent of GDP at market prices)		
1958–62 average	0.9	1.2	−2.3
1963–67 average	2.3	−0.1	−2.8
1968–72 average	1.6	0.0	−0.6
1973–77 average	4.7	−1.1	−5.5
1978	5.3	−0.4	−4.9
1979	6.1	−2.4	−4.4
1980	7.4	−0.8	−5.0

Sources: 1958–72, *Wilson Committee Report*, Table 12; 1978–80, *Blue Book*, 1980; *Financial Statistics*, April 1981, Table 1.1

balance in 1968–72, is the main deficit sector, with the high deficit in recent years corresponding to the high personal sector surplus.[2] It will be recalled that the sectoral financial surpluses and deficits reveal only part of what goes on in the system; in addition, intra-sector lending and borrowing takes place on a substantial scale.

Inflation has also affected the maturity structure of assets and liabilities, particularly in the private sector. Medium-term loans have replaced long-term stocks for industry. In the personal sector, over the 20 years as a whole, there has been a tendency for mortgage terms to lengthen in an attempt to keep down the capital element in mortgage repayments so that higher interest rates did not price so many potential house-purchasers out of the market.

The government has become the chief issuers of long-term fixed-interest financial instruments, with the result that an increasing proportion of the funds accruing to life assurance and pension funds has been channelled into government debt. At the same time the public sector has relied much less heavily on the banks for finance, which have directed their funds instead mainly to the private sector.

INFLATION AND THE RATE OF INTEREST

In Chapter 5 we noted that inflation tended to raise nominal rates of interest, so that in principle the nominal rate would equal the real rate of interest plus the expected rate of inflation. Table 16.3 shows

TABLE 16.3   INFLATION AND INTEREST RATES, 1958–80

	Annual averages; per cent per year						
	1958–62	1963–67	1968–72	1973–77	1978	1979	1980
Price inflation[1]	2.5	3.3	6.6	16.4	8.3	13.4	18.0
Treasury bill yield	4.5	5.3	6.7	10.2	8.8	13.6	13.5
Long-dated gilts yield[2]	5.7	6.3	8.7	13.5	12.6	13.0	13.8
Equity yield[3]	5.3	4.9	3.7	5.9	5.5	5.8	6.3

Source: Wilson Committee Report, Table 17; *Financial Statistics*, April 1981, Tables 13.6, 13.8 and 13.9; *Economic Trends*, April 1981
[1] As measured by the retail price index
[2] Calculated gross redemption yield on 20-year stocks
[3] Dividend yield on FT-actuaries all-share index (from 1963)

the course of inflation and a selection of yields on financial instruments since 1958. For the first period (1958–62) price inflation averaged 2.5 per cent per year, the Treasury bill yield was 4.5 per cent, long-dated gilts yielded 5.7 per cent and the dividend yield on ordinary shares was 5.3 per cent. Thus Treasury bills had a real yield of 2 per cent, long-dated gilts about 1 per cent more, and the real equity yield amounted to nearly 3 per cent (plus an allowance for the anticipated growth of real dividends in future). In 1963–67 inflation was a little higher, but the real yields on Treasury bills and long-dated gilts were little changed while the equity yield fell slightly. By 1968–72 inflation had accelerated to over $6\frac{1}{2}$ per cent per year; on average the Treasury bill yield was much the same as the rate of inflation, but gilts continued to provide a positive, though lower, real yield. The dividend yield on equities had fallen, one reason perhaps being a growing preference for equities in the increasingly inflationary environment. The last 5-year period in Table 16.3, 1973–77, shows negative real yields on Treasury bills and gilts. Inflation in that period averaged over 16 per cent per year, with peak rates which were clearly not fully anticipated in financial markets. Treasury bills had a negative real yield of some 6 per cent, long-dated gilts a negative yield of about 3 per cent, and the dividend yield on equities rose to nearly 6 per cent, higher than in any of the previous periods.

These figures illustrate the tendency for nominal yields to rise with inflation, but they show too that the correspondence between nominal rates and realized inflation is by no means exact, even when 5-year averages are considered. On a year to year basis the fluctuations in real yields are even greater, as the last three columns in Table 16.3 shows. In 1978 inflation had moderated considerably and a positive real Treasury bill yield was restored, while the gilts yield exceeded 4 per cent in real terms. The dividend yield on equities remained at about $5\frac{1}{2}$ per cent. Inflation accelerated again in 1979, and both Treasury bills and gilts had real yields of virtually zero, while the equity yield rose slightly. In 1980, with inflation yet higher on average for the year, the real yields on both Treasury bills and gilts were negative, and the dividend yield on equities climbed even higher.[3]

It is not only the failure to anticipate the rate of inflation correctly that accounts for the variations in the real yield on assets: the *equilibrium* real yield may itself have been affected by inflation. High private saving combined with low private investment implies that a surplus of funds will be available in the capital market, and other things equal, a fall in interest rates would be required to restore balance. In fact, of course, other things were not equal – there was a rise in government borrowing which mopped up a substantial part of the surplus saving. But in a recession of the depth experienced in 1980 and 1981 it is hardly convincing to argue that the government absorbed all the surplus saving and that aggregate demand (at high employment) was not deficient – a persistent recession is a symptom of surplus saving at the going rates of interest. Why then did real interest rates not fall farther?

There are several reasons why inflation may cause interest rates to be too high, when judged by the standard of the rates which would be consistent with a high level of economic activity. The first is that, as part of its policy to reduce the rate of inflation, the government may follow a tight money policy. The effects of such a policy will be felt as high interest rates, particularly on short-term assets. A second, connected reason lies in the behaviour of long-term savers, particularly the managers of investing institutions. We have already alluded to their concern with the possibility that inflation may rise in future. It may therefore be necessary for borrowers to pay a risk premium to persuade them to buy long-dated stocks, and a falling rate of inflation may not be followed swiftly by a decline in long-term rates of interest. A government committed to a restrictive monetary policy may have little option but to acquiesce in the long-yields demanded by these savers, because failure to sell long-dated stocks implies a build-up of liquid assets in the institutions' hands, which contributes to monetary expansion.[4]

The high nominal rate of interest on gilts may also help to explain why equity yields have remained so high. In comparing the dividend yield on equities with the yield on gilts investors take account of the expected growth of dividends due to both inflation and real growth. But growth of income for either reason is problematical and in a period of rapid inflation the uncertainty concerning the rate of inflation may lead to this element in the rate of return being to some extent discounted. Thus high inflation may itself put up the real cost of equity capital to companies.[5]

MITIGATING THE EFFECTS OF INFLATION

It is the fact that inflation is unpredictable that causes the most intractable problems for the financial system. Interest rates on ordinary financial instruments cannot simply be adjusted by adding on an allowance for inflation, because no one knows in advance exactly what allowance should be made. This does not matter very much for short-term financial instruments, because a reasonable guess can usually be made of the rate of inflation in the short-run and errors in one period are probably matched by offsetting errors in others. But there is no remotely reliable means of predicting inflation in the medium or long runs. Any adjustment in the financial system to mitigate the effects of inflation must therefore reduce the risk associated with this uncertainty.

One approach is for borrowers to make less use of debt instruments, by substituting equity for debt or rental for ownership. The equity holder can hope that in the long run his income and the value of his asset will move approximately in line with any changes in the general price level; the company seeking funds avoids the uncertain burden in real terms of a commitment to pay a high fixed rate of interest. On both sides therefore uncertainty is reduced. Rental rather than ownership of industrial property has a similar effect. The saver holds property as an asset, from which the rental income can be expected to increase with inflation, rather than a bond on which the income would be fixed in nominal terms; the company has a commitment to pay a rent which will rise with inflation but which will not prove unduly burdensome if the rate of inflation falls. However, both these solutions have limitations. Only a fraction of industrial investment is suited to long-term rental contracts, with the balance having to be financed in other ways; and while in principle issues of equity shares could provide sufficient capital for medium-sized and large companies, in practice there are few countries where equity issues account for as much as 20 per cent of companies' external financing, and it seems unlikely that habits would change to the extent necessary to resolve the financing problems created by inflation in this way. Moreover, the tax bias in favour of owner-occupation makes rental undesirable for many households, and the issue of equity is of course impossible for the personal sector.

A second approach for companies lies in altering the maturity of their borrowing, i.e. in going farther along the route which many have already followed, of borrowing at short- or medium-term from the banks at variable rates of interest. This borrowing is less satisfactory for companies than long-term borrowing at a reasonable rate of interest, but in the circumstances it gives them access to finance on terms which they find acceptable. The problem with this approach is that it throws the bulk of companies' demands for external financing onto the banks, to an extent that is greater than they may be able to supply, whilst leaving a deficiency in the demand for funds from the investing institutions – short- and medium-term variable-rate loans are not attractive assets for long-term investors. There is consequently an imbalance within the capital market.

One solution would be for the government to act as an inter-mediary, borrowing at long-term from the institutions and employing the funds raised to refinance bank loans. Something of this kind was already taking place in 1980 and early 1981, when the Bank of England reduced the extent to which the banks were required to hold various forms of government debt, and obtained the necessary government financing elsewhere in the financial system. The Bank also increased its own portfolio of commercial bills, thereby effec-tively refinancing part of the banking system's lending to the private sector. Much of the finance for the government was found by issuing conventional gilt-edged securities and through index-linked national savings. The index-linked securities matched the personal sector's desire for security as to the real value of part of their savings with companies' desire to be able to benefit from lower interest rates if inflation fell; while conventional gilts involved the government taking the risk that falling inflation would make their borrowing seem in retrospect to be an expensive form of finance.

Finally, an extension of index-linking in the financial system offers the possibility of reducing the inflation risks. Borrowers would issue index-linked loans, whose capital value and interest payments would be linked to a price index. The coupon on the loan, i.e. the per-centage rate of interest, would be fixed, but it would be applied to capital whose monetary value would be adjusted to take account of inflation since the date of issue. An example is the index-linked gilt-edged security issued by the government in March 1981 (to be held only by pension funds) on which the coupon is 2 per cent.

Indexed loans have several important advantages.[6] First, and most important, they eliminate the uncertainty about the real cost of borrowing and the real return on saving. That in itself would be likely to act as a stimulus to both investment and saving through the capital market. Secondly, the rate of interest would be low – at much the same level as used to prevail in periods of price stability – the 2 per cent paid by the government in March 1981 is by no means unrealistic. This would eliminate the problems of front-loading, and so be conducive to more long-term investment. Thirdly, index-linked loans would ensure the viability of funded occupational pension schemes, since they would permit such schemes to guarantee the real value of pensions (see Chapter 11). Without some assurance that pension funds will be able to earn a positive real return the present system of pension funding in the UK must be vulnerable. These are powerful arguments in favour of index-linking, which apply throughout the economy: personal borrowers would benefit from index-linked mortgages, industry and commerce from index-linked debentures, and the government, or the taxpayer in future, from low-coupon index-linked debt rather than high-coupon gilts.

There are, however, a number of arguments against index-linking. One is the risk that indexation might spread through the economy, particularly to labour markets. It is not difficult to demonstrate that if everybody's income was index-linked the risks of runaway inflation would be increased. It is impossible for *everybody* to be protected from a fall in real income, and price inflation which is not matched fully by a rise in incomes is one means of bringing people to accept an inevitable decline. Secondly, it is often suggested that the risks to borrowers would be heightened by index-linked debts. An index-linked loan implies an open-ended commitment in money terms. Whether this is more dangerous than an ordinary loan depends on whether such an uncertain *monetary* commitment in a period of inflation is more dangerous than the uncertain *real* commitment implied by conventional debt. A third argument which is sometimes advanced against index-linking is that it would heighten the risks to lenders, who have become accustomed to seeing their capital repaid quickly in a period of inflation as a result of front-loading. If this is a genuine problem it could be remedied by adjusting the repayment schedule to bring forward some capital repayments. Fourthly, it is argued that index-linking could give rise to disruptive flows of saving between index-linked securities and other as expectations of inflation fluctuated. There would be some force in this objection if index-linking applied to short-term financial instruments, such as deposits, unless it applied to all of them. If, however, index-linking was confined to long-term financial instruments, disruptive flows of the kind envisaged could not occur; instead, if there was a general desire to switch from one kind of financial instrument to another, relative yields would change to offset the potential movement of funds. Finally, it is suggested that index-linking would prevent borrowers from obtaining funds at a negative real rate of interest, and would weaken the anti-inflation lobby made up of those who see their savings being eroded, thus making it more difficult to control inflation itself. Whether it is desirable for borrowers to be able to use inflation to borrow at negative real rates is questionable, but the very possibility illustrates the strength of a pro-inflation lobby – borrowers who benefit from the effect of inflation on the real value of their outstanding debt. If these debts were index-linked borrowers' resolve to curb inflation would be strengthened.

Increased use of equity finance, rental of property rather than ownership, and the substitution of short- for long-term borrowing – with or without government assistance – are all palliatives which go some way towards ameliorating the damaging effects of inflation on the financial system. But only index-linking goes to the root of the problem, because only index-linking eliminates the effects of uncertainty about the future rate of inflation and enables borrowers and lenders alike to make contracts in real terms.

NOTES

1. Mortgages are usually repaid by level instalments, of capital repayment and interest together. In the early years the bulk of the instalment represents interest, while as time passes and the amount of the loan outstanding falls the capital repayment element gradually increases. When interest rates are high the maximum loan affordable changes almost in inverse proportion to the rate of interest.
2. The figures do not add across to zero because the overseas sector and the residual error in the national accounts are not shown.
3. Estimates of the real yields over short periods on long-dated instruments, such as those quoted for gilts and equities, must be treated with caution, since asset-holders take a view of trends for some years ahead, expectations of capital appreciation are important, and no allowance has been made for changes in capital values.
4. A reluctance on the part of savers to lower the nominal yield on securities due to fear of renewed inflation would have effects on the economy comparable to the 'liquidity trap' in Keynesian theory.
5. An alternative explanation of the high dividend yield – namely that savers were taking a more pessimistic view of the probable real growth of dividends – is not entirely convincing. It is difficult to reconcile with the very low level of company profitability at the end of the 1970s when equity investors must surely have expected some recovery in the long-run, rather than a further decline, to justify holding equities at all.
6. For a fuller discussion of indexation see *Wilson Committee Report*, Chapter 17.

17 PROMOTING INDUSTRIAL INVESTMENT

All recent governments have paid at least lip-service to the objective of promoting industrial investment. Measures intended to encourage investment abound, such as the tax allowances and grants discussed earlier, though when the needs of industry have conflicted with other policy goals the latter have often been given priority.

In spite of the advent of North Sea oil and its contribution to Britain's trading position, there is no reason to believe that promoting industrial investment will be less important in the future than in the past; indeed, there is a growing realization that an increased level of industrial investment should be accorded a higher ranking amongst the goals of government policy. There has been a *relative* shift of resources away from manufacturing in the UK, and North Sea oil has accelerated the pace of structural adjustment in the economy. But even if, for as long as the oil lasts, an economic structure giving less weight to manufacturing is to be expected, high productivity within the manufacturing sector is no less necessary than in the past, and a considerable expansion in the *absolute* level of manufacturing output is required to bring the standard of living in the UK up to that of other major industrial countries. Although this is not only, or even mainly, a question of increasing the capital stock through investment there is no doubt that changes in the quantity and character of industrial capital are essential.

Before considering the ways in which the financial system might foster investment we shall first consider briefly the nature of the investment process, in order to understand the points at which financing factors are brought to bear and the kinds of public policy which would be likely to promote investment. Then we shall consider in turn possible developments in the practices of some of the private sector financial institutions, particularly the banks and investing institutions, and ways in which the government might improve conditions for industrial financing. Our concern in this chapter is with the generality of private industry – the particular problems of small firms were discussed in Chapter 7, and investment by public sector enterprises raises different issues.

THE INVESTMENT PROCESS AND THE MARKET ENVIRONMENT

The investment process has three stages; identifying opportunities, researching returns, costs and risks, appraising proposals.

Some of the opportunities for investment are obvious. Most replacement investment comes in this category, as does investment for expansion to keep pace with growing demand. But investment which is connected with change demands considerable knowledge and insight to detect gaps in the market, conceive of and develop new products, or introduce new processes. New investment for the firm does not necessarily imply that it is embarking on something new in an absolute sense – it may simply be following the lead of its competitors. But knowing which products or processes to imitate itself requires some insight, at any rate until new products are widely available and new processes have become common practice.

Research involves estimating the extra revenue or saving in cost which is likely to result over the life of the investment. Initial capital costs, including any introductory marketing costs, have to be estimated, as do the manufacturing and sales costs subsequently. The risks attached to these estimates must be examined – what could go right or wrong, and how revenues and costs would be likely to be affected.

The final stage in investment decision-taking is appraisal. This entails comparing cost and revenue estimates, using standard techniques, such as discounted cash flow calculations, and employing variants to assess the risks involved. A decision on whether or not to implement an investment proposal is then taken on the basis of the expected return and risks. In general, high-risk projects will be undertaken only if the rewards of success are sufficiently attractive.

This investment decision-taking process may not be carried out explicitly, although the elements are contained in the standard procedures followed by most large firms. However, any firm which is seeking *external* finance for a project, whether from the banks or through the capital market, will find it necessary to go through some such procedure in order to convince potential suppliers of funds that their support is warranted.

The risk attached to an investment depends on many factors. First there is the nature of the investment: investment for replacement, gradual expansion, entry into a new market or a major expansion of facilities, and the introduction of new processes or new products, are in a roughly ascending order of risk. Next there is the time which must elapse before a return on the investment is received – the longer a return is delayed the greater the chance that something will go wrong. This is particularly true if new technology is involved, since cost estimates may be badly out, and the possibility of competitors developing a superior technology is ever-present. Thirdly, the scale of the project relative to the management and financial resources of the enterprise carrying it out is critical. A large project which goes wrong may endanger the continued independence of the enterprise. Finally, the risk attached to a project depends upon the receptiveness of customers, suppliers and workers to new ideas – adaptability in the economic system reduces the risks attached to investment.

Of the three elements entering into investment decisions – return, risk and cost – industry stresses the first two. These depend on the market environment within which industry operates. There is very little that the financial system as such can do to improve this environment, but there is more scope for government action.

First, a government which was successful in maintaining a high level of economic activity, avoided overvaluation of the exchange rate, and ensured that the cost of funds to industry was not burdensome would do much to enhance industry's profits and permit industry to function in a more stable economic environment.

Secondly, the government can help industry to obtain business. ECGD's activities are a good example of government assistance for exports, and the work of the Offshore Supplies Office in the earlier years of North Sea oil development helped UK firms to break into the oil supply business. More generally, through public purchasing policy the government can provide firms with reasonably assured markets. As well as raising profitability these policies help to reduce the risks firms face.

Thirdly, the government can assist industrial profitability by keeping to a minimum the costs imposed on industry by regulations. Examples are costly and time-consuming planning procedures, regulations governing conditions of work, and laws regarding redundancy payments and other benefits.[1]

By pursuing policies designed to restore industrial profitability and improve the market environment governments could do much to create a climate favourable to investment; and the general economic climate is of much greater significance for investment than marginal changes in financial conditions.

INVESTMENT AND THE FINANCIAL SYSTEM

Nevertheless, financial conditions do have some influence on investment, and may perhaps be more susceptible to change than some of the other factors mentioned. The main ways in which the financial system could promote industrial investment are by reducing the cost of finance, improving its availability, and altering the relationship between financial intermediaries and industrial borrowers. The financial institutions can do little to improve industrial profits or reduce the risks inherent in investment activity; neither can they make a serious contribution to identifying investment opportunities, the expertise for which lies in industrial companies and not in financial institutions.

In practice, the financial institutions do not have much influence on the cost of finance, because the main determinant is the general level of interest rates in the economy, and their own intermediation costs are a relatively small proportion of the total. The issues concern the terms and conditions on which finance is made available to industrial companies and the relationships between the providers and users of funds. The terms and conditions are not, of course, independent of the relationships which exist.

Before considering whether changes are needed, it is worthwhile recalling the normal relationships between financial institutions and industrial companies in Britain. Banks lend either on the basis of projects, in which case anticipated cash flows arising from the project are crucial, or on the strength of a company's balance sheet. Even when project loans are made, the bank will often have recourse to the remainder of a company's business. The banks have no pretensions to being experts in their customers' business – the development of oil resources being a partial exception – and unless the terms of loan agreements are breached, they have no control over their customers' activities. While they may in practice be able to bring a certain amount of informal pressure to bear before a default occurs, their only legal sanction is to demand repayment of a loan, and failing repayment to appoint a receiver or liquidator for the company.

The investing institutions are in a similar position when they provide long-term debt finance – they rely on the strength of companies' balance sheets and on covenants written into the loan agreements. As holders of equity shares they are not by and large privy to confidential information about the company's business.[2] The institutions have no particular expertise in the business of the companies whose shares they hold, and they are in a position to control them only in extreme circumstances, such as a takeover or if a company gets into difficulties. The result is that the institutions are not generally committed to particular companies as such, but regard a company's shares as something which may be bought or sold depending on their assessment of the likely return.

The situation just described differs both from the relationships within a large multi-divisional company and the relationships between financial institutions and industrial companies in some other countries. The divisions, or subsidiaries, in a large company normally rely on the centre to provide finance for major capital projects. They make investment proposals, which are appraised at the centre by people with experience of the business, and whose expertise enables them to judge the viability of the project itself with some confidence. Authorization of finance involves a commitment by the company as a whole to the particular project, and if a division should run into difficulties with a project it can reasonably expect to receive additional financial and/or managerial assistance from the centre. The performance of each division is monitored regularly from the centre, which retains ultimate control, and has the information and power to intervene long before a difficult situation has turned into a disaster. As a result the risk inherent in a project, both to the managers of the project itself and to those responsible for providing finance at the centre, is significantly reduced.

The relationships between financial institutions and industry in the UK are very similar to those which prevail in the USA. They differ, however, from those in Germany, where the banks have much wider functions in the financial system, being actively involved in the provision of equity and long-term debt as well as short-term loans, where the interchange of banking and industrial personnel is said to be greater than in the UK, and where bankers frequently occupy key positions on companies' (supervisory) Boards. In France the banks employ significant numbers of industrial experts, who can advise on the technical aspects of investment proposals for which finance is requested. In Japan the relationships between banks and large industrial companies are often extremely close, with the banks and companies joining together in broader industrial groups. These differences in structure and practice have important implications for the ways in which the financial systems of these other countries work.

We turn now to the question of whether it would be desirable for the banks in Britain to go further than at present in providing loan finance for industry – whether they should be prepared to accept higher levels of gearing, funds should be provided for longer terms, and they should be prepared to lend on riskier projects, with less security than they normally require. Banks in Britain are often criticized for their conservatism in these respects.

We have already referred to some of these issues in Chapter 7. At this point it is important to stress the argument developed above: the risk to the lender depends on his expertise – his ability to discriminate between sound and potentially unsound proposals – and on his control, as well as on any security he may be able to take. Moreover, with the borrowing ratios regarded as normal for banks, it is proper for them to seek a low degree of risk in their lending. Higher gearing, longer-term lending, or riskier projects all increase the probability of loss.

The tasks for the banks, and the lending policies which it is appropriate for them to follow, cannot be viewed in isolation from the other facilities which exist in the financial system. If other sources of finance were not available companies would perforce rely more heavily on the banks. This has often been the case in other countries, and helps to explain some of the international differences in banking practice to which we have referred. But if external equity is readily available, neither company managements nor banks gain from high gearing – the managements because they give up the security of a strong equity base and leave themselves more vulnerable to misfortune, and the banks because their exposure to the risk of loss rises. The same argument applies to the finance of risky projects: in principle what is required is equity capital, which is not the province of the banks. Again while, for reasons which have been discussed earlier, long-term loans have seemed too expensive for industry, in recent years there has been no evidence of a deficiency in supply through the capital market, from investing institutions or from special credit institutions. Industry's understandable reluctance to take on new long-term obligations has increased the pressure on the banks to make medium-term loans at variable rates of interest, but they have responded to these demands and, in an area of banking in which competition is intense, it is difficult to believe that banks generally are unduly restrictive.

In normal circumstances most UK industrial companies[3] are in a position to augment their equity capital if they wish. The argument that banks should permit higher gearing or finance riskier projects does not therefore carry a great deal of force. But even if external equity could not easily be obtained it would not necessarily follow that the banks should change their priorities. A more effective approach might be to seek improvements elsewhere in the financial system to remedy deficiencies in the supply of equity capital. Moreover, if the banks were to be asked to increase their exposure to risk, this could not reasonably take place unless companies were prepared to accept a much closer involvement of the banks in their affairs than has been customary in this country (as indeed occurs when companies in difficulties obtain an exceptional degree of support from their banks). Closer links of this kind might well be beneficial for some companies, whose managements might value the greater certainty of bank support more highly than the limitations on their independence it entails. But it should be noted that the arguments are not all on one side, and strong links between banks and industry in some countries (e.g. Germany) have been the subject of severe economic and political criticism, on the grounds that they create monopolistic bonds between companies and contribute to an excessive concentration of economic power in the banking system.

If greater risk-taking by banks is deemed inadvisable we must look at the factors inhibiting industry from seeking or obtaining extra equity finance. While the capital market can be tapped for additional equity by reasonably profitable quoted companies at most times, conditions can and do sometimes exist when companies either could not, or would not wish, to raise new equity capital. If profitability in the economy as a whole is poor, with the company in question being no worse than average, so that stock market prices are low, or if stock market prices seem to undervalue companies' equity generally, responsible company managements are reluctant to make rights issues. If the company itself is in difficulties, conventional rights issues become impossible. Unlike the division of a major company which can look for support from a single, permanent provider of funds, the quoted company does not have permanent committed shareholders on which it can rely.

The lack of commitment by the shareholders of most quoted companies makes the management particularly vulnerable to adversity. If profits fall, there is a possibility that the share price may overreact – some shareholders are likely to see the fact that profits have fallen as a reason for selling, while potential share purchasers have to base their decision on the mere possibility of a recovery. Bearing in mind the considerable uncertainty which surrounds business and the fact that the detailed information and expertise needed for proper assessment of future potential is seldom available to the market, it would not be surprising if share prices were strongly influenced by recent profit performance. But if the share price falls, a company becomes vulnerable to a takeover bid – putting the careers of its management at risk – and new equity capital appears more expensive. Faced with these possibilities, management may be reluctant to embark on investment projects likely to cause a short-run drop in profits, and may adopt a more cautious attitude to the taking of risks.

The source of these problems is the arms-length relationship between shareholders and industrial companies. To some extent this relationship is an unavoidable consequence of dispersed share ownership; individual shareholders cannot all be provided with confidential information,[4] and they cannot be given direct control over a company's business. Indeed, one of the strengths of the securities markets is that they enable firms to attract capital from many sources without putting these obligations on shareholders (who are mostly ill-qualified to discharge them). Nevertheless, some changes in the present system, which encouraged shareholders to have a greater commitment to the companies whose shares they held, and permitted them a greater measure of control in return for heavier obligations, would be advantageous if it gave companies the assurance of support when it was required. The growth of institutional shareholdings presents opportunities for the development of closer links, because some institutions control very substantial amounts of funds and the institutions as a whole are in a much better position than large numbers of unconnected individual shareholders to create machinery for concerted action.

One possibility would be for an institution to acquire strategic stakes of, say, 10 per cent or more of the equity capital of a limited number of small or medium-sized concerns. Board representation might be involved, but in any event the institution would keep in close touch with the company's management, have access to information, be consulted on major decisions and exert a measure of control. The company would have the advantage of knowing that its shareholders were committed to attempting to make the company successful, that they would not lightly dispose of their shares purely for short-term portfolio management reasons, thus perhaps weakening the share price at an inconvenient time, and that they could be called on for additional financial support if necessary. When taken into a company's confidence the institution would, of course, have to accept limitations on its freedom to deal in the company's shares; and a policy of holding strategic stakes has implications for the skills and experience of the institution's own staff.

Strategic stakes in giant companies are not a practical possibility. Very few institutional investors in the UK have shareholdings in giant companies which are significant in relation to the total value of the company's shares, and it would not be sensible for a company's management to attempt to maintain close relationships with a large number of investors. How, in these circumstances, are the problems due to the separation of ownership from control to be overcome? How are the institutions to ensure that company managements do not needlessly refrain from capital investment which the institutions would be prepared to finance, and that a satisfactory standard of management is maintained?

One approach is to increase the number of qualified non-executive directors in large companies. Non-executive directors are of course responsible to all the shareholders, not only institutional investors, and they are appointed by the shareholders as a whole. But if the non-executive directors on the Board of a company have the confidence of institutional investors, and if they act as watch-dogs over, and an informed sounding board for, the company's management, the shareholders have some check on the quality of the company's management and control over its activities. Thus, if the non-executive directors, who have access to the necessary information, are satisfied that an investment proposal is sound, the institutional investors may be prepared to accept their judgment and provide the necessary funds.

Another possibility would be for the institutions to make more use of ECI or FCI in a central role, with ECI or FCI holding some equity capital in a company themselves but also providing a co-ordinating and monitoring service for other institutional investors who would, in total, have much larger shareholdings in the company. By ensuring that ECI or FCI was properly staffed to carry out these functions on their behalf the institutions would avoid having to acquire their own staff for this purpose.

Arrangements of this kind were included in a recent rescue operation for a major industrial company.[5] A conventional rights issue was out of the question, but by arranging for major institutional shareholders to take their due proportions of a rights issue, and for these along with ECI and FCI to underwrite the remainder, it proved possible to find the new equity capital required. It was also necessary to create a new class of shares, which gave those who had put up the risk capital when the company was in difficulty a prior claim to a return on their investment.

This scheme might well be taken as a precedent for companies in less dire financial situations but which nevertheless find their access to new equity finance restricted. Facilities provided by ECI and FCI might be the foundation on which larger strategic stakes by major institutional shareholders could be built, with the closer links between these shareholders and the company recognized by offering a new class of shares to those shareholders who were prepared to undertake the greater responsibilities of a long-term commitment to the company.

ROLE OF THE GOVERNMENT

There are three ways in which the government might help to promote industrial investment through its influence on the financial system: its monetary and fiscal policies affect the general level of interest rates in the economy, and so the cost of finance for industry; it can take action to minimize the effects of any structural defect in the supply of funds for industry; and it can engage in a variety of forms of selective intervention.

The general level of interest rates governs industry's cost of funds, and has a pervasive effect on industrial investment. It depends on the balance between saving and investment in the economy, to which the public sector deficit makes an important contribution. A reduction in the deficit would help to lower interest rates and stimulate private investment. Indeed, it seems clear that if Britain is to emerge as a high-saving/high-investment economy in the 1980s a substantially lower proportion of GDP than in the late 1970s will need to be absorbed by the public sector deficit.[6] More saving must be found somewhere and it is unrealistic to expect any substantial increase in the proportion contributed by the private sector; a recovery in company profitability would enable companies to increase their retentions, but personal sector saving is likely to fall back from its recent peak level. A reduction in the public sector deficit does not necessarily imply that public sector investment should be reduced – such investment could legitimately share in an increase in the level of investment overall – but it does mean that saving by the public sector must rise, through higher retentions by public corporations, higher tax revenue or a reduction in the proportion of GDP spent on public sector *current* expenditure. Monetary policy also has a part to play. It cannot permanently reduce the equilibrium real interest rates consistent with high activity in the economy, but it must not be so tight in the short-run as to prevent a fall in real interest rates justified by the balance between high employment saving and investment.

The only major structural defect in the financial system is a consequence of industry's reluctance to borrow long-term funds at high nominal rates of interest, with the resulting diversion of the weight of loan demand onto the banks. Some means of relieving this pressure must be found. Possible techniques include a refinance scheme operated directly by the government itself, as suggested by the Wilson Committee; a similar scheme involving FFI, with the government guaranteeing FFI against any loss occasioned by long-term borrowing at fixed rates of interest to finance shorter-term loans at variable rates; altering the techniques of monetary control in a way which will enable the banks to reduce their holdings of public sector debt or off-load part of their private-sector lending onto the Bank of England;[7] and an extension of indexation to company securities in the long-term capital market – a structural reform which would enable industry to return as a long-term borrower. Unless the inflation of the 1970s proves to be a temporary phenomenon, and indeed is swiftly recognized as such so that long-term interest rates fall substantially, only a structural reform of this kind will avoid the need for some refinancing arrangements.

The third means by which the government can promote investment is through selective intervention, which comes in two forms – passive and active. When acting passively the government announces the terms on which funds will be provided and the categories of borrower to whom these terms will apply; it then awaits applications. This is the practice with selective financial assistance under Sections 7 and 8 (regional and general industrial assistance) of the Industry Act 1972. Rescue operations for companies in difficulty fall in the same category, since it is generally the companies or their advisers who make the approach to government. And one function of the NEB and regional development agencies is to respond to requests for assistance. Arrangements of a passive kind for selective financial assistance already exist, and could readily be extended through new Section 8 schemes if the government wished.

The alternative would be for the government to attempt to play a more active, or promotional, role. To do this effectively the government, or some agency acting on its behalf, would need first to identify industrial investment projects which warranted support.

However, merely identifying projects would be unlikely in itself to bring about the desired change, and it would usually be necessary for the government also to provide some kind of financial carrot, e.g. a grant or funds on concessional terms.

In principle, civil servants employed by the Department of Industry could fill this promotional role, but in practice there is considerable advantage in having investment decisions of this kind separated as far as possible from short-term political considerations, and this is most likely to be achieved if the investment function is carried out by a separate agency or institution, like the NEB or one of the regional development agencies. Within these agencies it is possible to build up teams who are well-informed concerning the state of industry, competent to select projects for support from amongst those submitted to them, and who, from their knowledge of industry, may also be in a position to suggest new developments, which no existing firm on its own might otherwise choose to pursue. An example is the developments in microelectronics promoted by the NEB.

There is no reason to believe that a government organization would necessarily be better qualified to carry out these functions than private institutions, but a public agency, or a private agency with public funds to disburse, might nevertheless be more successful than a wholly commercial private organization because some special financial assistance – grants or funds on comparatively soft terms – may be needed as a catalyst. Moreover, the knowledge that an agency with funds available could be approached might help to create a bias in favour of investment in the private sector.

THE NEED FOR NEW INSTITUTIONS

Proponents of a more active and interventionist government role are usually in favour of creating new institutions, which would provide funds on terms which were in some respects easier than those demanded by private financial institutions. While half of the Wilson Committee[8] were opposed to new developments of this kind, the remainder recommended the setting up of a new institution, either a public sector investment bank, or a much more substantial investment facility on the lines advocated by the TUC. The proposed public sector investment bank would have a structure and functions similar to that of the NEB. It would be expected to promote new

developments as well as helping to provide finance for existing companies, and it would insist on the application of strict commercial
criteria in assessing projects for support – though the finance might
be provided on softer terms. But it differed from the NEB in that
it would not have a legacy of rescue cases to look after and would
not be expected to take on such cases in future; its supervisory board
would lay down policy guidelines and hire and fire management, but
would not be involved in detailed investment decisions; day-to-day
decisions would be removed as far as possible from short-term
political pressures; and private as well as public funding might be
sought. It was intended that the scale of the investment bank would
build up gradually as its own resources (particularly in the form of a
skilled management team) grew and opportunities for investments
became apparent.

The proposed TUC facility was on an altogether grander scale.
Its initial funding was to be about £2 billion per year, half derived
from the investing institutions (who were to be guaranteed a return
not less than they could earn on gilt-edged securities) and half from
the government. Control was to be in the hands of a tripartite body –
representatives of employers and employees drawn from both
finance and industry and representatives of relevant government
departments – who would act as a policy council but who would
have reserve powers to intervene in detailed decisions. Finance for
projects would be provided at a spectrum of interest rates, depending
on the individual project, but long-run viability would be an essential
criterion for support. The TUC stressed the importance of involving
the institutions in the running of the facility, and saw it as a two-way
channel for communication between the institutions and industry.

Any arrangements to provide funds on concessional terms, whether
through schemes such as those under the Industry Act or through
special institutions, encounter a major difficulty: it is virtually
impossible to ensure that the subsidized funds are directed only, or
even mainly, to projects that would not be undertaken otherwise.
The provision of subsidized funds on a large scale is all too likely to
lead to only a marginal increase in investment at a very considerable
cost in terms of public expenditure; and there is a considerable
danger that public sector agencies with funds available on concessional terms will become the lenders of first, rather than of last,
resort. The proponents of the TUC facility have not indicated how
they would deal with the problem of ensuring that a major part of
the investment it financed was additional to what would have been
undertaken anyway, and it seems very likely that in current condi-

tions much of the finance provided by the facility would simply be a relatively cheap substitute for bank loans. It is also questionable whether the facility would in fact achieve its objective of bringing institutional investors and industrial managers tgether. Very few institutions could actually be represented on the policy council, and contact for the others would be, at best, indirect and remote. Moreover, if it is thought desirable to separate investment decisions from short-term political considerations, the proposed facility seems unlikely to achieve this objective.

The public sector investment bank seems to combine some of the functions of the NEB and some of the functions of ECI and FCI, particularly if ECI and FCI were to develop a co-ordinating role within the private financial system. The specifically 'public' elements in the proposal are its ability to draw on the central government for funds and to provide some finance on soft terms. Beyond this the proposal does not appear to involve activities which could not be carried out by ECI or FCI, though neither has in fact actively *promoted* investment in the past. The question which must be asked, therefore, is whether a new institution is needed, or whether the objectives could not be pursued more satisfactorily through developing the activities of existing institutions, without the need to set up a new organization from scratch and duplicate facilities.

The NEB and the regional development agencies in Scotland and Wales already carry out some of the functions of a public sector investment bank, though there is not yet any counterpart for the latter in England, and all are subject to day-to-day political intervention. Nevertheless, by changing their guidelines so that they could play a more active promotional role, by providing them with a limited amount of funds to employ on soft terms, and by placing the responsibility for investment on their Boards or managements – without the need of continual review by government departments and approval by Ministers – the advantages of the proposed public sector investment bank could be achieved within the existing framework. Alternatively, if the activities of the NEB and regional development agencies are inextricably interwoven with those of government departments, an attempt could be made to build on the existing functions of ECI and FCI, using them as agents to carry out government-approved programmes of financing. Arrangements of this kind have operated through the National Invesment Bank in the Netherlands and Crédit National in France.

In the author's opinion the case for a new public sector investment bank has not been made. While some agency with a promotional role is desirable, it already exists – this function is clearly stated in the NEB's present guidelines. Finance on concessional terms for investment, other than through Industry Act schemes, is not intended to be available from public sector agencies at present, and some relaxation of the NEB's and regional development agencies' guidelines in this respect would help them to promote investment more vigorously; but no new institution is required for this purpose. In theory the existing public sector agencies are also supposed to be free of day-to-day political control over their ordinary investment activites, though in practice much greater independence would be desirable. But if the existing agencies are not left to get on with their job without political interference it is difficult to believe that a new *public sector* agency could be assured of any greater independence.

There is, however, a case for giving official encouragement and support to steps to strengthen ECI and FCI in order to equip them to occupy a more central place in the financial system. So long as share ownership is dispersed amongst hundreds of institutions a gulf between shareholders and company managements will remain. Without some co-ordinating mechanism it is difficult in practice for shareholders to ensure that the quality of company managements is monitored effectively, that any necessary remedial action is taken, and that new developments are not held back through a lack of commitment or failures of communication.

In the earlier chapters of this book we examined the functions of both markets and institutions in the financial system. We saw how sometimes they act as alternative means for satisfying the needs of savers and investors, while in other respects their functions are complementary. So far as *risk* capital for industry is concerned, Britain at present relies heavily on markets, rather than direct contacts between companies and the suppliers of funds. The ability to call on the market for large sums of capital is one of the strong points of the British system. But the arms-length relationships, on which markets depend, make it difficult for the owners of companies, who have the ultimate responsibility for control, to discharge their responsibilities effectively. The economy would benefit from closer links between companies and their institutional shareholders. Some of the means by which these links might be forged have been discussed – strategic stakes are an example. But the possibility of further *institutional* development, founded on the existing special credit institutions, to complement and co-ordinate the working of the market, should not be ruled out.

284   *Issues*

NOTES

1. This is not to suggest that governments are wrong to legislate in these areas, and to impose costs on industry (which will often be passed on to customers in the form of higher prices); it is intended merely to point out that regulations are likely to have effects on industrial profitability and investment, considerations which must be borne in mind when the benefits of regulations are assessed.
2. Exceptions occur when an institution has a large shareholding and is represented on a company's Board or when formal discussions between a company and a group of major institutional shareholders are taking place.
3. With the exception of small firms.
4. Even if there were no implications for the working of the securities markets.
5. Stone-Platt Industries.
6. What happened to the **PSBR** would depend on how much of the capital needs of the private sector were provided through the public sector as an intermediary.
7. Changes in the monetary control arrangements at the end of 1980 and in early 1981 allowed the banks to reduce their holdings of public sector debt; and the Bank of England purchased a substantial volume of commercial bills.
8. Including the author.

SELECT BIBLIOGRAPHY AND FURTHER READING

GENERAL REFERENCES

H. Carter and I. Partington (1979), *Applied Economics in Banking and Finance*, Oxford: Oxford University Press, Chapters 1–5.
Economic Trends (April 1981), Central Statistical Office.
Financial Statistics (April 1981), Central Statistical Office.
Kenneth Midgley and Ronald Burns (1977), *The Capital Market: Its Nature and Significance*, London: Macmillan Press.
National Income and Expenditure (Blue Book), 1980 edition, London: HMSO.
Jack Revell (1973), *The British Financial System*, London: Macmillan Press.
Committee to Review the Functioning of Financial Institutions (Wilson Committee), *Report* (1980), Cmnd 7937, London: HMSO (hereafter WC *Report*), especially Appendix 3.

Chapter 1: The financial system

B. J. Moore (1968), *An Introduction to the Theory of Finance*, New York: The Free Press, Chapters 1–5.
Paul F. Smith (1970), *Economics of Financial Institutions and Markets*, Homewood, Illinois: Richard D. Irwin.

Chapter 2: Finance in Britain

Bank of England (1978), *United Kingdom Flow of Funds Accounts: 1963–1976*, London: Bank of England.
Sandra Mason (1976), *The Flow of Funds in Britain*, London: Elek Books.

Chapters 3 and 4: Mobilizing saving
                              Asset transformation

Richard Coghlan (1980), *The Theory of Money and Finance*, London: Macmillan Press, Chapters 6–8.

Chapter 5: Interest rates

Paul F. Smith (1978), *Money and Financial Intermediation*, Englewood Cliffs, New Jersey: Prentice-Hall.
WC *Report*, Chapter 11.

Chapter 6: Personal saving and investment

Christopher Johnson (1976), *Anatomy of UK Finance, 1970–75*. London: Longman Group, Part 1.

Chapter 7: Company financial behaviour

Christopher Johnson (1976), *Anatomy of UK Finance, 1970–75*, London: Longman Group, Part 2.
WC *Report*, Chapters 10, 15, 16.
Wilson Committee Interim Report (1978), Cmnd 7503, *The Financing of Small Firms*, London: HMSO.

Chapter 8: Public sector investment and financing

Christopher Johnson (1976), *Anatomy of UK Finance, 1970–75*, London: Longman Group, Part 5.

Chapter 10: Deposit-taking institutions

Wilson Committee, *Evidence on the Financing of Industry and Trade*, London: HMSO (hereafter WC *Evidence*). Vol. 5, Committee of London Clearing Bankers; Vol. 6, Committee of Scottish Clearing Bankers.
Wilson Committee, *Second Stage Evidence*, London: HMSO (hereafter WC *Second Stage Evidence*). Vol. 3, Committee of London Clearing Bankers, Building Societies Association.

Chapter 11: Investing institutions

WC *Evidence*, Vol. 3, Insurance Company Associations, National Association of Pension Funds; Vol. 7, Association of Investment Trust Companies, Unit Trust Association.
WC *Second Stage Evidence*, Vol. 2, Insurance Company Associations.

Chapter 12: Financial markets

R. J. Briston (1970), *The Stock Exchange and Investment Analysis*, London: George Allen and Unwin.
WC *Report*, Chapters 7, 13, 15, 16.
WC *Evidence*, Vol. 3, The Stock Exchange.
WC *Second Stage Evidence*, Vol. 4, The Stock Exchange.

Chapter 13: Special credit institutions

WC *Evidence*, Vol. 1, Department of Industry: Government Support for Industry; Vol. 4, The National Enterprise Board, Finance for Industry, Equity Capital for Industry; Vol. 6, Scottish Development Agency; Vol. 8, Welsh Development Agency.

Chapter 14: Regulation and control

WC *Report*, Chapters 21–24.
WC *Second Stage Evidence*, Vol. 1, Panel on Take-overs and Mergers; Vol. 4, The Stock Exchange, Bank of England; Vol. 5, Department of Trade.

Chapter 15: The efficiency of the financial system

WC *Report*, Chapters 13, 14.

Chapter 16: Inflation and the financial system

WC *Report*, Chapter 17.

Chapter 17: Promoting industrial investment

WC *Report*, Chapters 19, 20.

INDEX